HUGUENOTS IN BRITAIN AND THEIR FRENCH BACKGROUND, 1550–1800

Huguenots in Britain and their French Background, 1550–1800

Contributions to the Historical Conference of the Huguenot Society of London, 24–25 September 1985

Edited by
Irene Scouloudi

Honorary Editor and Vice-President
The Huguenot Society of Great Britain and Ireland

MACMILLAN
PRESS

First published 1987

Published by
THE MACMILLAN PRESS LTD
Houndmills, Basingstoke, Hampshire RG21 2XS
and London
Companies and representatives
throughout the world

Printed in Hong Kong

British Library Cataloguing in Publication Data
Huguenots in Britain and their French background,
1550–1800: Contributions to the Historical
Conference of the Huguenot Society of London, 24–25
September 1985.
1. Huguenots—England—History 2. Huguenots
—France—History
I. Scouloudi, Irene II. Huguenot Society of
London, *Historical Conference (1985 : Royal Society
and British Museum, London)*
284'.5'0942   BX9458.G7
ISBN 0-333-39669-3

Contents

List of Plates   vii

List of Tables, Map and Figure   xv

Acknowledgements   xvi

Notes on the Contributors   xvii

Preface by Randolph Vigne   xxi

PART I   HUGUENOTS IN BRITAIN

1   A Huguenot Historian: Paul Rapin
    Hugh Trevor-Roper   3

2   Huguenot Contributions to England's Intellectual
    Life and England's Intellectual Commerce with
    Europe, *c.* 1680–1720
    Graham C. Gibbs   20

3   The Stranger Community in the Metropolis,
    1558–1640
    Irene Scouloudi   42

4   The Canterbury Walloon Congregation from
    Elizabeth I to Laud
    Anne M. Oakley   56

5   Jacob David: A Huguenot London Merchant of the
    Late Seventeenth Century and His Circle
    Henry G. Roseveare   72

6   London Huguenot Silver
    Hugh Tait   89

7   Huguenot Upholsterers and Cabinet-makers in the
    Circle of Daniel Marot
    Gervase Jackson-Stops   113

8   Huguenots in the English Silk Industry in the
    Eighteenth Century
    Natalie Rothstein   125

PART II   THE FRENCH BACKGROUND

 9   Great Britain as Envisaged by the Huguenots of the
     Seventeenth Century
     Elisabeth Labrousse   143

10   The Huguenots and the Edict of Nantes, 1598–1629
     N. M. Sutherland   158

11   The Huguenots under Richelieu and Mazarin,
     1629–61: A Golden Age?
     Menna Prestwich   175

12   Louis XIV and the Persecution of the Huguenots:
     The Role of the Ministers and Royal Officials
     Roger Mettam   198

13   Patterns in the Study of Huguenot Refugees in
     Britain: past, present and future
     Robin D. Gwynn   217

Index   237

List of Plates (between pages 140 and 141)

CHAPTER 6   LONDON HUGUENOT SILVER

I   Figure 1   Design for a tazza by Hans Holbein the Younger, probably circa 1525, shortly before his first stay in England (1526–8). The highly original form of the stem, with its bulbous knop and 'frill' above a broad spreading foot, is unparalleled, except on the two Rochester Cathedral tazze (see Figure 2). The Basel Museum of Art.

Figure 2   The two silver-gilt tazze from Rochester Cathedral: the tazza on the left bears a maker's mark and is fully and spaciously hallmarked, London, 1528; the cover is equally well marked, with the hallmarks, London, 1532, and a different maker's mark. The tazza on the right is poorly marked in one small area below the rim but too indistinct for definite identification. Perhaps by a Continental goldsmith and subsequently copied in 1528 by a London goldsmith. Purchased in 1971.

Figure 3   Detail of the unidentifiable marks on the rim of the Rochester Cathedral Tazza without a cover. Perhaps made by a foreign craftsman before 1528.

II   The Wyndham Ewer: fully hallmarked (twice): London, 1554. Maker's mark: a star of intersecting triangles. This silver-gilt ewer, together with its matching basin made by Symon Owen in 1607 in London, passed by descent in the Wyndham family until the Second World War. H. 11¾ in. Purchased in 1977.

III   The Devonshire Ewer: fully hallmarked, London, 27th March – 29th May, 1697. Maker's mark: Pierre Harache Senior. This silver-gilt ewer, together with its basin *en suite*, was made for the 1st Duke of Devonshire and passed by descent,

vii

remaining at Chatsworth until 1958. H. 12 in. The
Wilding Bequest, 1969.

IV Figure 1   The Croft Cup: fully hallmarked, London, 1685.
Maker's mark: Benjamin Pyne. This silver
covered cup, together with another very similar
cup, passed by descent to Sir Herbert Croft, of
Croft Castle, Herefordshire, who, in 1719, gave
them to his two daughters; the cups were reunited
before 1911. This pair are the earliest known
examples of this type of monumental covered
cup. H. 15 in. Purchased in 1973.

Figure 2   Two-handled silver-gilt Cup and Cover: fully
hallmarked, London, 1705. Maker's mark: Simon
Pantin. H 8⅛ in. The Wilding Bequest, 1969.

V Figure 1   Two-handled silver Cup and Cover: fully hallmarked London, 1709. Maker's mark: David
Willaume. H. 11 in. The Wilding Bequest, 1969.

Figure 2   Two-handled silver-gilt Cup and Cover: fully
hallmarked London, 1723. Maker's mark: Paul de
Lamerie. Engraved with the arms of the Hon.
George Treby, MP, the first owner. H. 11 in. The
Wilding Bequest, 1969.

VI Figure 1   Two-handled silver Cup and Cover: fully hallmarked London, 1699. Maker's mark: Pierre
Platel. Probably this maker's earliest extant work.
This maker used this form of handle on more than
one occasion, as in the 1706 covered cup (in the
British Museum), probably cast from the same
mould. H. 9¾ in. The Wilding Bequest, 1969.

Figure 2   Two-handled silver Cup and Cover: fully hallmarked London, 1702. Maker's mark: Louis
Cuny. Probably the earliest known piece of plate
by this maker, who had adapted English decorative elements, such as the fluting, into his design.
H. 9½ in. The Wilding Bequest, 1969.

VII   Figure 1   Detail of handle on the Philip Rollos II Wine-
               cooler.

      Figure 2   Wine-cooler: fully hallmarked London, 1712.
               Maker's mark: 'R.O.' with an anchor between,
               previously thought to belong to Philip Rollos I
               but now recognised as belonging to his son, Philip
               Rollos II (made a freeman in 1705). This silver
               wine-cooler, engraved with the Royal Arms of
               Queen Anne, was in the Earl of Home's family.
               L. 28 in. The Wilding Bequest, 1969.

VIII Figure 1   Coffee-pot: fully hallmarked London, 1700.
               Maker's mark: Jean Chartier. H. 8½ in. The
               Wilding Bequest, 1969.

      Figure 2   *Ecuelle*: fully hallmarked London, 1704. Maker's
               mark: Pierre Platel. This silver vessel is a
               Continental type, apparently introduced by the
               Huguenots into English silver plate and normally
               reserved as a present to a nursing mother. Neither
               the form nor the custom seems to have become
               widely adopted in England. L. (including hand-
               les) 11 in. The Wilding Bequest, 1969.

IX   The Germain Vases: fully hallmarked London,
               1711. Maker's mark: David Willaume. Silver-gilt
               with ivory 'sleeves' carved by a Netherlandish
               artist, perhaps François Langhemans, in the late
               seventeenth century. Formerly in the collections
               of the Lady Betty Germain (d. 1769), the
               Margravine of Anspach (sold in 1818), William
               Beckford at Fonthill, and perhaps at Lansdown
               Tower, Bath. H. 16.7 in. The Wilding Bequest.
               1969.

CHAPTER 7   HUGUENOT UPHOLSTERERS AND CABINET-
            MAKERS   IN   THE   CIRCLE   OF   DANIEL
            MAROT

  X   Figure 1   The State Bed at Blair Castle, Perthshire.

Figure 2   Frontispieces of Daniel Marot's *Second Livre d'Appartements*, published about 1701.

XI   The State Bedchamber at Drayton House, Northamptonshire, showing the bed by the upholsterer, Guillotin, with embroidered hangings by Rebekah Dufee and Elizabeth Vickson, and the table and candlestands attributed to Gerrit Jensen.

XII Figure 1   Queen Elizabeth's room at Penshurst Place, Kent, showing the wall-hangings *en suite* with the day-bed and chairs, possibly made for Leicester House in London, about 1698–1700.

Figure 2   Day-bed from the Hornby Castle suite, atttributed to Philip Guibert, now at Temple Newsam House, Leeds.

XIII Figure 1   Part of a valance from a state bed at Dunham Massey, Cheshire.

Figure 2   Carved walnut bench at Dunham Massey, with a central cartouche representing the Infant Hercules.

XIV Figure 1   Painted looking-glass, attributed to Jean-Baptiste Monnoyer at Melbourne Hall, Derbyshire.

Figure 2   Looking-glass, table and candlestands, possibly by John Guilbaud, at Hopetoun House, West Lothian.

XV Figure 1   Marquetry dressing-table attributed to Gerrit Jensen, at Lennoxlove, East Lothian.

Figure 2   Carved and gilt table with a boulle top and frieze, Petworth House, West Sussex.

XVI Figure 1   Carved and gilt picture-frame by Jean Pelletier, at Boughton House, Northamptonshire.

Figure 2   Carved and gilt firescreen by Jean Pelletier, at Knole in Kent.

XVII Figure 1 Silvered gesso looking-glass and table at Erddig in North Wales, attributed to John Pardoe.

Figure 2 Pier-glass in the saloon at Erddig, attributed to John Belchier.

CHAPTER 8 HUGUENOTS IN THE ENGLISH SILK INDUS-
TRY IN THE EIGHTEENTH CENTURY

XVIII Figures Papers assembled by James Leman for the
1–4 campaign to prohibit the import, use and wear of printed calicoes. Figure 3 bears notes in Leman's hand about current work. Copyright Guildhall Library, by permission of the Worshipful Company of Weavers.

Figure 5 Inscription by James Leman on the back of a design for a flowered lustring brocaded with colours. Isaac Wittington, the Wheatsheaf, Ludgate Hill, was the mercer commissioning the design. Ben Manckey, apprentice or journeyman, who was to weave it, came from a distinguished family of Canterbury weavers. This was his first work on the drawloom.
E. 4460–1909 (neg. V.IOII)

Figure 6 Detail of design by James Leman. The inscription referring to Peter Rozee, his journeyman, may be compared with that on the adjacent 'Case of the Manufacturer'.
E. 4492–1909 (neg. HE.4599)

XIX Figure 1 Design by James Leman, 1719. Point repeat, only half is drawn as it would repeat mirror fashion.
E. 4449–1909 (neg. R.1176)

Figure 2 Inscription by James Leman on the back of this design. A 'paduasoy or tabby tissue' was a heavy silk, requiring two warp systems.
(neg. HE. 4591)

Figure 3   Design by Christopher Baudouin, almost certain-
            ly intended for gold or silver thread, perhaps on a
            lustring ground.
            5973.19 (neg. HE. 4597)

Figure 4   Inscription on back of Figure 3. Together with
            Lauzun (Charles Lansoon?) and Mariscoe (Peter
            Marescoe) Monceaux was reputed by J. S. Burn
            (in 1846) to be a founder of the English silk
            industry and to be associated with the designer
            Baudouin. The handwriting and flourish are
            characteristic of Baudouin. Monceaux may have
            come from Canterbury.
            5973.19 (neg. HE. 4592)

XX Figure 1   Design by Christopher Baudouin, almost certain-
            ly intended for gold or silver thread. One of the
            'Patterns by Different Hands' belonging to Anna
            Maria Garthwaite (1690–1763).
            5973.17 (neg. HE. 4595)

Figure 2   Inscription on the back of Figure 1. James Leman
            and Peter Lekeux (II) (1684–1743) were the first
            Huguenots on the Court of the Weavers' Com-
            pany. Lekeux's uncle of the same name was Peter
            Marescoe's son-in-law. Like him, Peter Lekeux
            joined the City Trained Bands and is referred to
            by Garthwaite as 'Capn. Lekeux'. Several silks
            woven by the Lekeux family survive.
            5973.17 (neg. HE. 4596)

Figure 3   Sleeved waistcoat, designed by Anna Maria
            Garthwaite, 1747, woven by Mr Peter Lekeux
            (1716–68), the third of his name in the industry,
            Upper Bailiff of the Weavers' Company, 1764.
            Copyright Metropolitan Museum of Art (Cos-
            tume Institute) New York. C.I. 66.14.2.

XXI Figure 1   Detail from a pattern book of Batchelor, Ham
            and Perigal, c. 1755. John Perigal was described
            in 1765 as 'a weaver of silks from the slightest to
            the roughest'. Two colourways survive, others
            have been ripped out.   T. 375–1972, p. 306.

Figure 2   Detail of dress, the silk woven by Batchelor, Ham and Perigal in a different colourway to the sample. Copyright Museum of London, Z.661 (neg. 14759).

Figure 3   Detail of silk designed by Anna Maria Garthwaite, 1752, woven by Simon Julins (1687/8–1774), Booth Street, Spitalfields. There is a slightly different motif in the upper half of the design, giving a repeat 43¼ in. long. In the Museum of Fine Arts, Boston there is a pale blue version from an American family. A specialist in damasks, more silks woven by Simon Julins have appeared than those of any other weaver. T.346–1975 (neg. GF. 5336)

XXII   Figure 1   Dress, the silk designed by Anna Maria Garthwaite, 1747, woven by Mr (probably Daniel) Vautier. Her best customer, he bought 106 designs between 1741 and 1751. He offered forty-seven men to serve against the Young Pretender in 1745. T. 720–1913 (neg. R.1111)

Figure 2   Silk, watered tabby, designed by Anna Maria Garthwaite, 1752, woven by John Sabatier (c. 1701–80) who bought ninety designs between 1742 and 1756. He gave evidence on the silk industry to Parliament in 1750, 1765 and 1766 and was equally active in the Christ Church, Spitalfields, vestry. T. 10–1962 (neg. X. 1330)

XXIII   Figure 1   Sample, c. 1770, probably woven by the Duthoit family in Canterbury or London since they had branches in both cities. Copyright, Canterbury City Museums, 4967. Given by Miss Duthoit.

Figure 2   Waistcoat, silk and linen, woven by Maze and Steer, summer, 1788, identified from their pattern book now in the Victoria and Albert Museum (T. 384–1972, p. 152). Which member of the Maze family was Steer's partner is unknown. Copyright, Exeter City Museums. 71.1958.3. Given by Mrs Boger.

XXIV

Design by Anna Maria Garthwaite 1748. 'Mr Godin' was almost certainly James Godin (c. 1697–1762) an active Assistant in the Weavers' Company and partner in Godin & Ogier, of Spital Square, living in a house 'finished in a grand manner'; Governor of the French Hospital, 1742; one of the first contributors to the London Hospital, 1747, and later its Treasurer. His firm offered sixty men to fight the Young Pretender in 1745.

5986.2 (neg. V.1044.)

List of Tables, Map and Figure

TABLES

4.1 Baptisms of foreign children in Canterbury city
parishes, 1591–1600   63

4.2 Figures for aliens and natives in Canterbury Wards,
1599   64

4.3 Collections for poor relief in Canterbury, 1631–47   64

4.4 *Passants* through Canterbury, 1630/1–1647/8   65

8.1 Huguenots in the Weavers' Company of London   126

8.2 Huguenot families on Canterbury quarterage lists,
1703–63   131

MAP

11.1 Geographical distribution of Calvinists in France,
c. 1603–70   174

FIGURE

13.1 British interest in the Huguenots: a visual impression   225

Acknowledgements

Plate I, Figure 1, by courtesy of the Basel Museum of Art. Plate I Figure 2 – Plate IX inclusive, by courtesy of the Trustees of the British Museum. Plate X, Figure 1; Plate XII, Figure 1; Plate XIII, Figure 1; Plate XIV, Figure 1; Plate XV, Figures 1–2; Plate XVI, Figure 1 copyright Country Life. Plate XI; Plate XIII, Figure 2; Plate XVI, Figure 2; Plate XVII, Figures 1–2 copyright National Trust. Plate XII, Figure 2 copyright Leeds City Art Galleries. Plate X, Figure 2; Plate XIV, Figure 2, copyright Victoria and Albert Museum. Plate XVIII by courtesy of the Worshipful Company of Weavers and the Guildhall Library. Plate XX, Figure 3 copyright Metropolitan Museum of Art (Costume Institute) New York. Plate XXI, Figure 2 copyright Museum of London. Plate XXIII, Figure 1 copyright Canterbury City Museum 1967. Plate XXIII, Figure 2 copyright Exeter City Museums. All remaining plates copyright of and reproduced by courtesy of the Trustees of Victoria and Albert Museum.

Notes on the Contributors

Graham C. Gibbs is part-time Lecturer in History at Birkbeck College and Reader Emeritus in History at the University of London. He has written articles and essays on British foreign policy in the early eighteenth century and on Huguenot contributions to the intellectual life of England and the Dutch Republic in the same period. He is currently working on European sources for the parliamentary history of the reign of George I and on a study of Abel Boyer, a Huguenot man of letters, contemporary historian and journalist, who was active as a writer in the period 1694–1729. Mr Gibbs has undertaken, under the auspices of the Huguenot Society, the co-ordination of British participation in the Huguenot Refugee Research Project (*Enquête sur le Refuge Huguenot*), which will computerise records of the Huguenots in the European countries in which they mainly found refuge, from 1680 to 1715.

Robin D. Gwynn is Reader in History at Massey University, New Zealand. During 1985 he was Director of Huguenot Heritage, the national tribute (under royal patronage) to the Huguenot refugees who settled in Britain between the sixteenth and eighteenth centuries. He has made a special study of the Huguenot refugees in England, especially in the latter part of the seventeenth century and on this subject has published work in a number of journals including the *Proceedings of the Huguenot Society*. He is the author of the *Calendar of the Letter Books of the French Church of London, 1643–1659* and *Huguenot Heritage: the History and Contribution of the Huguenots in Britain*.

Gervase Jackson-Stops is Architectural Adviser to the National Trust. He held a Museums Association Studentship at the Victoria and Albert Museum before joining the staff of the National Trust in 1971. He is also a regular contributor to *Country Life* and has written for many other periodicals, including the *Burlington Magazine, Architectural History* and *Furniture History*, as well as editing National Trust Studies. He was the curator of a major exhibition, *The Treasure Houses of Britain: Five Hundred Years of Private Patronage and Art Collecting*, held at the National Gallery of Art in Washington, DC, in the winter of 1985–6, and wrote the text of a book to coincide with the exhibition entitled *The English Country House – A Grand Tour*. His previous publications include an architectural history of New College, Oxford, written for its sixth centenary in 1979.

Elisabeth Labrousse is *Maître de recherche honoraire* at the *Centre National de la Recherche Scientifique* Hon. B Litt Paris, Oxford and Geneva, and Honorary Fellow of St Hilda's College, Oxford. She is an authority on Pierre Bayle and on the history of French Protestantism of the seventeenth century. She is the author of *Une foi, une loi, un roi?* and, together with E. D. James, has in progress a critical edition of the correspondence of Pierre Bayle under the auspices of the Voltaire Foundation. She is also one of the contributors to *International Calvinism, 1541–1715*, edited by Menna Prestwich.

Roger Mettam is Senior Lecturer in History at Queen Mary College, University of London, and Chairman of the Publications Committee of the Historical Association. His books include *Government and Society in Louis XIV's France* (also published by Macmillan), *French History and Society from the Wars of Religion to the Fifth Republic* (with Douglas Johnson), *Louis XIV and the Illusion of Absolutism, Images of Power: Social and Political Propaganda in Louis XIV's France* and an edition of Voltaire, *Le siècle de Louis XIV*.

Anne M. Oakley is archivist to the Cathedral, City and Diocese of Canterbury. She is in charge of the archives of the French Church at Canterbury, which date back to the sixteenth century. As such, she is familiar with the organisation and life of that community. She has also edited volume II of the *Actes* of the French Church Threadneedle Street, London, covering 1571–7.

Menna Prestwich is Emeritus Fellow of St Hilda's College, Oxford, and was Fellow and Tutor in Modern History at the College from 1947 to 1983. Her special field is English and French seventeenth-century history. On the English side her publications include *Cranfield: Politics and Profits under the Early Stuarts*; 'English Politics and Administration, 1603–25' in *The Reign of James VI and I*, edited by A. G. R. Smith. On the French side, a book is in preparation on 'The Making of Stability in Seventeenth-century France, 1630–85'. Among her essays on this period is 'France:

Monarchy and People from Henri IV to Louis XIV' in *The Age of Expansion, Europe and the World, 1559–1660*, edited by H. R. Trevor-Roper. The tercentenary of the Revocation of the Edict of Nantes has led to her writing the introduction to, as well as editing, a book of fourteen essays by specialists, entitled *International Calvinism 1541–1715*.

Henry G. Roseveare is Reader in History at King's College, University of London. He is author of *The Treasury: The Evolution of a British Institution* and *The Treasury, 1660–1870: The Foundations of Control*. He is currently completing *Markets and Merchants*, a study of European trade in the late seventeenth century, based on extensive mercantile correspondence from Sweden, Germany, the Netherlands and France directed to Protestant immigrant merchant-houses in London.

Natalie Rothstein is Deputy Keeper in the Department of Textiles and Dress at the Victoria and Albert Museum. She is widely known to be an authority on the silk industry and production of silk materials. Whilst working on the dated and inscribed eighteenth-century silk designs in the Victoria and Albert Museum she has studied, for many years, the contributions of Huguenots to that industry and has written the captions for this subject in the catalogue, *The Quiet Conquest*, for the exhibition commemorating the Revocation of the Edict of Nantes at the Museum of London in 1985.

Irene Scouloudi is Vice-President of the Huguenot Society of London and has been Honorary Editor of the Society since 1951. She was Honorary Editor of the British Archaeological Association from 1951 to 1974 and has, for many years, studied the stranger-communities in the metropolis between 1558 and 1640 (in this she was helped by her training at the London School of Economics and also by her work as Assistant Librarian at Guildhall Library, London). Her publications include an annotated list of the *Panoramic Views of London 1600–1666; French Protestant Refugees Relieved through the Threadneedle Street Church 1681–1687* (with A. P. Hands) and *The Returns of Strangers in the Metropolis 1593 and 1627, 1635, 1639*, which completes the publication of all known Returns and includes a description of the legal, economic and social life of the strangers. She has also published numerous articles and notes in the *Proceedings of the Huguenot Society*.

N. M. Sutherland has had a varied career coming later than usual to a University post. She became Assistant Lecturer in the History Department of Bedford College, London, in 1962; Lecturer in 1964, Reader in Early Modern History in 1980 and, finally, Professor of Early Modern History at Royal Holloway and Bedford New College in 1984. Her published books include *The French Secretaries of State in the Age of Catherine de Medicis; The Massacre of St Bartholomew and the European Conflict 1559–1572* and *The Huguenot Struggle for Recognition*. She is now planning to work on the French marriage negotiations of Queen Elizabeth I.

Hugh Tait is Deputy Keeper of the Department of Medieval and Later Antiquities at the British Museum. He was trained at Cambridge University and subsequently at the Courtauld Institute. He has published in many learned art journals on various aspects of the metallurgical crafts such as clocks, watches, jewellery, as well as on glass and porcelain. He is an authority on Huguenot silver.

Hugh Trevor-Roper (Lord Dacre of Glanton) is Master of Peterhouse, Cambridge, and includes among his many publications *Archbishop Laud, The Last Days of Hitler, Religion, the Reformation and Social Change* and *Renaissance Essays*.

Randolph Vigne, President of the Huguenot Society of London from 1979 to 1986, is Treasurer of the French Hospital, La Providence, and Chairman and a Trustee of the Spitalfields Centre for the Study of Minorities. He has written on numerous subjects of Huguenot interest, including the links between British and Cape of Good Hope Huguenots.

Preface

'I have always been interested in the conversation of anyone who could tell me anything about the Huguenots; and, little by little, I have picked up many fragments of information respecting them'. Thus began the writer of an article entitled 'Traits and Stories of the Huguenots' in *Household Words* on 10 December 1853. Managing Dickens's weekly journal for him at the time was a young man who later became a great popular educator and, as Professor Sir Henry Morley, a founder-member of the Huguenot Society in 1885. He later wrote lives of Palissy – a hero to the Victorians – and Clement Marot. At a similar level, the general public rediscovered the Huguenots from Samuel Smiles in 1867, the gentry their Huguenot forebears from the Rev. D. C. A. Agnew in the previous year, and for scholars there were works by J. S. Burn and Reginald Lane Poole, where Morley had only conversation and Sir Samuel Romilly's posthumously published memoirs (1840) as his sources.

The late Victorians also became deeply interested in the Wars of Religion in France, in the guerrilla campaigns in the Cévennes and in the sufferings of the Vaudois for their faith – even more so, indeed, than in the story of the Huguenots in Britain. Popular interest in the Vaudois pastor Félix Neff and material aid for his indigent flock in the Haute Savoie was far greater, as is the way of the English, than in the starving poor of Spitalfields, many of them of Huguenot descent, after the collapse of the silk industry which the refugees had built up. It seemed very proper that the good old General Beckwith, who had lost a leg at Waterloo, should settle among, and devote his later life to, the welfare and evangelical faith of the Vaudois in Piedmont, whose woes had been lamented by the English, off and on, since the days of Milton's sonnet.

Then in 1885 a London civil engineer called Arthur Giraud Browning, proud of his family's eighteenth century Vaudois roots and involved at first hand with the distressed Huguenot community of east London through his directorship of the senior Huguenot charity, the French Hospital, La Providence, called together some fellow-directors and, over dinner, constituted with them the Huguenot Society of London.

Their enthusiasm carried the Society into the new century: since 1892 the membership had been over 400 and included most of the specialists in the field. By 1902 eighteen Quarto volumes of Huguenot church registers and other original records, and twenty-two parts of *Proceedings* had been published. For reasons suggested in the concluding essay in this collection, public, and hence scholarly and academic, interest in the Huguenots had suddenly come to an end and silence seems to have greeted the labours of these researchers into the Huguenot past. Though the Huguenot Society has survived a century's pursuit of its founders' objects, the chief of which is the 'publication and interchange of knowledge' about the Huguenots, the silence outside has scarcely been broken.

Until 1985, that is. That year saw an unexpectedly positive response to the efforts of the Huguenot Society to reawaken in the British public an awareness of the *circa* 40 000 subjects of Louis XIV who came here as part of the *Grand Refuge* in the years around 1685 as well as of the earlier waves of strangers escaping religious persecution in Flanders and France from the mid-sixteenth century.

The 1980s equivalent of Smiles readers may be seen as those who watch improving television programmes early on Sunday evenings: over 2000 letters reached the Huguenot Society in response to an excellent programme of that description shown in December 1985. Can it also be that the essays in this collection mark, with two or three other scholarly works, the return of the Huguenots to the study of history in this country?

If they do, the Society, as conveners of the historical conference on 'Britain and the Huguenots' held at the Royal Society and the British Museum (both institutions fully conscious of the major role played by Huguenot refugees in their development) on 24 and 25 September 1985 may have confidence that these participants' contributions will help to maintain the study of the Huguenots by historians and their students in Britain. They will not be the only gainers. The indifference that we met, before 1985, when seeking to interest British publishers, producers, editors and many academics in plans for commemorating the tercentenary of the Revocation of the Edict of Nantes was matched by the ignorance and scepticism about Britain's share in the Huguenot Diaspora that some of us found, even among historians of the subject, when attending functions on the continent during the tercentenary year.

These essays are offered by teachers and researchers who have worked at times in neglected fields where work cannot make its mark merely by being modish or in step. Each one is a delight in its own way, and the whole has gained much from the editorship of Miss

Irene Scouloudi, in the year of her retirement as one of only four Honorary Secretaries who have nurtured the Huguenot Society, while Presidents have come and gone, through its hundred years. In her thirty-four years in this office she has also produced some of our most valuable Quarto Series volumes. As well as filling the role I have described, this book is her well-earned *Festschrift*.

RANDOLPH VIGNE
PRESIDENT

President, Huguenot Society   *May 1986*

Part I
Huguenots in Britain

1 A Huguenot Historian: Paul Rapin

Hugh Trevor-Roper

Anyone who studies the historical writing of the eighteenth century soon becomes aware of the great contribution – great at least in bulk – of *émigré* Huguenot scholars, the victims of the Revocation of the Edict of Nantes in 1685. Driven out of France, dissidents from the established culture of the *grand siècle*, and yet, at the same time, self-consciously French, refusing to be assimilated – at least for so long as they might hope to return with dignity to France – into the society of their host-countries, they became the representatives of an alternative France, the intermediaries between the two cultures of Europe: the firm classical–Catholic–Cartesian synthesis of the France of Louis XIV and the diversity of Europe.[1]

If we ask what was the general intellectual characteristic of the Huguenot Diaspora, the answer must be that it was essentially critical, not constructive. The Huguenots had always rejected the Catholic synthesis, the grand scheme of history set out by the greatest of their persecutors, Bishop Bossuet; but in exile they also escaped from their own. As long as they had been a depressed minority in France, they had been dominated by their clergy, preaching doctrines of self-defence: fundamentalist, prophetic, apocalyptic – the expression of a siege-mentality. But in exile the situation changed. Some of their pastors, like Pierre Jurieu, 'the Grand Inquisitor of the *Refuge*', tried hard, by anathemas and persecution, to keep their flocks faithful to the old doctrines and discipline; but that was now difficult. In the new open pastures to which they had escaped, many of the sheep – and some of the pastors themselves – ran riot. They faced the necessity, or discovered the luxury, of doubt.

The two most famous of the *émigrés*, Pierre Bayle and Jean Leclerc,[2] adversaries in almost everything else, agreed in one thing: that there was no certainty, no possible system, in history. Of Bayle's great *Dictionaire Historique et Critique*, 'there is not a single page' says Voltaire 'which does not lead the reader to doubt, and often to disbelief',[3] but he would also add that it was 'the first work of this kind from which one can learn to think';[4] and Leclerc, attempting to formulate the rules of history, concluded that it was so difficult to arrive at historical truth, which was nevertheless so important, that very few persons should be allowed to write it: for to get it wrong could be fatal. On this his fellow-Huguenot Henri Basnage de Beauval commented that 'his reflexions tend to fortify historical Pyrrhonism'.[5]

'Historical Pyrrhonism', scepticism, distrust of all great schemes of history – that was the chief contribution of the Huguenots to the study of history in the half-century after the Revocation. Because they had not been assimilated into French culture, and because they refused, for that time, to be assimilated into the culture of their host-countries, they became a distinct, coherent 'third force' dissolving the certainties of the previous century. Thereby they gave a new character to historical philosophy: 'Pyrrhonism' was to be its chief characteristic throughout that period – a period in which the great systems of the past were dismantled in preparation for the new synthesis of the Enlightenment.

However, the work of the Huguenot historians was not entirely destructive. They responded to their own challenge. For if the historical systems of the past were inadmissible, and had to be disintegrated, how was the historian to begin again? Obviously he must go back to first principles, re-examine the sources, collect and test the facts, eliminate the conjectures and prejudices, and so provide a new basis on which, perhaps, a more accurate system could afterwards be built. So the Huguenot scholars took to the study of detailed, factual, objective history with the same scrupulous technical exactitude which their more practical co-religionists devoted to jewellery, enamelling, clock-making, and other delicate mechanical crafts. Serious-minded, industrious collectors and compilers, pedestrian writers, critical not constructive, judicious not elegant or vivacious, they compiled great 'lexicons', edited huge collections of documents. Their enemies complained that thereby they smothered all thought and drove men, through despair, even deeper into Pyrrhonism. But stronger minds knew how to use their labours, and today we can still detect their relics pickled in the footnotes of Gibbon or half-dissolved in the easily-flowing prose of Voltaire.

I have spoken of the Huguenot historians as a coherent 'third force' in the intellectual world. Their cohesion came from the French language, which they insisted on using, and from their ubiquitous international journalism. Bayle's *Nouvelles de la République des Lettres*, Leclerc's *Bibliothèque Universelle et Historique* with its successors – both of them the single-handed work of their editors – were but the most famous of a whole series of international periodicals which disseminated the critical scholarship of the Huguenot Diaspora throughout Europe. There was also Henri Basnage de Beauval's *Histoire des Ouvrages des Savants* and the *Journal Littéraire de la Haye*. There was the *Bibliothèque Germanique* through which the Huguenot circle in Berlin – a very active circle, thanks to the patronage of Queen Sophie Charlotte and then of Frederick the Great – sought to make the literature of Northern Europe (and of course their own works) known throughout Europe. There was the *Bibliothèque Anglaise* which did the same for English literature, and its successor the *Journal Britannique* of Matthew Maty, the friend, incidentally, of the young Gibbon, whose own short-lived periodical, *Mémoires Littéraires de la Grande Bretagne* is a late entrant in the competition. Nearly all these periodicals were published in Holland – in Rotterdam, Amsterdam or the Hague. Holland remained to the end their intellectual and publishing centre, the place where, since the last years of Charles II, English Whigs had taken refuge and English ideas were translated into French by exiled Huguenots and thus supplied to the European Republic of Letters.

This conference is concerned with the Huguenots and Great Britain, and having thus prepared the ground, I shall devote the rest of this lecture to the Huguenot writer who did most to explain English history and the English political system to Europe. In so doing, he had a considerable influence both in England and in Europe; for in England he provided the first systematic 'Whig interpretation' of its history and in France he gave ideas to Montesquieu and Voltaire. I refer to Paul Rapin de Thoyras, described by Erich Haase as the only Huguenot historian 'who knew how to combine the objective collection of facts with a clear opinion of his own'.[6]

Paul Rapin came of a Savoyard family which, having been converted to Protestantism, had emigrated to France in the reign of François I and had settled in Huguenot Languedoc.[7] His father, Jacques Rapin, sieur de Thoyras, was a lawyer at Castres and later at Toulouse; his mother, Jeanne Pellisson, also came of a Huguenot legal family and was the sister of that Paul Pellisson who, having been converted to Catholicism and put in charge of the notorious *caisse de conversions*, played a significant, not to say sinister, part in the conversion of his co-religionists before the Revocation of the Edict. Paul Rapin studied at the Huguenot academy of Puylaurens, where Pierre Bayle had been before him, and then at the more liberal academy of Saumur, where

Leclerc had studied. He was destined for the law, but in 1679 the suppression of the *Chambres de l'Edit*, in which his father pleaded, closed that prospect, and he was pressed by his now famous uncle to change his religion in order to open another. This he did not do, and in 1686, a year after the Revocation, his father being now dead, he left France and, with his younger brother Salomon, went to England.

Rapin had personal reasons to choose England; but once there, he soon found that the England of James II was not much more comfortable, for an obstinate Huguenot, than the France of Louis XIV. There too the *convertisseurs* were now at work, and Rapin discovered that he had escaped the attentions of his uncle Pellisson only to incur those of the French Ambassador Paul Barillon and Pellisson's persuasive friend the abbé de Denbeck. He therefore moved on to the Netherlands where his cousin, Daniel de Rapin, commanded a company of French – that is, Huguenot – volunteers. Rapin enlisted in this company, and it was as an officer of the Prince of Orange that he found himself returning to England to take part in the great adventure of 1688.

Rapin landed with William at Torbay, served him in England throughout the revolution there, and then accompanied him on his expedition to reconquer Ireland. There he fought in the battle of the Boyne, was wounded in the assault on Limerick, and took part in the capture of the supposedly impregnable citadel of Athlone. Then he was stationed at Kinsale. William's governor of Kinsale was James Waller a son of the regicide Sir Hardress Waller, and it was he (as Rapin would afterwards write) who first turned his thoughts towards the historical significance of these events in English as well as in European history. It was in Kinsale that he first entertained the idea of studying the history of this mysterious island, which had suddenly become so important, and explaining it, as only a Huguenot was qualified to do, to the inquisitive but baffled observers in Europe.

They had good reason to be baffled by recent events. In 1686, when Rapin had first visited England, Louis XIV was at the height of his power, the master, it seemed of Europe, and James II, having defeated all attempts to prevent his succession or challenge his authority, was securely established as his willing puppet. When Rapin moved on to Holland, that impression could only be confirmed. In Holland – *'la grande Arche des fugitifs'* as Bayle called it – he found not only the Huguenots driven from France but also the English Whig statesmen and thinkers who, since 1680, had found it prudent to escape from England. Among them were famous names – Algernon

Sidney, Gilbert Burnet, John Locke. All these men pinned their hopes on the half-English *stadhouder* William of Orange. To the Huguenots, he was the only leader of European resistance to their oppressor, Louis XIV, the only man who might secure their return to France. To the English Whigs he was the only practical alternative to James II as King of England. But how chimerical these hopes must have seemed in face of such securely established power! Then suddenly, less than two years later, the revolution in England changed everything. By 1691 William of Orange was effective ruler of all three kingdoms, ready to throw their resources into the war against France. Seen from Kinsale, after the collapse of resistance in Ireland, the revolution in England might well be a turning-point in European history.

However, first things first. If Rapin were to pursue his historical studies, he must exchange his accidental military career for some more scholarly employment. Luckily, in 1693, while he was still at Kinsale, an opportunity presented itself. William's Dutch friend, Hans Willem Bentinck, Earl of Portland, needed a tutor for his eldest son, Lord Woodstock, then 11 years old. William's Huguenot general in Ireland, the Marquis de Ruvigny, recommended Rapin, praising him not only for his intellectual gifts but also for '*un certain air du beau monde et ces manières nobles et aisées qu'on n'attrape qu'avec gens de qualité*'. William urged Rapin to accept the post; and he accepted it.[8] For the next thirteen years Rapin was employed by Portland, living sometimes in England but mainly, it seems in the Bentinck house at the Hague. He does not seem to have written much, if anything, in these years. No doubt he was reading; but the time of a tutor in a great nobleman's house was not his own, and it was liable to inconvenient interruptions.

One such interruption occurred in 1698, after the Treaty of Ryswick, which ended the War of the Grand Alliance, begun in 1689. By this treaty Louis XIV was forced to concede failure and to recognise William III as King of England. William thereupon sent Portland as his ambassador to Paris. It was a very splendid embassy, and the envoy of so formidable a ruler was treated with great deference: Louis XIV himself, according to Saint-Simon, welcomed Portland '*comme une espèce de divinité*'. Rapin accompanied Portland to Paris and, in the two years that he spent there, could observe the interest in England and in the mysterious strength which it had drawn from revolution. Then, in 1700, with the resumption of the war, the embassy ceased; Portland returned to Holland, taking Rapin with him; and next year Rapin was required to complete his service by accompanying his pupil, now 18 years old, on a Grand Tour. Because of the war, France was excluded from the itinerary, which was confined to allied or neutral countries: Germany, Austria and parts of Italy. The letters in which Rapin reported to Portland on the plans and progress of the tour do not suggest that he enjoyed it much.[9] He was not, I think, a man given to enjoyment. But they are interesting as showing, among other things, his attitude towards England, the country whose history he undertook to interpret to Europe.

Ever since the Reformation, the Huguenot exiles in England had been ambivalent towards their host-country. On the one hand, as Protestants and victims of oppression, they admired its Protestantism and its liberty. On the other hand, as Frenchmen, and rather priggish Frenchmen too, they looked down on its lack of civilisation. When planning the tour, Rapin urged Portland on no account to yield to his son's desire to begin it in England. At present, he explained, Lord Woodstock was docile; but if he were to start a European tour in a country 'where he will see so many bad examples', all would be over: 'the air and manners of *les jeunes seigneurs anglais*', their shocking conversation and barbarous behaviour, were only too catching, and they would undoubtedly incite him 'to shake off the yoke of an inconvenient tutor'.[10] These observations were, alas, only too true, as Mr Graham C. Gibbs has shown in the case of the unfortunate Huguenot tutor of Lord Wharton.

However, it may be some consolation to our national pride that during the tour (which did not include England) Rapin found almost all other peoples almost as disagreeable. The Austrians, he observed, are insufferably proud and stuffy, the Germans unsociable, pompous and ignorant; Italians look down on all other nations as stupid and easy to cheat and treat them with contemptuous *insouciance*: cardinals, who had been so liberal with their invitations in the freedom and safety of the carnival at Venice, forgot all about them when back in their palaces in Rome; etc., etc. Rapin also complained that everything everywhere was very expensive; that Lord Woodstock's valet, undermining his careful tutor, encouraged him to wasteful largesse; that Lord Woodstock himself preferred the company of flighty girls to that of grave elderly statesmen; and that Italy, in this time of war, was not at all safe for any of them: if Lord Woodstock should be captured by brigands, he would be very expensive to ransom. It was all very trying, and by the end of the tour Rapin was regretting that he had ever accepted his present position: if he had stayed in the army, he wrote, he would have been a major by now.

From these exasperating travels Rapin returned with relief to the Hague. He was back before the end of 1702, and remained for another two years in the Portland household. Then, in 1704, Lord Woodstock married and established himself in England: his wife was English, and he became a Member of Parliament – Whig of course – for Southampton. Rapin's employment by the family therefore came to an end: now at least he was his own master, and being now married – to a Huguenot lady of course, who, we are told, was *'jeune, riche et surtout vertueuse'* – he could settle down to a life of scholarship and literature.

Rapin's life in the Hague, in these years, was agreeable enough. He had the stimulus of learned and congenial – that is, other Huguenot – society: for in Holland, as in England, he lived, as most of the *émigrés* lived, in a small Huguenot circle. He was in touch with Leclerc, whom he had known in Saumur, and through him with the Huguenot Republic of Letters. His closest friends in the Hague were Abel Rotolp, sieur de la Devèze, the author of an *Apologie pour les Refugiés*, and Jean Rou, a scholarly lawyer whose splendid and costly compilation of chronological and genealogical tables had been seized in proof and burnt in Paris at the instigation of Bossuet. The bishop, it seems, had detected in it some whiff of heresy. Rou was now – thanks to the patronage of William III and the Grand Pensionary Francis Fagel – official interpreter to the States General. Rapin had introduced him to the Portland family to teach Lord Woodstock law, and did his best to have Rou's *Tables Chronologiques* published in Holland; but the Dutch printers boggled at the cost. Rou, in turn, helped Rapin with his historical studies, which, from now on, were his main preoccupation: it was in 1705, on his release from his employment in the Portland family, that he began at last to write his *History of England*.[11]

Rotolp de la Devèze and Rou were founder-members of a scholarly Huguenot club which met every week for learned discussion. This *'petite academie'* as Rou called it, had been founded when Rapin was abroad; but when he returned, they made him a member of it. Others who were co-opted into it were Henri Basnage de Beauval, the author of the *Histoire des Ouvrages des Savants*, and his brother, the clerical statesman Jacques Basnage. At first, having seven members, this club was called *la Plëiade*; afterwards, having increased its numbers, it became *la Féauté*. After Rapin had joined it, it met regularly in his elegant house in the Hague.[12]

Alas, this idyllic existence did not last long. Life at the Hague was expensive. Rapin's means, now that he was no longer maintained by Lord Portland, were limited. The pension somewhat belatedly granted to him by William III had expired with the King in 1702 and was not renewed by the States General. His wife's income was evidently inadequate to maintain their accustomed style; so, in 1707 he moved to Wesel in the Duchy of Cleves. Since Cleves was now under Prussian rule, he was still in approved Huguenot territory, and could communicate easily with the Huguenot scholars in Berlin. He spent the rest of his life at Wesel concentrating on his literary work.

For several years Rapin kept his work secret. Only Rou, it seems, knew of his plans; and Rapin insisted that Rou was to mention them to nobody: any publicity on this subject, he said, could only damage him.[13] Why he was so secretive, we do not know. Perhaps it was a personal trait, perhaps merely the suspiciousness of an *émigré*. Perhaps also it was through fear of competition. For there was a competitor in the field. This was Isaac de Larrey.

Isaac de Larrey, seigneur de Grandchamp et de Commesnil, was a Huguenot from Normandy who, like Rapin, had been trained as a lawyer. After the Revocation he had left France for Berlin, been patronised by Queen Sophia Charlotte and employed as counsellor to the Prussian embassy at the Hague. There he had become aware of the demand for a history of England, and in spite of discouragement from British friends, who doubted his capacity, he set to work, and in 1697–8 – the time of the peace of Ryswick – he published, at Rotterdam, two huge volumes covering the period 1485–1625. Two more volumes, he announced, would cover the medieval period and the period 1625–88. The third – the most modern – volume in fact appeared in 1707. Fortunately for Rapin, the work of his rival, after initial applause, sank to its true level, and by the time the last volume – the medieval – was published in 1713, it was clear that the great gap was still unfilled.[14] Then Rapin came out of his secret closet. In 1714 the Huguenot *Journal Litteraire* of the Hague, deploring the absence of any good history of England, announced, *en passant*, that such a work was at last in preparation, that it would be far more exact than anything published hitherto, and that the author was 'a very able man who has been working on it for several years'. This very able man was Rapin, to whose slow and secret work, first in the Hague, then in Wesel, we may now turn.

Rapin's plan of work was not consistent.[15] At first, he tells us, he had planned to begin with the Norman Conquest, but then, seeking for causes and origins, he moved back to the Anglo-Saxons. Soon he was in love with the Anglo-Saxons. This, of course, was a sound Whig romance: English Whigs saw the Anglo-Saxons as the inventors of

Parliament, and even Tories like Clarendon accepted the view that William the Conqueror had not subverted but continued the good old Anglo-Saxon constitution. It was also, *mutatis mutandis*, a sound Huguenot doctrine: the sixteenth-century Huguenot publicist François Hotman had similarly insisted that the Germanic Franks had brought into Roman Gaul the free institutions which later French kings, with their revived Roman ideas, had subverted. Having fallen for the Anglo-Saxons, Rapin decided to stay with them and to go no further forward than the reign of Henry II, in whose reign the Norman conquest was rounded off by the conquest of Ireland. This would have been an elegant close to a study inspired by Rapin's own part in the reconquest of Ireland by William III.

It seems that this decision was inspired partly by mere fatigue: that Rapin's original impetus was failing. For clearly he was becoming bored in Wesel. Life there might be cheap but it was also very dull. As he wrote to his fellow-Huguenot in Berlin, Paul-Emile de Mauclerc, one of the editors of the *Bibliothèque Germanique*, he was starved of intelligent conversation and had no one who could encourage him or criticise his work. If only he were back in the Hague, he sighed, or even in Berlin! But in Wesel he met only soldiers, talking endlessly of war ... However, just as he was about to give up, a fresh wind from England filled his sagging sails. It was like that timely 'Protestant wind' which had carried William of Orange into Torbay. Now it carried Rapin forward to the completion of his work. This timely assistance was the arrival on the continent of Rymer's *Foedera*.

Rymer's *Foedera* is a massive compilation of all the treaties entered into by the Crown of England since the Norman Conquest. It had been commissioned by Charles Montagu, Earl of Halifax, the Whig minister of William III, in imitation of Leibniz's *Corpus Juris Gentium Diplomaticum*. The chosen editor, Thomas Rymer, was a sturdy Whig whose father had been hanged for treason under Charles II. The work began to appear in 1704. By then William III was dead and had been succeeded by the Tory Queen Anne, who hated his memory and could not bear to hear his name; but this little dynastic accident, which might have disconcerted a more sensitive editor, had no effect on the hardy bigot Rymer. Indeed it only stimulated his Whig zeal. In an unctuous dedication of his fourth volume to the Queen he drew her attention to the interesting parallel between the reign of her father James II and that of another deposed King, Edward II. In particular he invited her to rejoice that during that 'most unprosperous and disastrous administration ... amidst the greatest confusion and dismal jumble of affairs', Almighty Providence had sanctioned an alliance with 'William III, surnamed the Good, Count of Holland ... whereby those measures were concerted which, in the next succeeding reign carried English arms victorious into France'. Luckily Queen Anne is unlikely to have read this insolent dedication.

In order to promote Rymer's work abroad, Halifax had copies of it sent to Leclerc in Rotterdam, for review in his *Bibliothèque Choisie*. Leclerc duly published an abstract of the first volume in 1708; but then, 'having so many other important engagements in the Republic of Literature', passed on the remaining volumes, as they came in, to 'a gentleman of merit who is working on the history of England'. This gentleman was of course Rapin, now bored beyond endurance by the conversation of colonels in Wesel.

The arrival of Rymer's *Foedera* restored the drooping spirits of Rapin. He made abstracts of each volume as it arrived – fifteen volumes had been published when Rymer died in 1713 and the sixteenth was in the press – and these abstracts were duly published by Leclerc. They were so admired that the Grand Pensionary Heinsius caused them to be collected together and printed as an official document for the use of the States General. For this edition Rapin also wrote an abstract of the first volume to replace the more superficial review by Leclerc. This volume was afterwards translated into English and published in England as *Acta Regia*.

Rymer's *Foedera*, with its original documents, reanimated Rapin's *History*, offering it a firm and continuous spinal cord. He now worked on both concurrently, abstracting the one and composing the other, in order, as he wrote, 'to show the relation which the documents bear to the events which we meet in his *History* and to illustrate the one by the other'. It was an application of the new historical method of Mabillon and Leibniz. But it was also more than that. For Rapin also had a thesis: a thesis which he derived from his Huguenot predecessors of the sixteenth century and which had been fortified by his contact with the English Whigs. This thesis he was enabled to ventilate, even before he had completed any part of his book, by a fortunate incident in 1714.

For in 1714 Queen Anne died. Her last government – the high Tory government of Lord Bolingbroke – had just ended the war against France by the Treaty of Utrecht. That treaty marked the final frustration of Louis XIV's grandiose ambitions and left Great Britain the arbiter of Europe; but it was also regarded by the English Whigs and their Dutch and Huguenot allies as a betrayal: a 'shameful precipitate peace', Rapin would call it, 'which has filled all Europe with amazement and indignation'.[16] Now the Queen's death brought a sudden and welcome reversal. The new German dynasty came in; the Tories were removed from power; and the old Whigs came back. Naturally all Europe was excited by this sudden change – excited but also perplexed: what, men asked, did it mean?

At Wesel, at the house of the Prussian governor of Cleves, Field-Marshall Count von Lottum, the conversation one day was all about these extraordinary English parties: what on earth were Whigs and Tories? Rapin was there, but did not think, from what he heard, that those present 'had a very distinct knowledge of those two parties'. So, to clarify his own ideas, he wrote a paper on the subject. Some time afterwards he was visited at Wesel by a courtly Whig virtuoso, Sir Andrew Fountaine, to whom he showed the paper. Sir Andrew was greatly impressed by it and urged that it be published. It was published at The Hague in 1717, in French, as *A Dissertation concerning the Whigs and the Tories*.

This pamphlet was a huge success in Europe. Translated into English, Dutch, Danish, Spanish and German, it was frequently reprinted. Of the French version alone there were ten editions in the next hundred years. This journalistic triumph was well-deserved, for it was a lucid, temperate, sensible explanation, by means of history, of otherwise unintelligible politics. Whether that history was correct is another matter, which we can leave for the moment. The essential fact was that it became 'the standard textbook on the subject, accepted as authoritative even in England'.[17] 'These few pages', says a Swiss historian, 'place their author in the forefront of modern publicists'.[18]

Meanwhile Rapin pressed on with his *History*. By 1722 he had reached 1640 and there he thought that he would stop; for how, he asked, could he compete with 'milord Clarendon', whose classic account of the Great Rebellion had now been published? Nor were the years after 1660 any easier: 'in view of the present state of parties in England', he doubted whether he could handle *'un morceau si délicat et si difficile'*.[19] However, pressed by his friends in Berlin and Rotterdam, he overcame his doubts and persevered until 1649, the execution of Charles I. Then at last he broke covert. In 1723, having whetted the appetite of his readers by extracts published in the *Bibliothèque Germanique* and in Leclerc's *Bibliothèque Ancienne et Moderne*, he published the whole work so far written. It was published at the Hague in eight volumes, fulsomely dedicated to the Hanoverian King of Great Britain, the client and patron of the Whigs, George I.

It was the right moment, for just at that time the English Whigs were taking steps to recover the historiographical initiative, lost to the Tories in the reign of Anne. Next year they established the Regius Chairs of History in the British universities: an act prompted by the Whig Bishop of London, Edmund Gibson, and hailed with absurd rapture by the pushing young Whig clergyman William Warburton.[20] In the same year the first volume of Bishop Burnet's posthumous *History of his own Time* was published, giving a sound Whig account of the reigns of Charles II and James II. This last work was particularly timely: it spurred Rapin to further efforts, and when he died, in 1725, he left the manuscript of two more volumes which carried his *History* down to the coronation of William and Mary in 1689. These last two volumes were prepared for the press by his fellow-Huguenot David Durand, a minister first in the Hague, then in London, and were published in 1727. Simultaneously an English translation was published in London.

'*1723, voilà une date vraiment importante dans l'histoire des idées*', exclaims Joseph Dedieu: Rapin has captured French public opinion and from now on he will be, for Frenchmen, the teacher of English history, the interpreter of English liberty.[21] That, of course, was what he set out to be: it was the function of the Huguenot scholars. But he also did more than this. He captured the Protestant world too. In particular he captured England itself.

For the next generation Rapin's work was the standard history of England. It was accepted as a classic throughout Europe. Catholic and Protestant, English and French, Whig and Tory vied to praise it. Even the Jesuits of Trevoux printed an edition of this Huguenot work, adjusting the text where expedient. In England, it was praised, even by Tories, for its judiciousness. Bolingbroke was a subscriber to it. Six editions of the French text, five of the English translation, were printed in the next thirty years. An English historical catechism based on it ran through twenty-four editions in the remainder of the eighteenth century. It was, men said, the only impartial history of England.

That indeed was Rapin's own claim. Being quite independent of English parties or English patrons, and writing only for foreigners, he was, he said, 'free from all party passion and prejudice'. (The same claim had been made by the unfortunate Isaac de Larrey, but he was now quite forgotten.) Rapin's claim was endorsed by Voltaire, who wrote that his was the only complete and impartial history '*d'un pays où l'on n'écrivait que par esprit de parti*', the nearest thing to a perfect history in all Europe. And Voltaire's praise was echoed by the editor of the sixth French edition, who explained that he had republished the work of this Frenchman because the English themselves, owing to their party spirit, were incapable of historical impartiality.

Rapin was certainly different from the English writers of his time. He was certainly judicious, cautious, temperate. But was he in fact impartial? Of course he was not. How could he be when his life had been spent – in so far as it was spent among Englishmen – entirely among Whigs? For neither Rapin nor any other Huguenot historian was able to transcend the limits of their situation. They were intermediaries, interpreters, critics, not thinkers. If they contributed to the thought of Europe, it was by demolition, not construction. Rapin tried to construct, but as he had no originality of mind, as he was essentially a journalist, not a thinker, he only interpreted and systematised the Huguenot history that he had read in France and the Whig theories that he had heard in England. So he produced, just as the Whig Ascendancy was being consolidated in England, the classic exposition of the Whig – the 'old whig' – interpretation of history.

It was the doctrine of the ancient English constitution, with its guarantee of liberty through the separation of powers. Such a constitution (said Rapin, following Hotman) had once been common to all the Germanic nations, but in all the other nations it had succumbed to royal usurpation. Only in England had it been preserved intact. So English history became the history of its preservation, and Rapin described in turn the German origins of the parliamentary constitution, its introduction into England by the invading Saxons, the absorption of the Norman Conquest, the Whig principles of the medieval barons, the constitutional propriety of the Lancastrians and Tudors, the Stuart betrayal. It was a story of aristocratic virtue, of conservatism, of continuity: the English nobility, the ancestors of the grandees who had called William of Orange and the Hanoverians to the throne, had been the guardians of their constitution (how different from the domesticated Catholic nobility of France who had betrayed theirs!): 'more Kings since the Conquest have mounted the throne by virtue of Acts of Parliament, or some other means' (he prudently adds) 'than by hereditary right'; and the four English kings who, with the support of the high Tories of their time, had attempted to break the constitution – Edward II, Richard II, Charles I and James II – had all come, deservedly, to sticky ends.

Such was the historical philosophy which a Huguenot historian, uniting the theories of sixteenth-century French Huguenots and seventeenth-century English Whigs, presented to eighteenth-century

Europe. It was a philosophy of idealist conservatism. There is no suggestion in it that change has occurred or should occur in history: no reference to economic life or to ideas. The English constitution that was vindicated in 1688 was, according to Rapin, the identical constitution which the Anglo-Saxons had brought with them from Germany. In 1729, when Montesquieu came to England and was bowled over by his experience of English liberty, Rapin's work was the classic explanation of it; and he swallowed it. We have only to read that splendid work, the *Germania* of Tacitus, he wrote, to see that there lies the source of the English government: *'ce beau systeme a été trouvé dans les bois'.*[22] Voltaire, who came a few years later, was less certain: *'la Chambre de Pairs et des Communes, la cour d'Equité, trouveés dans les bois!'* he exclaimed, *'on ne l'aurait pas deviné'.*[23]

Of course there were dissenting voices in England too, especially from Tories and Jacobites, who were particularly enraged that a foreigner should take it upon himself to interpret their history. The Tories were now the national party, defenders of true-born Englishmen against interloping Dutchmen and Germans; and French Huguenots, they thought, were no better. The Jacobite Thomas Rawlinson even approved of the Whig Regius Chairs at the universities since at least they would save the sons of English noblemen from being taught history and languages by 'ignorant French Huguenots and Scotch pedlars'.[24] The Jacobite, Samuel Jebb, a doctor of medicine, accused Rapin of 'all imaginable want of accuracy and judgment' in whatever concerned Mary Queen of Scots,[25] and the Jacobite antiquary Thomas Carte (who described himself provocatively as 'an Englishman') found him 'utterly unacquainted with our constitution, laws and customs', having picked up his meagre knowledge of them in 'coffee-houses, the common habitation of his countrymen in this city'. Carte particularly disapproved of Rapin's thesis that the national constitution of England was the 'Whig' system brought in by the Anglo-Saxons. The Anglo-Saxons, to him, were foreign invaders from Germany, like the Hanoverians, and their constitution was an improper German innovation. The true national constitution (he said) was that of the ancient Britons; and that was High Tory and clerical, having been devised for them by their clergy, the divinely ordained and universally respected Druids, who had 'their ordinary abode in colleges, retired from the world'.[26]

The Jacobites, the Tories, the modern Druids in their Oxford colleges, were unable to dethrone Rapin. Just as the Whig ascendancy itself was beginning to crumble, he was dethroned by a far greater man who, unlike him, was capable of original thought and could base his historical writing on radically new ideas – in short, by a man of genius: David Hume. Though Hume never cites Rapin's work in his *History of England*, it is clear that he had it continuously in his eye; and indeed, our considerable pleasure in reading Hume's *History* is increased if we are aware of the unspoken controversy which lurks behind it: if we recognise the sacred cows of Rapin's Whig orthodoxy – the virtuous Anglo-Saxons, the early Parliament, the medieval barons, Magna Carta, Simon de Montfort, the Reformers, the Scotch Covenanters, the Whig patriots – tumbling one by one to that exquisite marksmanship. To Hume the whole idea of history as the defence of a static system through the centuries was absurd. History, to him, was historical change, the transformation of the economy, the sophistication of manners, the improvement of life and thought, not the stubborn defence of an unchanging inheritance from the Dark Ages. His view of his predecessor, implicit in his *History*, emerges openly from the private letters which he wrote while at work on it. 'You know', he wrote, while engaged on his first volume, 'that there is no post of honour in the English Parnassus more vacant than that of History. Style, judgement, impartiality – everything is wanting to our historians, and even Rapin, during this later period' – for Hume began his work with the Stuarts – 'is extremely deficient'. A little later, he would express himself more strongly:

> the more I advance in my undertaking, the more I am convinced that the History of England has never yet been written, not only for style, which is notorious to all the world, but also for matter; such is the ignorance and partiality of all our historians. Rapin, whom I had an esteem for, is totally worthless.[27]

Nearly a century later, when Macaulay set out to restore Whig history it was Hume whom he set out to dethrone; but he dethroned him by accepting the essence of his thought – the central concept of material progress – and changing its political implications. He did not attempt to restore the obsolete Whig conservatism of Rapin.

Nevertheless, at a less sophisticated level, Rapin's thesis detached from his name, survived. Englishmen have generally been proud of their history and like to emphasise its continuity, and that sense of continuity, which Hume had temporarily disintegrated, was strengthened in the nineteenth-century. Then the middle classes took over the aristocratic institutions of the past and, while transforming their substance, gave their forms a new lease of life. The romantic movement, the Gothic Revival, the rebuilding of the Palace of Westminster, and its decoration with frescos and statues commemorating – sometimes very inappropriately – the continuous history of Parliament, all supported the old Whig thesis, which at one level, the level of forms, is real enough. It is agreeable to think that the classic and most extreme version of that patriotic thesis was expressed not for Englishmen or by an Englishman but for foreigners by an author who had no great love for the English: by a French Huguenot who, having come over with Dutch William and served him in Ireland, afterwards retired to Germany and wrote in French, for publication in Holland, the first complete history of England.

Notes

1. For the general character of Huguenot literature and scholarship, I am much indebted to the posthumously published work of Erich Haase, *Einführung in die Literatur des Refuge* (Berlin, 1959).
2. At the conference, Madame Elisabeth Labrousse objected to my inclusion of Leclerc among the Huguenots on the ground that he was an Arminian who left Calvinist Geneva because of its intolerance. However, exactly the same could be said of Isaac Casaubon a century before; and we generally regard him as a Huguenot. The Huguenot Diaspora, for me, consists of all those French Protestants who were forced, or preferred, to live outside France.
3. Voltaire, *Siècle de Louis XIV (catalogue des ecrivains)*.
4. Voltaire, *Oeuvres Complètes* (Paris, 1825) Vol. XXXIV, pp. 326–8.
5. J. Leclerc, *Parrhasiana* (Amsterdam, 1699–1701) I, p. 137, cited in E. Haase, *Einführung*, pp. 433–4.
6. E. Haase, *Einführung*, p. 400.
7. For Rapin's biography see Raoul de Cazenove, *Rapin–Thoyras, sa famille et ses oeuvres* (Paris, 1866).
8. This is stated by Jean Rou, who no doubt had it from Rapin: '*c'estoit sa Majesté même, le grand Guillaume, qui l'avoit obligé de se charger de cette commission*'. (Jean Rou, *Memoires inédits et opuscules*, edited by F. Waddington, (Paris, 1857), Vol. II, p. 226.
9. The originals of these letters, the property of the Duke of Portland, are deposited in the Nottingham University Library. There are copies in the British Library (Egerton MS, 1706).
10. Rapin to Portland, 2 March 1701, in N. Japikse, *Correspondentie van Willem III en ... Portland* (Hague, 1927–37). Vol. I, p. 529.
11. This is clear from a reference in Leclerc's *Bibliothèque Ancienne et Moderne* (1722) Vol. XVIII, where Rapin is said to have been working

on his *History* for seventeen years quoted in Joseph Dedieu, *Montesquieu et la Tradition Politique Anglaise en France* (Paris, 1909), p. 87.

12. For an account of the life of Rapin in the Hague, and *la Féauté*, see Rou, *Mémoires* Vol. II. pp. 258–9.

13. Rou, *Mémoires* Vol. II. p. 269.

14. On Larrey (apart from his own prefaces in his *Histoire d'Angleterre*) see Dedieu, *Montesquieu*, pp. 78–84.

15. Rapin's motivation and methods are documented partly in his correspondence (quoted by Rou and Cazenove), partly in the prefaces to his *Dissertation sur les Whigs et les Torys*, *Acta Regia*, and the successive volumes of his *History*.

16. 'A Dissertation concerning the Whigs and Tories', in *Memoirs and Secret Negotiations of John Ker of Kersland, esq.* (1727) Vol. III, p. 120.

17. R. Shackleton, *Montesquieu* (Oxford, 1961) pp. 292.

18. P. A. Sayous, *Le 18ᵉ siècle a l'étranger* (Paris, 1861), Vol. I, p. 52.

19. Rapin to Mauclerc, quoted in Cazenove, *op. cit.*

20. See Waburton's effusion in S. Parr (ed), *Tracts by Warburton and a Warburtonian* (1789) pp. 138–9.

21. Dedieu, *Montesquieu*, p. 89.

22. Montesquieu *de l'Esprit des Lois*, livre XI, ch VI. For Rapin's influence on Montesquieu see Dedieu, *Montesquieu*. Nelly Girard d'Albissin, *Un precurseur de Montesquieu, Rapin-Thoyras* (Paris, 1969) adds little to Dedieu.

23. Voltaire, *Dictionnaire Philosophique* s.v. 'Lois'.

24. *Reliquiae Hernianae* edited by Philip Bliss (1869) Vol. II, p. 311.

25. Samuel Jebb, *The History of the Life and Reign of Mary Queen of Scots* (1725).

26. *A Collection of Several Papers published by Mr Thomas Carte in relation to his History of England* (1744); *The General History of England by Thomas Carte, an Englishman* (1747–55); cf. *A Defence of English History against the Misrepresentations of M. de Rapin-Thoyras* (1734).

27. *The Letters of David Hume*, edited by D.Y.T. Greig (Oxford, 1932) Vol. I.

2 Huguenot Contributions to England's Intellectual Life, and England's Intellectual Commerce with Europe, c. 1680–1720

Graham C. Gibbs

England, as an island, and in part because she was an island, had always been accessible to European, or at least to Western European cultural influences. In a cultural sense the Channel had been a highway and not a moat. English culture was not insular but Western European long before the arrival in numbers of the Huguenot Diaspora of Louis XIV's reign.[1] The English constitution, it is true, was very different from that of any other European country, and it became increasingly different after 1689. The English became convinced that they had no political lessons to learn from any foreigner. Nor did European travel, in the form of the increasingly fashionable Grand Tour, do anything to diminish in Englishmen their sense of the superiority of the English political system; indeed, it seems often to have confirmed that sense of superiority, narrowed the English political mind, and reinforced national prejudices and stereotypes about foreigners.[2] Moreover, if the Grand Tour in many cases did little to broaden the political horizons of those English aristocratic young bloods who were obliged to engage in it – and greatly irked some of them – the real sufferers seem usually to have been their French tutors, frequently Huguenots. A tutorship in a noble household may have constituted a lifebelt to a literate and penurious Huguenot of good family, but it also constituted for some an intolerable yoke. Being the bear-leader on the Grand Tour of Philip Wharton turned out to be a much more precise job-description than his French Protestant tutor had bargained for, and a very sick joke. When Wharton slipped his tutor's reins at Geneva, he left behind him a bear-cub which he had acquired in the course of the tour, and the following note: 'Being no longer able to bear your ill-usage, I have thought proper to begone you. However, as you may not want company, I have left you the bear as the most suitable company in the world for you'.[3]

However, if in the political field, the grass always seemed greener at home, in other areas this was not so. In intellectual and cultural matters, not only was there virtual free trade between England and Europe, at least in times of peace, but English imports were heavy. Free trade in ideas was facilitated during the last quarter of the seventeenth century by a novel and important addition to the intellectual life of Europe, the emergence and upsurge of erudite journalism. The fashion was set in the 1660s by the French *Journal des Savants* and the *English Philosophical Transactions*. Soon after, many cities, scattered all over Europe, followed the examples of Paris and London. It was an aspect of the institutionalisation of European life evident in the establishment of academies in the same period, an accompaniment to, and an extension of, that process, and it proved of enormous importance in easing the lives of individual scholars, and to the circulation and advancement of European scholarship.[4] In this new intellectual communications system, which proliferated throughout Europe in the last quarter of the seventeenth century, Huguenots played a large role, as designers, directors, switchboard operators and subscribers. Three of the most influential of these journals, particularly important for the part they played in making possible a regular two-way intellectual trade between Britain and Europe were Pierre Bayle's *Nouvelles de la république des lettres* (1684–7), Jean le-Clerc's *Bibliothèque universelle et historique* (1686–93), and Henri Basnage de Beauval's *Histoire des ouvrages des savans* (1687–1709). All were published in the Dutch Republic, and all owed their inspiration and their direction, wholly or in large part, to Huguenot refugees from the France of Louis XIV. Le Clerc, it is true, was a refugee from Genevan Calvinism, but his periodical was inspired by what he considered shortcomings in Bayle's periodical, and his editorial collaborators, Jean Cornrand de la Crose and Jaques Bernard, took flight from the religious persecution of Louis XIV, the former in the aftermath of imprisonment for allegedly seditious dealings, and the latter to escape the death penalty for involvement in a skirmish with French troops deployed to break up a Huguenot service, which resulted in the deaths of a number of royal troops.[5]

I give one example of this two-way intellectual trade, which illustrates not only the exchange of information facilitated by these periodicals, but the function they performed in bringing scholars into direct contact with each other. I take it from the *Histoire des ouvrages des savans*, until recently the least studied of the three periodicals. In the 1690s Henri Basnage de Beauval, its editor, received an appeal from Dr John Mill, the Oxford biblical scholar and Oxford literary correspondent of the periodical. Mill wrote to ask for a particular work thought to be in the hands of the Bollandist fathers at Antwerp, in order to enable him and another scholar, Henry Dodwell, to complete their edition of the Epistle of St Barnabas. An abbreviated version of Mill's letter to Basnage, translated from the original Latin, appeared in the letter section of the *Histoire*. Basnage himself wrote to Daniel Papenbroek, the Bollandist father, repeating Mill's appeal. Papenbroek, pleased at the opportunity thus provided to be put in contact with Dodwell, answered the call for help, and Mill and Dodwell were sent the precious work they required to finish their task.[6] In this, as in other matters, Basnage acted as a kind of secretary to the Republic of Letters.[7] His periodical, like other such periodicals, helped to lubricate the wheels of contemporary scholarship, making use of a network of correspondents all over Europe. In England he had three; the most assiduous was another Huguenot refugee, the contemporary biographer of Bayle, Pierre Desmaizeaux, who acted as a literary correspondent for a number of European periodicals.[8] Thus, through periodicals such as that of Basnage, Huguenots performed an important function as cultural intermediaries between Britain and Europe.

Britain's intellectual imports from Europe were also enriched by the activities of Huguenots as translators and commentators. Many Huguenots with a knowledge of French and Latin, or who developed fluency in other European languages, were able to win a temporary meal-ticket, and sometimes to make the vital, initial breakthrough into the world of letters, and into more settled and better-regarded employment as writers, by taking on work as proof-correctors, as devils for scholars, and as translators. Opportunities for translating work were numerous, not only translating books, but in the expanding world of journalism, translating the foreign news that made up the bulk of news in all contemporary newspapers, constituting its indispensable ballast as well as a highly prized cargo.[9] In the world of books and the world of newspapers, economic considerations contributed to the contemporary addiction to translation. It was cheaper for a bookseller to secure a copy of the latest French novel and pay for a hack-translation than it was to pay for the rights to an original work of fiction.[10] It was cheaper and less troublesome for those who conducted newspapers to pillage foreign news from foreign newspapers than it was for themselves to collect foreign and domestic news: indeed, a proper system of news collection would not have been possible given the meagre resources available to contemporary newspapers.[11] In the field of the learned periodical, economic considerations of a fundamentally similar kind – the problems involved in operating a shoe-string enterprise in a highly competitive market – led to heavy dependency on material pillaged from other periodicals. When in 1691, Cornrand de la Crose, having broken with Leclerc and the *Bibliothèque universelle*, and having moved on to England in the conviction that the Anglican church would provide him with the religious liberty he could not find in the Dutch Republic, set out to supply the world of learning in England with a periodical analogous to those appearing on the continent, and to fill the gap left by the cessation since 1688 of the *Philosophical Transactions*, he was soon obliged to engage in systematic plagiarisation of Basnage's *Histoire des ouvrages des savans*, and even reduced to the straits of 'borrowing from our enemies the matter of a philosophical entertainment' – a reference to borrowings from the *Journal des savans* and *Mémoires de mathématiques et de physique*.[12]

Much of the contemporary translation of books was denounced at the time as demeaning and degrading, the companion and prostitute of every miserable creature that wants a meal and had the least smattering of a language.[13] However, if much translation was hack-work, and deserved the opprobrium heaped upon it and its practitioners, by writers of the day, some of it was highly regarded in its day, survived the test of time, and at least made accessible, or more accessible, jewels from Europe's cultural treasury that would otherwise have been inaccessible, or less widely accessible.[14]

The translations by Pierre Motteux, a Huguenot from Rouen who took out letters of denization in England in 1686, of Rabelais in 1694, and of Cervantes in 1700, belong to the category of translation work that was highly regarded in its day, and for long after; and they are regarded as Motteux's principal claim to remembrance.[15] Certainly they have a better claim to remembrance than his other translations of works by Pidou de St Olon, Malebranche, and Fontenelle,[16] but they are not his only claim to remembrance. Before he became noted as a translator, he was a journalist, something of an *avant-garde* journalist.

His short-lived *Gentleman's Journal* (1692–4), which was changed into the *Lady's Journal* in October 1693, was the first miscellany journal in England, and was one of the first periodicals in England to be written by a professional writer. It brought together, and adapted, a number of recently introduced journalistic techniques that were to become familiar features in the repertoire of journalists. Significantly, given the chronic economic difficulties of contemporary journalism, these included regular appeals for material from readers. What is further significant in the case of Motteux is the response these appeals elicited from men of letters and musicians.[17] It underlines the surprising rapidity with which he gained a footing for himself in the world of letters and of music.[18]

The *Gentleman's Journal*, though essentially a periodical of amusement, in direct descent from the *Mercure Galant*, also looked occasionally at the world of learning and, more frequently, at happenings in contemporary science, where, as has been noted, there then existed a temporary gap in public news coverage in England.[19] But, if it looked back to the *Mercure*, the *Gentleman's Journal* also looked forward to the *Spectator*, not least in its explicit address to women readers, who were being wooed by publishers in Europe as well as in England in the 1690s.[20] But Motteux soon found the going too hard as a professional journalist in sole charge of the conduct of a monthly publication. There was too much for one person to do, and the rewards were not commensurate with:

> the charges of correspondence abroad and at home, consulting, writing to, and waiting upon great numbers of persons daily, many times for a single piece, perhaps at last not proper: the running or sending from one extremity of this long fatiguing town to the other, several times each day, the answering many importunate letters, etc.[21]

There was also, though Motteux did not mention it, the translation of Books 4 and 5 of Rabelais, which appeared in July 1694, produced frantically against a deadline.[22] This did more than revise and complete the translation begun by Sir Thomas Urquhart.[23] Motteux added a lengthy preface, in which he gave an account of the design and nature of Rabelais's work, and what he described as a key to its most difficult passages. Deciphering and annotating Rabelais were made more difficult by a lack of books, though Motteux seems to have had access to some of the favourite sources of French Protestant controversialists of the seventeenth century. He made the obligatory references to Jacques-Auguste de Thou, whom he saluted as 'the great Thuanus, the best of all our modern historians'; and he referred to the *Histoire ecclésiastique*, attributed to Théodore de Bèze, and a preferred source among seventeenth-century French Reformed controversialists for information on the establishment of the Reformed churches in France.[24] But at times, as he admitted, he was forced to quote from memory. That is an important admission: not so much a criticism of the reliability and standing of Motteux's commentary and historical annotations, in which, indeed, a later Huguenot *érudit*, Le Duchat, found much to praise,[25] as a tribute to the extent to which, in common with other contemporary literate Huguenot refugees, Motteux was drawn to, and was familiar with, French humanist culture, and French history, particularly the history of the emergence and establishment of Protestantism in France, and of the French religious wars. In the Huguenot ideological campaign against Louis XIV, the sixteenth century was an arsenal of ammunition. Capturing Rabelais for Protestantism, as a crypto-proto-Protestant, a Protestant in head and heart, and in all save name, was a Huguenot concern in that campaign, perhaps a means of combating the accusation of French Catholics that the Reformed were not, and never had been, true Frenchmen.[26] Motteux seems to have shared that concern. In the dedication of his translation of Rabelais to Edward Russell, he described Rabelais as the greatest genius that France had ever produced, and he likened translating Rabelais into English to taking a French prize of war, and setting it out in English colours.[27] In Motteux's English colours, Rabelais sailed into the eighteenth century and beyond, and into the English-speaking world. With revisions by John Ozell in 1737, it became the standard English translation, and was published six times between 1737 and 1843. To Motteux's Huguenot compatriots, however, it was not the translation, but the commentary and the historical annotation that commanded attention. Bayle, who played a major role in persuading Le Duchat to edit Rabelais, alerted him to the existence of Motteux, more than once advised him to consult Motteux, and searched for a copy of Motteux for him. Le Duchat, in his turn, not only paid tribute to Motteux's work, but when his own edition of Rabelais appeared, emphasised the importance of a translation into French of Motteux's commentary and notes. This duly appeared in 1740, from the hands of another Huguenot, César de Missy, thus completing a remarkable circle of translation.[28]

Motteux's translation of Rabelais was followed shortly by his translation of Cervantes, which attracted a score of subscribers – wits, fellow-translators, painters, politicians of both parties, nobility and gentry, and one woman – and established him as one of the most versatile linguists of his day.[29] Not the first English translation, and not the only English translation of the eighteenth century, it was, in terms of editions, the most popular of the eighteenth century, and was paid the high compliment of plagiarisation in 1742.[30] It was the basis of further translations which appeared in the 1880s, and as recently as 1930, there was a reprint of the seventh edition of 1743.[31]

Translation and journalism, and other writing, did not provide Motteux with a secure or sufficient livelihood, though his knowledge of Rabelais seems to have formed the main thrust of a letter of recommendation from Sir Godfrey Kneller to the Huguenot Maecenas, Sir William Trumbull, in which Kneller described Motteux as 'a French protestant ... well acquainted with that book [Rabelais] which exposes the superstition of popery'.[32] That Motteux enjoyed 'favours' from Trumbull seems certain: Motteux gratefully and publicly acknowledged them.[33] What the favours were is not known. But the patronage of Trumbull may have been the beginning of the road, which turned out to be a cul-de-sac, leading to Motteux's appointment in 1700 to 'a very genteel place in the General Post Office, relating to the Foreign Letters', another translating job.[34] By 1702 Motteux was in receipt of £40 p.a. as a clerk, a salary which placed him among the lower clerical proletariat in government service.[35] It was a pretty miserable pittance on which to support a wife and two children, and although the Post Office did offer its executives good pickings in fees, as well as good salaries, Motteux did not stay long enough to graze upon its lush upper pastures.[36] In 1704 he began an eight-year apprenticeship to one Paul Franjoux, citizen and apothecary of the City of London to learn his art. Upon completing his apprenticeship in 1712 he was admitted freeman of the City of London, and he set up as an apothecary specialising in the sale of East Indian goods.[37] Writing to the *Spectator* in September 1712, he claimed that the foreign goods he sold were no less acceptable to his customers than the foreign books he had translated, Rabelais and Cervantes.[38] Apart from being a neat way of advertising both his books and his wares, the claim seems to have been justified on both counts: 1712 saw the third edition of his translation of Cervantes, and a puff for his business from his friend Steele, who, describing a visit to Motteux's spacious warehouses, exulted in the success of a former brother of the quill now become an industrious and successful man of trade.[39] In truth, Motteux had not so much abandoned the quill for a trade, as abandoned one form of the importing business for another in which the financial rewards proved much greater. He prospered quickly and greatly. His warehouses in Leadenhall Street became a centre of fashion, so fashionable as to have conferred upon them in 1716 Addison's seal of approval as the lodgement for his proposed Sisterhood of Loyalists, a voluntary assocation of 'the consorts, relicts and spinsters of the Isle of Great Britain', engaged to do their all for the good and safety of the Protestant and Hanoverian succession.[40] That proved a singularly infelicitious conceit when, two years later, Motteux died violently, at the hands – or in the arms – of prostitutes, whom Addison, in common with other Whig writers of the day, depicted as High Church sympathisers and Jacobite supporters.[41]

As a translator and a journalist, Motteux typifies a good deal that is conspicuous in the Huguenot contribution to the intellectual life of England and Europe in the period 1680–1720. Further, his failure to earn his bread by writing, and the manner in which he did prosper, by attaching himself to a rising proto-professional group like the apothecaries, are illustrative of the difficulties and the opportunities which faced Huguenot intellectuals obliged to shift hard for their livelihood in England.[42] Nor does the interest of Motteux for the student of Huguenot history end there. As an apothecary, Motteux belonged to a society which included many men of culture with a keen interest in the developing sciences of botany, chemistry and medicine. Indeed, at the time Motteux completed his apprenticeship, the apothecaries could claim five Fellows of the Royal Society.[43] Although none was a Huguenot, Huguenots were numerous in the Royal Society, thus adding substantially to Britain's intellectual imports from Europe.

Between 1680 and 1720, sixteen Huguenots were elected Fellows of the Royal Society – seventeen if the converted Catholic, Michel Le Vassor, is included. There were four elections in the reign of Charles II; there was one at the end of the reign of James II, elected after the Second Declaration of Indulgence; six elections in the reign of William II (seven if Le Vassor is included); two elections in Anne's reign; and, in the reign of George I, up to my arbitrary cut-off point of 1720, there were another three elections.[44] As is evident from Dr Michael Hunter's invaluable recent work on the morphology of the Royal Society, this large constellation of Huguenot Fellows was part of a wider contemporary tendency towards its increasing Europeanisation.[45] It is a remarkable phenomenon, the more remarkable in view of the estimated size of the Huguenot influx into England – put most recently at about 40–50 000 during Louis XIV's reign – and when it is noted that the Huguenot elections between 1660 and 1700 constituted the second largest group of elected 'persons of other nations' during those years.[46] Remarkable though it is, it is a phenomenon eclipsed in some respects by the thirteen elections to the Berlin Academy of Sciences made during the thirteen years of the rule of its royal founder, Frederick I, especially since one of the elections was that of Jean Henri Samuel Formey, who became the permanent secretary of the Berlin Academy, as well as an honorary member of St Petersburg Academy of Sciences, and a powerful force in establishing Russia as a province of the Republic of Letters.[47] It is another illustration of the rapidity with which the Huguenot grape-vine grew, and the great distances it travelled, to produce a goodly crop not only of academicians, but of official historiographers to the courts and estates of Europe.[48]

It would take more expertise than I possess to evaluate the contribution made to the intellectual life and standing of Britain by these Huguenot Fellows of the Royal Society, but they do typify some of the important features of contemporary Huguenot intellectual endeavour. The first of the Fellows, Henri Justel, was the first of a formidable line of Huguenot librarians in Britain.[49] Described by Evelyn as a great and knowing virtuoso, and by a modern scholar as a well-informed and conscientious mediocrity, Justel was an early Anglophile.[50] Before he was made Keeper of the Royal Library by William III, he was an occasional correspondent of Locke, Leibnitz and Bayle, whom he kept *au courant* with English intellectual life, and furnished with letters for publication in the *Nouvelles*.[51] He also seems to have been instrumental in setting in train a French translation of Burnet's *History of the Reformation*, a work which had particular interest in France in the 1680s, when Louis XIV was embroiled with Rome as well as with the Huguenots.[52] The translator, J. B. de Rosemond, was a Huguenot, a naturalised English subject, and an ordained priest of the Anglican church.[53]

Of the medical Fellows among the Huguenots, two, Paul Buissière and Pierre Silvestre, were active in England and in the Dutch Republic in promoting, by means of private lecture courses in anatomy, the general quality of the surgeon's art, and his standing as a professional man.[54]

Abraham de Moivre was one of the great mathematicians of an age which has been described as one of the greatest periods of progress in mathematics, and in which mathematical knowledge had the greatest impact upon life in general.[55] He was a great admirer of Newton: without his assistance in translating Newton's *Optics* into French, Maty his first biographer (the Huguenot librarian of the British Museum) argued, the work would have been full of errors.[56] If de Moivre saved Newton from error, he also seems to have saved him from the importunings of an inquisitive public. It is alleged that he became so trusted a friend that Newton's favourite method of dealing with questions about the *Principia* in his old age was to refer the questioner to de Moivre.[57]

But de Moivre was more than Newton's intellectual minder and publicist. He was one of the pioneers of probability theory. His *Doctrine of Chances*, the first edition of which appeared in 1718, and was dedicated to Newton, was the most important textbook on probability theory until the nineteenth century.[58] Part of it, *Annuities upon Lives* (1725) enjoyed more than half a dozen editions in the course of the eighteenth century, as well as the bitter-sweet experience of being plagiarised, and is held to have laid the foundation of modern actuarial science, and hence of life assurance.[59] It is tempting to observe that de Moivre's work on probability theory fitted naturally into an age of political arithmetic, concerned with the quantitative study of vital statistics and economic facts, and concerned also with arguing the usefulness of mathematical knowledge.[60] It would be misleading, however, to leave things there; the retrospective tidying-up operations of historians not infrequently distort as much of the historical reality as they reveal. The pioneers of probability theory were concerned initially with the chances involved in various games of cards and dice, and, fundamentally their concern was religious, to combat the widespread view – the superstition, as they termed it – 'that the distribution of good and evil, and generally all the happenings in the world could be attributed to a fatal power which works without order or rule ... this blind divinity, that one calls Fortune'.[61] De Moivre approached probability theory from the same starting-point, and with the same overriding religious concern. In dedicating his *Annuities* to the Earl of Macclesfield, he stressed its entertainment value, and in the preface he attempted to entice readers by minimising the degree of mathematical expertise that would be required to master its practical rules, and by holding out the prospect of 'more useful discoveries if they would take the small pains of being acquainted with the bare notation of algebra, which might be done in the hundredth part of the time that is spent in learning to read short-hand'.[62]

Moreover, in so far as he professed a concern with the usefulness of his work on probability theory, it was to draw attention repeatedly to the importance of its underlying principles in constituting the most convincing refutation of the contemporary argument that the creation of the universe was the result of a random conjunction of atoms.[63]

A similar concern with summoning science to the support of God is to be found in the work of another Huguenot Fellow of the Royal Society, Jean Theophilus Desaguliers.[64] Like de Moivre, and in co-operation with him in the translation of Newton's *Optics*, Desaguliers played a part in transmitting Newtonian science to Europe. But, in addition to acting as a cultural intermediary between England and Europe, Desaguliers acted as a cultural intermediary in England itself, doing much to popularise Newtonian science via itinerant public lectures in experimental philosophy. Though not the first in the field, he was among the first, and he proved an assiduous and influential practitioner in the field, training others to follow in his footsteps. In 1734 he claimed that eight of the ten or eleven persons then engaged in providing such courses were his students, and he further claimed that between 1710, the year of his first course in Oxford, and 1734, he had given 121 courses.[65] In 1734 he published his lectures, and he declared that they had been, and were, intended for persons with little mathematical knowledge, and of all ranks and professions and even the ladies.[66] If – and it is a big 'if' – given the multiplicity of pressures that could lead someone publicly to advance money for a publication,[67] the 264 subscribers listed in the book can be held to indicate the audience for his lectures, then his intention was partly achieved. Those listed were persons of all ranks and professions, and of both sexes, among those who could afford the fees. These were not only relatively high, but payable in full, well before the completion of the course – which may say something about the expected commitment and staying-power of those who enrolled.[68] Beginning with George I, George II and Princess Caroline, all of whom had attended lectures which Desaguliers had given at George I's command at Hampton Court, the list went on to enumerate members of the nobility and gentry, MPs of both political parties, merchants, industrialists, divines, lawyers, military officers, teachers, actors, Fellows of the Royal Society and fellow Freemasons. There were thirteen women in all, and subscribers were attracted from all over the British Isles, and from outside it, most numerously from the Dutch Republic, where long before 1734 Desaguliers had made important intellectual contacts.[69]

At one level, Desaguliers' lectures, published as *A Course of Experimental Philosophy*, were a form of do-it-yourself science, of rational amusement for gentlemen and ladies, an appropriate leisure activity in an age when the commercialisation of leisure and the diffusion of science went hand-in-hand, when some scientific and medical knowledge had come to be expected of a gentleman's education, and as part of a lady's reading, and when owning scientific instruments had become part of a gentleman's equipage.[70] But, as in the case of de Moivre, the desire to amuse did not exclude, but was intended to serve, profoundly serious purposes, defined by Desaguliers as 'to contemplate the works of God, to discern causes from their effects, and make nature subservient to the necessities of life ... a skill in joining proper causes to produce the most useful effects is the business of science'.[71] In popularising science, Desaguliers hoped to lead his listeners and his readers to a closer study of science, in the conviction that a little science was a dangerous thing, and that those tinctured with atheism as a result of a smattering of science, could be brought back to a religious sense of God's wisdom and providence by a deep search of nature.[72]

Both de Moivre and Desaguliers contributed to the process of making accessible to Europe the scientific achievements of England: indeed, for Voltaire, life – his life – could not go on without Desaguliers.[73] Both contributed significantly to England's intellectual export trade. In the over-all balance of intellectual trade between England and Europe in this period, English exports counted for more than imports. Huguenots in England, and elsewhere, were in the van, and in the train, of this process, giving Europe access not only to English science and English philosophy (most conspicuously in the translation of Locke by Pierre Coste) but also to English religious writings and controversies, English literature, English history, English politics, English current affairs, even English parliamentary affairs. The learned periodicals, to which reference has been previously made, were a major force in making accessible to Europe this variegated English achievement. Pierre Desmaizeaux, another Huguenot Fellow of the Royal Society, elected in 1720, to whom an earlier mention has also been made,[74] played a key role in this process of keeping Europe up-to-date with intellectual developments in England. He seems to have arrived in England in 1699, probably upon the advice, and with the recommendation of Bayle. Already in 1700, he was being hailed as '*L'homme le plus instruit de ce qui se passe de curieux dans la République des Lettres en Angleterre*'.[75] He soon became a regular, direct correspondent for the *Nouvelles*, and for a variety and succession of other periodicals; and, by virture of plagiarisation of his material, served indirectly as the source of English literary news for still more periodicals.[76] His letters to European periodicals conveyed a mass of information and appraisals on matters, intellectual and political, and are held to have had a direct bearing, and possibly influence, on the image of England on the continent.[77] English theology and religious debates occupied a large share of Desmaizeaux's letters, especially the writings of Tillotson, for which there was a ready market in the Dutch Republic, evidenced amongst other things by the appearance of an early translation of his sermons by the Huguenot émigré, Jean Barbeyrac, who took up this translation as a means of learning English.[78] But pride of space was accorded to publications in English *belles-lettres*, to English poetry (which Desmaizeaux found outstanding) and to the English theatre.[79]

For all his incessant scribbling, however, Desmaizeaux seems to have found the going hard. The combination of literary agent and tutoring affected his health, and although from 1710 he enjoyed a small pension of £40 p.a. on the Irish establishment, he had not enough to keep afloat.[80] His final years were passed in destitution and decrepitude, the victim, he wrote somewhere around 1739:

> of ye diseases and infirmities incident to studious and sedentary persons ... and being no longer capable of steddy labour on application, having almost lost use of my leggs and hands, and my wife being likewise sickly and infirm, I say, after above 40 years stay in this kingdom and being upward of 66 years old, I have ye misfortune to find myself and family destitute of a sufficient livelihood, and in a most distressed condition in so much that should I happen to dye to-morrow, my poor wife and child must go-a-begging in ye streets, a dreadful prospect, the thoughts of which overwhelm me with grief night and day, and are more painful than ye fits of ye gravel and rheumatism I am tormented with.[81]

Desmaizeaux fared much worse than a fellow Huguenot man of letters, a friend of long standing, Abel Boyer, who died in 1729 in comfortable circumstances created by his writings.[82] Boyer, by virtue of his experiences as well as his achievements, sums up a great deal of the Huguenot intellectual achievement in England and in Europe. Born at Castres in the Languedoc, like his strictly contemporary fellow-Castraisien, Rapin de Thoyras, the author of a highly influential history of England, Boyer fled to Holland in 1685 where he met Bayle. Perhaps through Bayle's good offices he proceeded to the university of Franeker in Friesland, where he attended courses in philosophy and history, as well as in mathematics and fortifications, given by Perizonius, an influential and innovative philologist and historian. From Franeker, he moved to England in 1689, carrying with him a letter from Bayle recommending him to Burnet, and asking Burnet to assist him. Once in England, he served as a devil for Dr Thomas Smith, assisting in preparing Smith's edition of *Camden's Life and Correspondence* for the press. Subsequently he kept himself afloat by taking employment as a French tutor, an experience which scarred him for life, as it scarred other Huguenots. In 1694, he produced his first published work, *The Compleat French Master for Ladies and Gentlemen*, which enjoyed great success in America as well as in England. In the same year he began work on his royal dictionary, French–English, and English–French. When it appeared in 1699, it established him as a lexicographer of international repute, and proved a work of enduring utility. By then he had several other works to his credit, and henceforth he never stopped writing.[83]

Boyer played a minor role in bringing to the attention of Europe the achievements of English culture by providing the first French translation of Addison's *Cato*, together with translations of more fugitive contemporary English poets. He also conducted literary traffic in the opposite direction with a translation of a play of Racine, and other translations from French into English. But his main claim to remembrance by historians is a series of works on contemporary English history. In 1702 and 1703 there appeared the first of these, the first complete account of the life and reign of William III. Amongst other things, it exemplified what was to become a notable Huguenot facility for being quick off the mark in producing histories of great contemporary public figures, a facility evidenced in instant histories of the reigns of Louis XIV, George I, Charles XII of Sweden, Peter the Great, and Catherine I.[84] Boyer's *William III* was paid the compliment, though Boyer did not regard it as such, of immediate pillaging in England and the Dutch Republic, and it was given a puff in the *Nouvelles*, which singled out for special commendation Boyer's coverage of English parliamentary affairs. The puff presumably came from Desmaizeaux, who seems to have puffed again in recommending to the readers of the *Nouvelles* Boyer's next major historical work, the *History of the Reign of Queen Anne* digested into annals, as suitable 'to all foreigners who desired to understand the developments and affairs in England'.[85] The first volume of the *Annals* appeared in 1703, and was carried through until 1713. The *Annals*, as Desmaizeaux had indicated, were more concerned with British affairs than with continental affairs. They made use of contemporary newspapers, English and foreign, including the *Post Boy*, for which Boyer began work as a translator of foreign news in 1705, acquiring a reputation as an authority on Spanish news. In the *Annals*, as in his *William III*, he took especial pride in his coverage of parliamentary affairs, especially the debates of parliament. Here he acknowledged obligations to unnamed members of parliament, who had communicated speeches to him, and procured him opportunities for being an occasional ear-witness to its debates. The *Annals* were abandoned in 1713, but in a sense were brought to a conclusion in 1722 with *The History of the Life and Reign of Queen Anne*. Boyer regarded this as his historical masterpiece. Today historians think more highly of his *Political State of Great Britain*. Launched in 1711, it continued in Boyer's hands until his death in 1729. A monthly compilation of domestic, foreign and colonial news, it contained pamphlets, and abstracts of pamphlets, as they were published, and before they were published; abstracts from books of current interest; documents, discourses and observations intended as essential background material for the understanding of current events. But, above all, from the historian's point of view, it provided regular information, scraps of parliamentary eloquence, from parliament's debates, usually published within a month of the debate. This was the periodical's crucial novelty, and constitutes its overriding importance for the historian.

To trace the provenance of these reports, and to assess their value, is not possible here. It must suffice to say that the information could not have come from the London newspapers, which conducted themselves for the most part as if parliament did not exist. Boyer himself claimed to have received some information, oral and written from MPs, some of whom he names, and to have obtained some himself as a result of personal attendance at debates. Further information probably came from persons who had somehow procured access to parliament's debates, which was not too difficult to procure in the early eighteenth century. But in whatever way Boyer procured his parliamentary intelligence he had achieved his best first. His extracts from parliament's debates have formed the substance of all subsequent collections of parliament's debates for the early eighteenth century.[86]

The matter does not end there. Extracts from English parliamentary debates – before, during, and after the reign of George I – found their way into contemporary monthly political periodicals · published predominantly in the Dutch Republic (mainly in French-language publications) and into Dutch-language newspapers. These monthly political periodicals were another largely Huguenot journalistic enterprise, compiled by them, and sometimes published by them, which further enriched the intellectual life of Europe from their beginnings in the Dutch Republic in the last decades of the seventeenth century.[87] Some of the information on English parliamentary debates in these periodicals, and in the Dutch-language newspapers, repeats what is to be found in the *Political State*. Where information in the European periodicals repeats what is in the *Political State*, it could have come from the *Political State*. But this cannot hold for any of the information appearing in the Dutch-language newspapers, since its appearance there invariably antedates the appearance of the same material in the *Political State*. Further, some of the information on debates to be found in these European publications, both periodicals and newspapers, is not to be found in the *Political State*, nor, indeed, in any other English publication. This information could only have come from manuscript newsletters. Boyer himself operated a newsletter service, which for a time at least ran concurrently with his compilation of the *Political State*. It seems reasonable to suppose that some – probably most – of the information on the English parliament that appeared in contemporary European publications, such as those I have mentioned, came from Boyer. In any case, whether or not Boyer was the sole spring and only conduit of this information, the fact remains that its diffusion throughout Europe was largely the consequences of the activities of Huguenot journalists and publishers in the Dutch Republic. It was another band in the beam of light transmitted by Huguenots, which both illuminated the English achievement, and the English scene for Europeans, and made the Huguenots England's cultural intermediaries *par excellence*.

Notes

1. Sir George Clark, *Three Aspects of Stuart England* (London, 1960) pp. 1–23.
2. Jeremy Black, *The British and the Grand Tour* (London, 1985) pp. 164, 170, 172, 178–80, 183, 186, 236–7, 239; and 'France and the Grand Tour in the Early Eighteenth Century', *Francia: Forschungen zur West-Europaischen Geschichte*, ii (1984) p. 415; C. C. Barfoot, 'A Patriot's Boast: Akenside and Goldsmith in Leiden', in J. van Dorsten

(ed.) *Ten Studies in Anglo-Dutch Relations* (Leiden/Oxford, 1974) pp. 204–8.

3. J. R. Robinson, *Philip, Duke of Wharton, 1698–1731* (London, 1896) pp. 11–13. For other cases, see G. C. Gibbs, 'Abel Boyer *Gallo-Anglus glossographus et historicus* 1667–1729; from tutor to author, 1689–1699', *Proceedings of the Huguenot Society of London*, xiv, pp. 48–55, and 'Some Intellectual and Political Influences of the Huguenot Emigrés in the United Provinces, c. 1680–1730', *B[ijdragen en] M[ededelingen betreffende de] G[eschiedenis der] N[ederlanden]*, 90/2 (1975) pp. 268–9; R. Sedgwick, *History of Parliament: The House of Commons, 1715–1754* (London, 1970) 2 vols, ii. p. 271; N. Japikse (ed.) *Correspondentie van Willem III en van Hans Willem Bentinck, eersten graaf van Portland* (Rijks Geschiedkundige Publicatien, Kleine serie, 23) ('s-gravenhage 1927) 2 vols, i, pp. 526–8, letter from Thoyras Rapin, 2 March 1701, relating to the Grand Tour of Lord Woodstock.

4. G. C. Gibbs, 'The Role of the Dutch Republic as the Intellectual Entrepôt of Europe in the Seventeenth and Eighteenth Centuries', BMGN, lxxxvi (1971) pp. 327–8.

5. For a comparative study of the three periodicals, see H. J. Reesink, *L'Angleterre et la littérature anglaise dans les trois plus anciens périodiques français de Hollande de 1684 à 1709* (Zutphen, 1931); for more detailed studies of two of the periodicals, see H. Bots (ed.) *Henri Basnage de Beauval en de Histoire des ouvrages des savans, 1687–1709; Verkenningen binnen de Republiek der Letteren aan de vooravond van de verlichting* (Amsterdam, 1976: Studies van het instituut voor intellectuele betrekkingen tussen de Westeuropese landed in de seventiende eeuw, 4) 2 vols, and H. Bots, H. Hillenaar, J. Janssen, J. van der Korst and L. van Lieshout (eds) *De 'Bibliothèque universelle et historique' (1686–1693): Een periodiek als trefpunt van geletterd Europa* (Amsterdam, 1981: Studies, 7) especially pp. 10–48, 61–74 (for information on Le Clerc's motives in launching the periodical, and on his editorial collaborators, de la Crose and Bernard).

6. *Henri Basnage de Beauval*, p. 37.

7. Ibid, p. 37.

8. Ibid, pp. 58–69. For Desmaizeaux, see J. H. Broome, 'An Agent in Anglo-French Relationships: Pierre Des Maizeaux 1673–1745' (unpublished Ph.D. thesis, University of London, 1949) parts of which have been published in 'Pierre DesMaizeaux, Journaliste: Les Nouvelles littéraires de Londres entre 1700 et 1740', *Revue de littérature comparée*, xxix (1955) pp. 184–204, and in 'Bayle's Biographer, Pierre Des Maizeaux', *French Studies*, ix (1955) pp. 1–17; J. Almagor, 'Pierre Des Maizeaux and his key-role as English Correspondent in the First Half of the Eighteenth Century' (Leiden, 1984: Werkgroep Engels-Nederlandse betrekkingen/Sir Thomas Browne Institute) pp. 41–5. For other references to correspondents, see Reesink, *L'Angleterre et la littérature anglaise*, pp. 106–10.

9. Gibbs, 'Some Intellectual and Political Influences', p. 273 (with the references cited in note 93). For foreign news in English newspapers see E.S. De Beer, 'The English Newspapers from 1695 to 1702', in Ragnhild

Hatton and J. S. Bromley (eds) *William III and Louis XIV: Essays 1680–1720* (Liverpool, 1968) pp. 124–5; G. C. Gibbs, 'Newspapers, Parliament and Foreign Policy in the Age of Stanhope and Walpole', in *Mélanges Offerts à G. Jacquemyns* (Brussels, 1968) pp. 298–302.

10. R. A. Day, *Told in Letters: Epistolary Fiction before Richardson* (Ann Arbor, Michigan, 1966) pp. 28–9.

11. De Beer, 'English Newspapers', p. 125; G. C. Gibbs 'Newspapers, Parliaments and Foreign Policy', pp. 301–2; M. A. Thomson, *Some Developments in English Historiography during the Eighteenth Century* (an inaugural lecture delivered at University College, London, 1956) p. 5.

12. De *Bibliothèque universelle et historique*, pp. 40–6; R.P. Bond (ed.) *Studies in the Early English Periodical* (Chapel Hill, North Carolina, 1957) pp. 33–4.

13. Day, *Told in Letters*, p. 30.

14. Reesink, 'L'Angleterre et la littérature anglaise, pp. 130–1; Erich Haase, *Einführung in die literatur des Refuge* (Berlin, 1959) pp. 401–4; E. S. De Beer, 'Huguenots and the Enlightenment', *Proceedings of the Huguenot Society of London*, xxi, p. 185.

15. R. N. Cunningham, *Peter Anthony Motteux 1663–1718* (Oxford, 1933) pp. 6, 85, 103–5; Huntington Brown, *Rabelais in English Literature* (Cambridge, Massachusetts, 1933) pp. 126–7.

16. Cunningham, *Peter Anthony Motteux*, pp. 69, 86, 91.

17. W. Graham, *The Beginnings of English Literary Periodicals* (New York, 1926) pp. 44–5, and *English Literary Periodicals* (New York, 1930) p. 57; Cunningham, *Peter Anthony Motteux*, pp. 9, 13–27, 50; Bond, *Studies*, pp. 20–1.

18. *Rabelais' Gargantua and Pantagruel: Translated into English by Sir Thomas Urquhart and Peter Le Motteux, Annis 1651–1694*, with Introduction by C. Whibley (London, 1900), Introduction, p. x.

19. Cunningham, *Peter Anthony Motteux*, pp. 13–14, 27, 42–8.

20. Ibid, pp. 24, 48; Bond, *Studies*, p. 21; J. Klaits, *Printed Propaganda under Louis XIV* (Princeton, 1976) p. 67; E. Sullert, *Histoire de la presse feminine en France des origines à 1848* (Paris, 1966), p. 9; H. Bots (ed.) *Pieter Rabus en De Boekzaal van Europe 1692–1702* (Amsterdam, 1974; Studies, 2) p. 42; Bertha-Monica Stearns, 'The First English Periodical for Women', *Modern Philology*, 28 (1930–1) pp. 45–59; G. E. Noyes, 'John Dunton's Ladies Dictionary, 1694', *Philological Quarterly*, xxi, April, 1942, pp. 129–45.

21. Cunningham, *Peter Anthony Motteux*, p. 23.

22. *The Works of F. Rabelais, MD* (London, 1694) Motteux's Preface, pp. lxxiii–lxxiv.

23. F. C. Roe, *Sir Thomas Urquhart and Rabelais: The Taylorian Lecture 1957* (Oxford, 1957) *passim*.

24. *The Works of F. Rabelais, MD*, Motteux's 'The Life of Dr Francis Rabelais', p. i, Preface, pp. xliv, cvi, cx, cxv; E. I. Perry, *From Theology to History: French Religious Controversy and the Revocation of the Edict of Nantes* (The Hague, 1973) pp. 26 and 30.

25. T. P. Fraser, *Le Duchat, First Editor of Rabelais* (Geneva, 1971) pp. 41, 71, 73–4.

26. Ibid, pp. 40, 147, 159–61, 189; M. de Grève, 'Les érudits du xviie siècle en quête de la clef de Rabelais', *Etudes Rabelaisiennes*, v (Travaux d'humanisme et renaissance, lxv) (Geneva, 1964) pp. 48–52; Perry, *From Theology to History*, p. 7.

27. *The Works of F. Rabelais, MD*, Dedication.

28. Fraser, *Le Duchat*, pp. 20–4; *Oeuvres de Maître François Rabelais ... avec ... des remarques historiques et critiques de Monsieur le Duchat, sur tout l'ouvrage*, 6 vols (Amsterdam, 1732) p. i. Preface; *Remarques de Pierre le Motteux sur Rabelais: Traduites librement de l'Anglois par C... d. M...* (London, 1740).

29. Huntington Brown, *Rabelais*, p. 126. The subscribers, in the order in which they subscribed, are to be found in the translator's preface, *The History of the Renown'd Don Quixote de la Mancha*, 4 vols (London, 1700–12) – the woman was the Viscountess of Weymouth; Cunningham, *Peter Anthony Motteux*, pp. 93–6, 104.

30. Cunningham, *Peter Anthony Motteux*, pp. 97, 103; G. Becker, *Die aufnahme der Don Quijote in die englische litteratur 1605 bis c. 1770* (Berlin, 1902) pp. 23–5 (plagiarism by Charles Henry Wilmot).

31. Information from the British Library Catalogue.

32. Cunningham, *Peter Anthony Motteux*, pp. 86–9.

33. Ibid, p. 89.

34. Ibid, p. 181.

35. Geoffrey Holmes, *Augustan England: Professions, State and Society, 1680–1730* (London, 1982) pp. 256–7; Cunningham, *Peter Anthony Motteux*, p. 181.

36. Holmes, *Augustan England*, p. 257.

37. *Corporation of the City of London Record Office: Freeman Admissions* March 1712/3.

38. *The Spectator*, no. 288, Wednesday, 30 January 1712.

39. *The Spectator*, no. 552, Wednesday, 2 December 1712.

40. Joseph Addison, *The Freeholder* (edited, with an Introduction and Notes by James Leheney) (Oxford, 1979) pp. 74–5, 89, 207.

41. Cunningham, *Peter Anthony Motteux*, pp. 191–2; *The Freeholder*, p. 48, note 4, and p. 52, note 3. For details of Motteux's trial, see A. Boyer, *The Political State of Great Britain*, 60 vols (London, 1711–40) XV, pp. 425–36. There was some doubt as to whether Motteux was strangled or died accidentally of self-strangulation resulting from an excess of physical effort. Even if it was an accident, César de Missy observed in 1740, it was an accident *'qui ne lui seroit jamais arrive s'il ne s'y fut exposé par une impuissance beaucoup trop volontaire'*. (*Remarques de Pierre le Motteux*, pp. 17–18).

42. For a good recent study of the apothecary in this period, see J. G. L. Burnby, *A Study of the English Apothecary from 1660 to 1760* (Medical History, Supplement no. 3, 1983, London Wellcome Institute for the History of Medicine, 1983).

43. Ibid, pp. 62–63, 88–91.

44. The Fellows were: Henri Justel, Denis Papin, Sir John Chardin and Frémont D'Ablancourt in Charles II's reign; Nicolas Fatio de Duillier in James II's reign; Louis Paule or Pau, Moises Pujolas, Abraham de

Graham C. Gibbs 39

Moivre, Basnage de Beauval, Paul Buissière, Pierre Silvestre and Le Vassor in the reign of William III; Jean Christophe Fatio de Duillier, elder brother of Nicolas, and the Rev. John Theophilus Desaguliers in Anne's reign; and, in the reign of George I up to 1720, Claude Amyand, Albert Henri de Sallengre, and Pierre Desmaizeaux. I derive this information from *The Record of the Royal Society of London* (London, 1897) (Chronological Register of Fellows, pp. 384–96.)

45. Michael Hunter, *The Royal Society and its Fellows 1660–1700: The Morphology of an Early Scientific Institution* (London, 1982) pp. 24, 107, and his 'Reconstructing Restoration Science: problems and pitfalls in institutional history', *Social Studies of Science (SAGE)* (London and Beverly Hills, 1982) pp. xii, 461; and J. S. Bromley, 'Britain and Europe in the Early Eighteenth Century', *History*, 66, no. 218 (October 1981) p. 394.

46. Robin D. Gwynn, *Huguenot Heritage: The History and Contribution of the Huguenots in Britain* (London, 1985) p. 5. The statement concerning Huguenot elections comes from figures in Hunter, *The Royal Society.*

47. *Die mitglieder der deutsche akademie der wissenschaften zu Berlin 1700–1950* (Berlin, 1950) pp. 10–14, 56–61; J. Kämmerer, *Russland und die Huguenotten im 18. jahrhundert* (1689–1789) (Wiesbaden, 1978) p. 100.

48. Gibbs, 'Some Intellectual and Political Influences', pp. 279–81. (To the names mentioned therein I would now add Frémont d'Ablancourt, historiographer of William III, and Charles Ancillon, historiographer of Brandenburg.

49. Gwynn, *Huguenot Heritage*, p. 79.

50. *Dictionary of National Biography*, xxx, pp. 231–2; René Ternos, 'Les débuts de l'anglophilie en France', *Revue de littérature comparée*, 13(1933) pp. 588–605.

51. E. R. Labrousse, 'Les coulisses du journal de Bayle', in Paul Dibon (ed.) *Pierre Bayle le philosophe de Rotterdam: Etudes et documents* (Paris, 1959) pp. 101, 102, 108.

52. P. Burke, 'The Politics of Reformation History: Burnet and Brandt', in A. C. Duke and C. A. Tamse (eds) *Clio's Mirror: Historiography in Britain and the Netherlands* (Zutphen, 1985) pp. 80–1; E. S. De Beer (ed.) *The Correspondence of John Locke* (Oxford, 1976) vol. II, pp. 109–10, Letter 506. Justel to Locke, c. 24 September/4 October 1679.

53. Georges Ascoli, *La Grande-Bretagne devant l'opinion française*, 2 vols (Paris, 1930), Vol. I, p. 231.

54. For Buissière, see *Dictionary of National Biography*, vii, p. 228; George C. Peachey, *A Memoir of William and John Hunter* (Plymouth, 1924) pp. 9–10; Holmes, *Augustan England*, pp. 168–235 (for an extended statement on the coming of the doctor and the medical profession, with a particular mention of Buissière on p. 198). For details of Silvestre's life, see British Library, Additional MS 4288 (Birch, Letter to M. Des Maizeaux) f. 178 (no date, signed B. Silvestre); Elisabeth Labrousse, *Inventaire critique de la correspondance de Pierre Bayle* (Paris, 1961) pp. 395–6; Randolph Vigne, 'Mayerne and his successors, some Huguenot Physicians under the Stuarts', lecture

delivered to the Royal College of Physicians, 1985, published abridged and unannotated in the *Journal* of the Royal College of Physicians of London, 1986, pp. 224–5.

55. For details of de Moivre's life, see *Dictionary of National Biography*, xxxviii, pp. 116–17; for a contemporary assessment of his work, see Maty, *Mémoire sur la vie et sur les écrits de Mr Abraham de Moivre de la Société Royale de Londres et des Académies Royales de Paris et de Berlin* (A La Haye, 1760); for the standing of mathematics in the seventeenth century, see G. N. Clark, *The Seventeenth Century* (Oxford, 1950) p. 233.

56. Maty, *Mémoire sur la vie... de Moivre*, pp. 29–30.

57. *Dictionary of National Biography*, xxxviii, pp. 116–17.

58. Carl B. Boyer, *A History of Mathematics* (New York, 1968) pp. 464–7; A. Hald, 'A de Moivre: 'De Mensura Sortis' or 'On the Measurement of Chance' (Philosophical Transactions, no. 329, for the months of January, February and March, 1711); Commentary on 'De Mensura Sortis', *International Statistical Review* (1984) pp. 52–3, 229–62. I wish to thank my colleagues at Birkbeck College, Dr E. H. Kronheimer and Professor P. Holgate for drawing my attention to these works, and for other bibliographical help with de Moivre.

59. F. N. David, *Games, Gods and Gambling: The Origins and History of Probability and Statistical Ideas from the Earliest Times to the Newtonian Era* (London, 1962) p. 172.

60. Sir George Clark, *Science and Social Welfare in the Age of Newton* (Oxford, 1970) 2nd edn, pp. 119–46.

61. David, *Games, Gods and Gambling*, p. 143.

62. *Annuities upon Lives* (London, 1725) Dedication and Preface. The quotation from the Preface is to be found in David, *Games, Gods and Gambling*, p. 166.

63. Maty, *Mémoire sur la vie... de Moivre*, pp. 29, 41.

64. The best account of Desaguliers is to be found in M. E. Rowbottom, 'John Theophilus Desaguliers, 1683–1744', *Proceedings of the Huguenot Society of London*, xxi, pp. 196–218.

65. J. T. Desaguliers, *A Course of Experimental Philosophy* (London, 1734) Preface.

66. Ibid.

67. W. A. Speck, 'Politicians, Peers, and Publication by Subscription, 1700–50', in I. Rivers (ed.) *Books and their Readers in Eighteenth-century England* (Leicester, 1982) p. 50.

68. Usually 2 guineas – 1 guinea down and the other on the third night after the course had begun.

69. The subscribers are listed after the preface in the 1734 edition. In addition to the contact with the Dutch mathematician, Nieuwentyt, (mentioned in note 72) another Dutch mathematician, W. J. s'Gravesande, attended Desaguliers's lectures whilst secretary to the Dutch Embassy in London in 1715–16, at which time he had also been elected a Fellow of the Royal Society. And in 1720, Desaguliers had translated from Latin into English, a work of s'Gravesande, entitled in English, *Mathematical Elements of Natural Philosophy* (London, 1720–1) two volumes.

70. R. S. Porter, 'Science, Provincial Culture and Public Opinion in Enlightenment England', *The British Journal for Eighteenth-Century Studies*, 3, no I, Spring 1980, pp. 20–46.
71. Desaguliers, *A Course* (the dedication to Prince Frederick).
72. *The Religious Philosopher: or the Right Use of Contemplating the Works of the Creator... by that Learned Mathematician, Dr Nieuwentyt. Translated from the original by John Chamberlayne, esq. FRS. To Which is Prefix'd A Letter to the Translator by the Reverend J. T. Desaguliers, MA, FRS* (London, 1718). The quotes are from Desaguliers's letter.
73. *Voltaire; Correspondence and Related Documents: Definitive Edition by Theodore Besterman*, (Toronto, 1969) v. February – December 1738, p. 338, Voltaire to Nicolas Claude Thieriot, c. 24 Octobre 1738.
74. See above and note 8.
75. Almagor, *Pierre Des Maizeaux*, p. 43.
76. See references cited in note 8.
77. Almagor, *Pierre Des Maizeaux*, p. 42.
78. Ibid, p. 44; Ascoli, *La Grande-Bretagne*, pp. ii, 66–7; N. Hodgson and C. Blagden, *The Notebook of Thomas Bennet and Henry Clements 1686–1719, With Some Aspects of Book Trade Practice* (Oxford, 1956) (Oxford Bibliographical Society. New series, vi (1953) pp. 15, 34.
79. Almagor, *Pierre Des Maizeaux*, p. 43.
80. *Calendar of Treasury Books*, 24(2) 1710, p. 258; Add. Ms. 4289 (Birch) f. 268 (His account of his life, written c. 1739).
81. Ibid, ff. 269–71.
82. G. C. Gibbs, 'Abel Boyer, *Gallo-Anglus glossographus et historicus*, 1667–1729: His Early Life 1667–1689', *Proceedings of the Huguenot Society of London*, xxii, pp. 87–98; ibid, 'Abel Boyer... from tutor to author', *Proceedings of the Huguenot Society of London*, xxiv, pp. 46–59; ibid, 'The Contribution of Abel Boyer to Contemporary History in England in the Early Eighteenth Century', in Duke and Tamse, *Clio's Mirror*, pp. 86–108.
83. I have covered the period up to 1699 in the first two articles cited in note 82.
84. Gibbs, 'The Role of the Dutch Republic', p. 342; 'Some Intellectual and Political Influences', pp. 23–4; Kämmerer, *Russland und die Huguenotten*, p. 103.
85. Gibbs, 'The Contribution of Abel Boyer', p. 95; *Nouvelles de la Republique*, July 1704, p. 103, and September 1710, p. 356.
86. Gibbs, 'The Contribution of Abel Boyer', pp. 95–102.
87. Gibbs, 'The Role of the Dutch Republic', pp. 347–9 (for a general statement about political periodicals). I have given the titles of the European publications containing regular extracts from parliament's debates in 'The House of Commons in the Early Eighteenth Century', in *The Welsh History Review: Cylchgrawn Hanes Cymru*, vii (1974) p. 231, note 23. To these titles I add the *Leydse Courant* (for the reign of George I) consulted at the University Library, Leiden.

3 The Stranger Community in the Metropolis 1558–1640

Irene Scouloudi

This paper aims at giving a poster-sketch of the life of the strangers in the metropolis, 1558–1640, during the Elizabethan and early Stuart period when the political, economic and social position was undergoing a fundamental change which in some senses meant consolidation and in others disintegration; when the concepts and policies established even in the Elizabethan period itself were altered, often radically modified by the early Stuarts and even by the Elizabethan government itself. It was an uneasy period in which to live and especially difficult for the strangers unfamiliar with the language and customs of the land of their settlement.

The term 'metropolis' includes the City of London and the areas under the control of the City authorities and its traditions. Added to this must be the City of Westminster, and the rapidly growing nearby suburbs of Middlesex and Surrey.[1]

But why this concentration on the metropolis when there were other stranger settlements, on the whole considerably smaller in numbers, in such centres as Sandwich, Canterbury, Southampton, Colchester, Norwich and a few other areas? The reasons are threefold.

First, London was the capital and largest city, the main centre of the economic life of the country at this period. Second, for centuries it had housed a large and active stranger community and as such attracted strangers coming to this country and further caused the peculiar set-up of the community in this area. Third, London was built on the Thames. The great *amateur* of the City, John Stow, proudly indicates the importance of the river in its development. He writes:

the Thames both for the streight course in length reacheth furthest into the bellie of the land, and for the breadth and stilnesse of the water is most navigable up and downe the streame: by reason whereof London standing almost in the middle of that course, is more commodiously served with provision of the necessaries, than

any towne ... This River openeth indifferently vpon France and
Flaunders our mightiest neighbours ... and this Citie standeth
thereon in such conuenient distance from the sea, as it is not onely
neare enough for intelligence of the affayres of those Princes, and
for the resistance of their attempts: but also sufficiently remoued
from the fear of any sodaine daungers that may be offered by them ...

a happy thought both for business men and refugees.[2]

Because of this age-old background the organisation of the stranger
community in London was unique. The position of the strangers had
evolved over the years in a fortuitous manner shaped by habit, custom
and immediate need. We find no founding sets of regulations or the
establishment of such bodies as *'les hommes politiques'* in Canterbury
and Norwich.

The sources from which one can obtain a picture of the strangers in
the metropolis are abundant, but it must be stressed that by their
nature the majority deal with the stranger community as a whole.
There certainly exists material for the individual Dutch–Flemish and
also French–Walloon communities but this is largely in the archives of
the Dutch and French Churches.[3] The archives for the French Church
are incomplete and the extant registers, published by the Huguenot
Society of London, only begin at 1600.[4]

Fortunately the material to be found in the State Papers, records of
the City of London, the City Companies,[5] various collections of wills
and so forth is vast since this paper is mainly concerned with the
stranger community as a whole. Basically the information is largely
drawn from an analysis of the *Returns* of which the Huguenot Society
has published all known Returns covering the Elizabethan period to
the end of the reign of Charles I. Volume 57, the centenary volume in
the Society's Quarto Series,[6] besides a general commentary on the
legal, economic and social position of the stranger community, also
contains an analysis of one of the most informative Returns, that of
1593, as well as the three less instructive and often incomplete Returns
of the reign of Charles I for 1627, 1635 and 1639. Unfortunately the
1593 Return got into the clutches of the antiquarian William Dugdale,
who mutilated and thoroughly muddled up the original when using it
as scrap paper upon which to scribble his history of Warwickshire.[7]

But why did this heterogeneous mass of strangers decide to come to
London? Life is a complex of threads which historians, often with
one-track minds following one particular thread, tend to forget the
whole woven cloth. These strangers were *not* all refugees for religion.

Some came for economic reasons, or possibly because their friends or relatives were living in the country. In the Parliamentary debate of 1593 which dealt mainly with the problem created by the stranger merchants, one speaker argued that those who had fled to England for conscience's sake should be pitied although not to the detriment of the native population.[8] In this connection in 1573, when the government was particularly anxious that no undesirable should penetrate into the country, an inquiry was initiated with the result that it was stated that out of 7143 strangers in the City and suburbs 2561 did 'confesse themselves that their coming hither was onlie to seeke woorke for their livinge' which indicates that about 36 per cent, or about one third, came for economic reasons.[9] England offered good economic prospects and furthermore was near to that part of Europe from which the immigrants – refugees for religion or not – came.

But what of the actual places from which the strangers came? As indicated by the membership of the Dutch and French churches as well as from an analysis of the information found in the 1593 Return, and also from the rather scrappy Returns of Charles I, the majority of strangers came from that part of north-western Europe near to England: that is, from the countries today known as Holland, Belgium, north-eastern France bordering on Belgium and a small area of upper north-west Germany touching on Belgium and the Netherlands. A negligible number came from districts farther away such as Italy, Spain, Greece, Hungary and Scandinavia. Interestingly the 1593 Return also mentions three unnamed 'blackamores', servants to Paul Banning, Alderman of Farringdon Ward. We do not know whence they came.

Unfortunately such information as exists today is difficult to interpret and is far from complete. Frequently we are only given the name of one individual with no mention of wife or husband, children or servants. However, taking the figures for Belgium and the Netherlands together, in 1593 there were 776 emigrants, and in the reign of Charles I, 911; from France there were 352 in the earlier period which in the latter rose to 1191. Germany showed the much lower figure of 107 which rose slightly to 152 in the latter period. But it must be stressed these figures are far from absolute and only show a tendency.[10]

An interesting reflection on the general political background and thought which prompted the government to call for the making of these Returns is illustrated by the information given in connection with church membership.

In Elizabethan times authorities anxious to suppress all dangerous sectarian groups kept a close watch on the membership of the stranger churches. Periodic estimates were made of the number of the different congregations which also proved useful when the government wanted to squeeze money out of the communities for financing some special effort such as the campaign in the Netherlands, for the relief of those seized by pirates, or for some forced loan.[11] By the Stuart period the emphasis of interest had changed. It lay in the political allegiance of the stranger rather than in his church membership. The vital question was whence he came and whether he accepted James as his sovereign.[12] With the Returns of Charles I, despite Laud's prepossession with conformity, we get no information on the numbers attending these churches. Was this an instance of the unco-ordinated policy and counter-pulls of the Stuart government? Whatever the reason the officials ordering the Returns were more interested in the general economic and demographical facts to be gleaned than with Laud's mania. It is significant of the line of interest of the Stuart government that in 1636 the aborted attempt to create a corporation to control the tradesmen and artificers inhabiting the City and Westminster and three miles thereof without the control of the city had just come into existence.[13]

But what of the membership of the stranger churches? It must be mentioned that it is impossible in this confined space to give a detailed breakdown of all the various figures indicating church membership. The general position during the period was that the numbers attending the Dutch Church were estimated to be slightly higher than that of the French Church. The Italian Church had a negligible number of members and those attending the English Church decreased considerably as time wore on.[14]

The Flemish-speaking refugees used the so-called Dutch Church and the Walloon immigrants the French Church since their languages were respectively closer to Dutch and French.

It is impossible to state the proportion of Flemings or Walloons attending either Church and from a general historical standpoint it is unimportant. This chapter is concerned with the stranger community as a whole. Further, the English authorities, as well as those of the Churches themselves, appear to have regarded the Churches from an administrative angle as Dutch and French respectively.

This leads to the vexed question to which there seems to be no clear-cut answer. How should we define the term 'Huguenot' and what is its connotation in an English context of the sixteenth and early seventeenth centuries? St Augustine wrote 'I know what time is, but if someone asks me, I cannot tell him'.[15] The author of this chapter knows what she means by the term Huguenot, but how and when it came to be used in an English context of the sixteenth and early seventeenth centuries, and even when in France at this period, she is uncertain and was rather surprised that in a recent publication some French immigrants of the Henrican period were described as Huguenots.[16] It is a difficult term to apply precisely, but it would be helpful if some precise and consistent attempt were made to state how and when the term came to be used, as well as to show why it is not today employed in connection with French Protestantism. Historically it is an evolution of one trend although varying considerably in place and time.

To turn to another question – what was the position of these strangers? Legally a stranger was said to be one born without the jurisdiction of the sovereign and broadly speaking one of his main disabilities was that, whilst he could rent or even buy 'real' property, he could not bequeath this property, except through very complicated subterfuges, to his foreign-born children.[17] Another disadvantage was that the government took measures to ensure that the stranger, as well as his children, even if English-born, paid the Lay Subsidy tax at the higher rate levied on strangers.[18]

In theory a stranger could legally free himself of the disadvantages of being a stranger by obtaining either a Patent of Denization or an Act of Naturalisation. Time prohibits the full description of the significance of these two measures and much more detailed work still needs to be done on this matter. Only a few general conclusions can be stated here:

1. It seems that it was the government, or its nominees, who through fees personally obtained, reaped the main advantages.
2. As far as can be ascertained the Acts of Naturalisation were far fewer than the number of Patents and were generally given to the foreign-born children of English persons.
3. Again as far as can be estimated from extant sources, during the period under consideration only a small number of strangers felt it worth their while to obtain these Patents. Between 1558 and 1640, a period of eighty-two years, only some 2778 Patents are today entered in the printed records as being granted to all strangers scattered throughout the country.[19]

This raises another point – should one look rather differently at the highly rated so-called bounty of Charles II for making free grants of Patents to the Huguenot refugees of the period of the Edict of Nantes?

Although it has not been estimated, one might even wonder if the crown lost much revenue by this gift.

However, to return briefly to the difficulties of the bequest of real property and the various legal subterfuges adopted, the position is well illustrated by two instances, that of William De Laune, who died in 1611, and that of the famous Elizabethan merchant, Sir Horatio Pallavicino.[20] Legally De Laune was unable to leave any of his real property in Blackfriars to his eldest son, Gideon, the famous apothecary, who was stranger-born. To circumvent this difficulty he left this property 'in the form of a sale' to a younger English-born son. Another example of real legal chicanery is well illustrated by the administration of the will of Pallavicino, described in such admirable detail by Lawrence Stone.[21] Pallavicino having established his financial position, made careful provision in his will for the distribution of his property and chattels. But his wife, Lady Anne, was a stranger-born, and his children although born after his denization, were young. To ensure their position he left the landed property in trust by the legal devise of a use. His chattels and wealth were in the charge of his executors, who included the Earl of Shrewsbury and Sir Robert Cecil. But within the shortest time possible after her husband's death, Anne married the Huntingdon Squire, Sir Oliver Cromwell, who managed to circumvent the intentions of the testator by marrying his young children to those of his new wife and, by the connivance of both Shrewsbury and Cecil, to inherit himself the wealth of the deceased.[22]

This stranger population covered a wide spectrum,[23] although small in proportion to the Eglish population in the Elizabethan,[24] as well as in the Stuart period,[25] there were a few who played an active and outstanding part in the life of the time such as the merchants, Sir Horatio Pallavicino and Philip Burlemachi, the engineers, Peter Morris and Sir Cornelius Vermuyden, the apothecary, Gideon de Laune, and the doctor, Sir Theodore de Mayerne, to mention only a few outstanding names. But the majority were small men as evidenced in the Lay Subsidy Return for the City of 1582.[26] In 1593 only 23 per cent were householders.[27] But the strangers were active with their own affairs and the Returns show that the majority ran their businesses as a family concern. Yet a few employed outside help. From the Ellesmere summary of 1593 we learn that in the metropolis there were 1671 English as against 686 strangers employed, a fact which must have delighted the government. The mutilated Dugdale manuscript gives some further information. Out of 1040 entries we gather that 516 families employed no workers, 212 had only English employees and 149 both English and stranger workers. Another interesting fact emerges: 264 of the English employees were separately described as being 'set on work' and not as being 'kept', to use the phraseology of the Returns. In other words they were presumably not living in the strangers' homes.[28]

We also get some slight information about the composition of the family unit. In 1593 there were 631 families which consisted of husband and wife. Of these 460 had children and the majority of these had between one and five children per family. 359 families were entered with only one parent and here again the largest majority of families had between one and five children per family.[29] It is of interest that out of a total of 2957 children by far the largest number, 2243, were English born and so legally well on the way to becoming integrated with the English population.[30]

The age variation of these stranger children was extreme. It ranged from a few months to over 20 years. Occasionally there is mention of twins as in the case of the families of John Futchett and Mathew Garrett. We also find a few instances of stranger women being married to Englishmen. Conversely there appears to be a few instances of stranger men being married to English women as with Barget Millor, Anthony Gyllam and John Harison.[31]

But what of the occupational grouping of the stranger population throughout the metropolis?

We find the strangers engaged in almost every possible occupation which could be found within an urban group. Some of these occupations – such as the various kinds of silk-making, glass-making, needle-making, etc. – were new to the country. A list of occupations in which the strangers engaged in the metropolis in 1593, found among the Ellesmere papers, shows six occupations with over one hundred persons employed. As expected cloth-making (which included a variety of silk-workers) easily headed the list with 502 persons. At a much lower level came those engaged in some aspect of clothes making such a tailors, button-makers, hat-makers, lace-makers and others, which occupied 202 persons. Those occupied in some form of mercantile activity accounted for 208 persons and at a lower level still came those concerned with metal-working, food production and leather-working. Other occupations engaged a smaller number. But, as was to be expected, the largest proportion of workers laboured in the City itself rather than without the City bounds.[32]

About forty years later the somewhat less-detailed Return of 1635 shows more or less the same trend, but with the total number at a lower level, with one outstanding exception, the cloth-making trades. It is significant of the trend of events that here the total of workers within the City was somewhat less than those without the City bounds – 317 as against 396. The localised establishment of silk-weaving and the ancillary industries, which characterised the suburbs of the later period, had already begun.

In passing it should be noted that the distribution of occupations within the Court suburb of Westminster somewhat illustrates the character of the area. Here cloth-making absorbed only 14 per cent. But 17 per cent of the total were engaged in making clothes, and this group included the more luxury occupations such as embroidery, periwig making, perfumery and tailoring, and involved 104 persons.[33]

Finally a few brief comments must be made on the vitally important subject, which still requires much study – the position of the strangers in the City. The most persistent restriction was on the open sale of wares by strangers in competition with Englishmen. Strangers were normally forbidden to keep 'open shop'. They were expected to work behind shuttered windows where the public could not see their wares. But at times this restriction was somewhat modified.[34]

Occasionally, upon some special request, strangers were permitted to become freemen of the City. An interesting case is that of Robert Thiery, for whom in 1609 James I lodged a special request that he be given his freedom on the grounds of his extraordinary skills and invention, being the first to weave material from the silk of silkworms nourished in England. In this instance the City fathers acceded to the request and he was admitted to the Weavers' Company on payment of 6s 8d to the Chamberlain of the City.[35]

At periodic intervals, in times of stress, attempts were made to restrict the employment of strangers by citizens of London. This limitation also included the English-born children of strangers as well as foreigners – English persons not free of the City. So in 1574, the City fathers took measures to make it unlawful for any citizen to apprentice the child of a stranger.[36] To exacerbate the situation it was argued that the children of these strangers, being born within the realm, were accounted English. But these children retaining a natural disposition to follow their parents had shown themselves hurtful to the common weal by secretly exporting victuals, leather, tallow and other necessitous commodities.[37] But the ruling was not rigorously observed for we find at times these restrictions had to be implemented by measures taken against individual offenders. For example in 1582 Cresfer Barker, stationer, had employed Edmond Francke as apprentice contrary to the act of Common Council. He was fined 20s and in addition, 'to make the punishment fit the crime', was appropriately ordered to print 'for service to the City' 200 copies of the Act restricting the employment of strangers.[38] It was against this background that the companies were ordered during 1582–3 to report on the number of strangers they had admitted during the past six years. The inquiry showed that some, but not all, of the companies had admitted strangers. Although these strangers do not appear to have held any high office, in some cases, such as that of Ascanius Renialme, who was admitted *gratis* to the Stationers' Company, they were held in some respect.[39]

There is also evidence that strangers had to pay certain local dues other than those exacted of merchants for package, scavage, porterage,[40] and for the weighing of goods at various beams.[41] For example in January 1599 the City authorities stated that by ancient custom strangers and foreigners living in the City were liable for the payment of the 'fifteenth' levied by Common Council. A cursory glance through parish records also affords examples of assessment of strangers for such local dues as the payment of the poor rate and rates for meeting the wages of the raker and scavenger.[42] On a higher level we find such instances as that of the reputable stranger, the apothecary Gideon de Laune, being fined. He had been elected Alderman for Dowgate Ward in 1626 but was discharged upon payment of a fine from taking office, on grounds that he was an alien.[43]

In passing it should be mentioned that the strangers did not always passively submit to restrictions imposed. For example when William Tipper, goldsmith and citizen of London, sought in 1576 to revive the restrictions enforcing the moribund regulations for hosting of merchant strangers and their payment of certain fines, he failed. His activities created a host of protests which reached minor international level.[44] If aggrieved, the strangers undoubtedly voiced their objections as evidenced in the protest against the rates and methods of administering such dues as package and the weighing of goods at the various beams and so forth.

The strangers however, were also molested by informers on every possible line of argument which could be found. There was also some doubt as to how far the famous Statute of Artificers of 1563 applied to the City in so far as clause 33 provided that the Act should not 'be prejudiciall or hurtfull to the Cytties of London and Norwiche or to the lawfull lyberties [etc] of the same Cytties for [etc] the havinge [etc] of any Apprentice'.[45]

The authorities of the Dutch Church, who were closely watching the problem, seized an opportunity to make inquiries. In May 1572 a Bill was under debate in Parliament for the explanation of doubtful clauses of the statute of 1563 concerning the lawful liberties and usages of the Cities of London and Norwich for taking apprentices. So the authorities of the Dutch Church approached a 'Parliament man' for an explanation, since, as they stated, many strangers, free denizens and others of the Dutch and French congregations in London, Norwich, Canterbury, Colchester, Sandwich, Maidstone and elsewhere had been molested by informers who stated that the strangers practised trades to which they had not been apprenticed for seven years and that they had sold their goods to non-freemen. Further, these informers, the Church authorities claimed, so troubled those of the 'true religion' that they dared not attend their churches especially at times of Communion. The strangers were anxious to discover whether they could practise occupations to which they had not been apprenticed for seven years or had served as journeymen. They pointed out that despite the Act of 1563, measures had been taken to stop them from exercising their occupations on the grounds that they had not been apprenticed. So the strangers wished to discover the purpose of the Bill under discussion.[46] Unfortunately we do not know the reply of the 'Parliament man'. The Bill, like so many others, did not become an Act.

Another point of some interest is that the character of the stranger settlements in the different areas of the metropolis varied considerably. The City, where of course the largest number was congregated, consisted mainly of those engaged in commercial and industrial activities. Westminster and the adjoining areas and parishes such as St Martin-in-the-Fields, reflected the atmosphere of the court and included luxury trades as already described. Here we find artists, musicians, cooks, many of whom were employed at Court, as well as victuallers keeping feeding establishments. Even some of the tradesmen were entered in the Returns preceded by the epithet *'monsieur'*, spelt in innumerable ways. For instance we find *'Monsier'* Jallyn, tailor; *'Monser'* Delagard, French dancing master; *'Monnsier'* Dulace, teacher of French.[47] The epithet *'monsieur'* had lost its old social significance.

The Returns covering the south bank of the river, including Bridge Ward Without, present a totally different picture. The population was sparsely scattered and of the 'meaner sort' to borrow a term from the Bounty Papers of the late seventeenth century. Here, in the Liberty of the Clink, was established the Dutch Almshouse, where in 1639 were housed fifteen old and impotent folk and here worked such individuals as the nine unnamed rope-dancers. It was here that Anthony Bancroft, the constable of Kent Street, who was unable to sign his name, rid himself of two Irish families consisting of two men and women and three children whom he sent to 'Westchester'. Isabell Barker, 'a poor helpless woman', with three children he sent on to Somerset and John Galland, with six other Frenchmen, he deposited in the house of correction.[48] So he passed on his problems to others at the expense of his victims.

It has been attempted here to give a superficial picture of the strangers in the life of the metropolis rather than as members of their individual congregations. Inevitably the chapter has been pestered with much detail and many figures. Nonetheless it is hoped it has succeeded in giving to some extent a living image.

Notes

1. For the area covered by the Returns see the maps in Scouloudi, *Returns of Strangers in the Metropolis, 1593, 1627, 1635, 1639: A Study of an Active Minority*, Huguenot Society of London Quarto Series (1985) vol. 57 pp. 78–9. Subsequently cited as 'Scouloudi (1985)'.
2. J. Stow, *A Survey of London Reprinted from the Text of 1603*, edited by C. L. Kingsford, (Oxford, 1908) vol. II, pp. 199–200.
3. See R. Smith, *The Archives of the French Protestant Church of London: A Handlist*, Huguenot Society of London Quarto Series, (1972) vol. 50 J. H. Hessels, *Ecclesiae Londino – Batavae Archivum*, (Canterbury, 1887–97) vols. II and III in two parts, an analysis of letters and other documents in the archives of the Dutch Church in London. The archives of the French Church are deposited in the French Protestant Church of London, and those of the Dutch Church in the Manuscript Department, Guildhall Library, Aldermanbury, London.
4. W. J. C. Moens, *The Registers of the French Church, Threadneedle Street*, (1896) Huguenot Society of London Quarto Series, vol. ix.
5. Many of the records of the City Companies as well as those of the City Parishes, are deposited in the Manuscript Department, Guildhall Library.
6. R. E. G. Kirk and E. F. Kirk, *Returns of Aliens Dwelling in the City and Suburbs of London from the Reign of Henry VIII to that of James I*. Huguenot Society of London Quarto Series, X in 4 parts (1900–1908). See also Scouloudi (1985).
7. Scouloudi (1985) pp. 73–5 where the manuscript is considered in some detail.
8. *Ibid*, pp. 64–6, where the debate is described.

9. Kirk, *Returns of Aliens* Pt. 2, p. 156.
10. Scouloudi (1985) pp. 84–5, 106–8. For Paul Banning see p. 149, entry 32.
11. *Ibid*, pp. 25–6.
12. Kirk, *Returns of Aliens* Pt. 3, pp. 180 ff.
13. Scouloudi (1985) pp. 96–7. The story of this corporation is told in detail by N. G. Brett-James, *The Growth of Stuart London* (London: Allen & Unwin, 1935) pp. 228 ff.
14. Scouloudi (1985) pp. 75–6.
15. Quoted D. S. Landes, *Revolution in Time: Clocks and the Making of the Modern World* (Harvard University Press, 1984).
16. During the subsequent discussion Professor Sutherland said that the term Huguenot does not appear to have come into general usage before about 1560 at the time of the Conspiracy of Amboise when it was generally an appellation for a French political military group. A little later it was applied to French Calvinists. See also Tollin 'Concerning the name "Huguenot"', *Proceedings of the Huguenot Society of London*, 6 (1902) pp. 327 ff.
17. For the legal concept of a stranger see Scouloudi (1985) pp. 1ff.
18. For the position of the stranger with regard to the Lay Subsidy see Ibid. pp. 17ff.
19. Ibid, p. 5.
20. Ibid, pp. 7–8, 23, where the wills and problems of administration of De Laune and Pallavicino are briefly considered, as well as those of Sir Noel de Caron, Nicholas Eyffler and Jacob Bancks.
21. L. Stone, *An Elizabethan: Sir Horatio Pallavicino* (Oxford, 1956) gives a lively and scholarly description of the activities and importance of this outstanding Elizabethan merchant.
22. Scouloudi (1985) p. 23.
23. Ellesmere MS 2514, in the Huntington Library, San Marino, USA.
24. R. Finlay, *Population and the Metropolis: Demography of London 1580–1650* (Cambridge: Cambridge University Press, 1981) p. 68; Scouloudi (1985) p. 76.
25. Scouloudi (1985) p. 101.
26. In the Lay Subsidy Return of 1582 out of a total of 1840 strangers taxed 1358 paid only the Poll Tax (Scouloudi (1985) p. 22). This is further exemplified in the Ellesmere MS 2514d where it is calculated that out of 2358 estimated to be taxable 1849 would only pay the Poll Tax (Scouloudi (1985) p. 90).
27. Ellesmere MS 2514d, shows that out of a total 7113 strangers only 1665 (or 23 per cent) were sufficiently well-to-do to be householders. See Scouloudi (1985) p. 90, where the manuscript is reproduced.
28. Scouloudi (1985) pp. 81–2 and p. 146 where the significance of the term is considered.
29. Scouloudi (1985) p. 83.
30. Ellesmere MS 2514d, (Scouloudi (1985) p. 90).
31. Scouloudi (1985) p. 84 and pp. 147ff for further information on the persons mentioned.
32. Ellesmere MS 2514e; Scouloudi (1985) Appendix V, pp. 131ff, analysis of the occupations mentioned in the 1593 Return.

33. Scouloudi (1985) Appendix VI, pp. 363ff, which gives an analysis of the occupations mentioned in the Return of 1635.
34. For example in 1556 the Chamberlain of the City was instructed to shut discreetly the shop windows of all strangers and foreigners, setting lattices before them; 'For as muche as the same [windows are] not onely much hurtful unto the citizens ... but also directly against the ancient laws ... of this citie ...' (London City Record Office, Letter Book V, f 35v). Occasionally the Court of Aldermen was more reasonable and considerate to the strangers and ordered that, whilst all the strangers in the City and Liberties should take care that passers-by should not see them at work, yet doors and windows could be of such sort to leave sufficient light for work to be carried on. (Hessels, vol. III, no. 1081). For further instances of the application of this restriction, see Scouloudi (1985) p. 42.
35. London City Record Office, Journal of the Court of Common Council 27, f. 385v. However the question of the admittance of strangers to the freedom of the City was far from clear-cut. There is no doubt that strangers were, upon occasion, admitted, but their acceptance was jealously watched by the City authorities and each case was tested on its own merits. See Scouloudi (1985) pp. 9–12, where numerous instances are mentioned.
36. London City Record Office, Repertory of the Court of Aldermen 18, f. 256.
37. Hessels, vol. III, no. 307.
38. London City Record Office, Rep. 20 f. 380. The right of the citizens to employ strangers and/or foreigners was far from clear-cut. In fact it would seem that it varied with each case and the mood of the moment. For example, in 1577 John Richardson, upon suit of the Chamberlain, was pardoned for setting 'foreigners' to work (Rep. 19 f. 382v). In 1582 Bryan Savell, clothworker, in ignorance apprenticed Bryan Marrowe, son of Peter Marrowe, 'stranger'. A fine of 20*s* was imposed and the apprentice had to be discharged. Further it was ordered that a precept was to be sent to the several Companies to be set up in their halls, and that thereafter no son of a stranger, or alien-born, should be apprenticed (Rep. 20 f. 360). In 1588 the Court of Aldermen, with certain dramatic irony, fined Henry Hewitt, clothworker, £20 to be used in the building of Blackwell Hall, for taking Willyn Troches, 'a stranger', as apprentice and retaining him for ten years (Rep. 21 f. 257v). See Scouloudi (1985) pp. 46–8, where further instances and the varying attitude of the City authorities are considered.
39. The report on the City Companies was included in the Return compiled during the mayoralty of Sir Thomas Blanck and is published by Kirk, part II, pp. 258ff. For reports by the City Companies see pp. 305ff. See also Scouloudi (1985) pp. 43ff.
40. There were continued disputes over the rates for and payments of package. Periodically there was a lull when merchant strangers were content to pay rates as listed in the time of Edward IV, but not on those goods not mentioned in the list. Upon being asked to name the objectionable goods the strangers refused (Rep. 23 f. 377v and

f. 562v). By September 1596 a committee was set up to consider the whole problem of scavage, baillage and porterage (Rep. 23, f. 577v). The report was compiled by November when the strangers agreed to pay on listed items but continued to be recalcitrant on those not entered. Upon being asked to appoint four merchant strangers to meet the committee they appeared reluctant (Rep. 24 f. iv). However by December the matter seems to have been resolved for a committee consisting of both Englishmen and strangers was named (Rep. 24 f. 17). This was not the end of the story. In the second decade of the seventeenth century the dispute over charges flared up again (Scouloudi (1985) pp. 31–2).

41. Merchants were supposed to take heavy goods to be weighed at the King's, or Great, Beam situated at a large house on the north side of Cornhill. In January 1582 the aldermen considered complaints of the merchant strangers about the method of weighing goods at the Great Beam. In the following year a lengthy report was made on the method of weighing and types of machines used not only at the Great Beam but also at other weigh houses (Scouloudi (1985) pp. 31–2).

42. See Scouloudi (1985) pp. 33–4 where the payments by strangers of local dues, parish rates, tithes due to the clergy are cited.

43. A. B. Beaven, *The Alderman of the City of London*, (London, 1908) vol. I, p. 140. Also F. N. L. Poynter, *Gideon de Laune and his family circle: The Gideon de Laune lecture, 1964* (London: Wellcome Historical Medical Library, 1965).

44. Scouloudi (1985) pp. 59–61.

45. R. H. Tawney and E. Power, *Tudor Economic Documents*, (London, 1924) vol. I, p. 349.

46. Hessels, vol. III, no. 156. Here the Bill is tentatively dated 1571, but thanks to the entry in the *Journal of the House of Commons*, it can be precisely dated 1572. See also Scouloudi (1985) pp. 49–50.

47. See Scouloudi (1985) pp. 103–5 for a description of the strangers in Westminster.

48. Ibid, p. 105.

4 The Canterbury Walloon Congregation from Elizabeth I to Laud

Anne M. Oakley

On 29 June 1561, two Jurats rode from Sandwich to London to see their counsel, Roger Manwood, to draw up Articles for the strangers 'that be mynded to come and Inhabit within this Toune of Sandwich'. It appears that the invitation to the foreigners came from Sandwich. The warrant under the great seal, dated 26 July 1561, directed the Mayor, Jurats and Commonalty of Sandwich to receive certain 'men of knowledge in sondry handy crafts' belonging to the Church of Strangers in London. The settlers were to be such persons whom the Archbishop of Canterbury and the Bishop of London deemed suitable to go there:

> for the exercise there of the facultie of making saes, bay and other cloth which hath not been used to be made in this our realme of Englonde, or for fishinge in the seas, not exceeding the nombre of twentie or five and twentie householders, accompting to every household not above tenne or twelve persons, that they and every of them may savely repaire to our said towne of Sandwich, and there by our consent and order inhabite and take houses for their habitacion, and to have as manie servants as shall suffice for the exercise of the said faculties there not exceadinge the number above expressed.[1]

The settlers arrived in December 1561. John Boys lists the original twenty-five families in his *History of Sandwich* though not in their entirety. He gives the whole family for Francis Bolle who appears first on the list with his wife Christina, his daughters Jacomina 18, Jorina 16, Christina 15, Caterina 14, and his sons Christian 13, Jacob 11, Peter 9, Francis 6, and George 3; but contents himself with naming only the householders for the other twenty-four which is a pity because some of them do turn up in Canterbury later on and it would have been useful to have been able to trace whole families from city to city. However, he does tell us the name of the workmaster, William

Hornenagel, a say maker; and also gives some interesting figures: married men and women, 180; widowers, 3; widows, 6; bachelors between 18 and 30, 23; maidens and servants, 17; children from one week to 18, 178. Their minister was Jacob Bucerus. These people numbered 407 in all and were Dutch and Flemish. A small number were Walloons from French Flanders, Artois and Picardy. All had been living in London for several years.[2]

In 1567 the Mayor, Aldermen and Commonalty of Canterbury also decided to accept a group of strangers in their city, despite the plea from Sandwich that no other town nearby should so benefit lest it harm Sandwich. On 15 July they recorded in their Burghmote Minute Book:

At this Court yt ys agreed that there may be a company of Straungers received to inhabytt within the Libertye of this Citty by Order from the Quenes majesties Counsell and upon orders to be devysed by this house.[3]

The order from the 'Quenes majesties Counsell' has never been found, nor is there any rough draft of it among the records of the Canterbury Walloon Church. If, however, it was a small scrap of paper such as the Maidstone order, it may easily have been lost.[4]

Nothing happened for some years. But what of Canterbury's reasons and hopes?

Canterbury at this time was not a thriving city. The dissolution of the monasteries, friaries and other religious houses had robbed it of finance and trade. It was in an economic backwater and seriously in need of impetus. Pilgrims still came to the city, but in very small numbers. The shrine of Thomas Becket had been destroyed and the vast lodging-houses which the Prior and Chapter of Christ Church had constructed in the city for the reception of visitors in the previous century were empty. Indeed the picture painted by the Court of Burghmote is one of desolation and decay. In a letter to the Privy Council the city offered one hundred houses for the use of the strangers, not out of sympathy for their plight, but out of pure selfish self-interst to boost its own economy.[5] The houses were empty. Nobody was to be turned out of his home. The whole idea of receiving a company of strangers is to be seen as a simple way out of present difficulties. Moreover, if Sandwich was so obviously benefitting from the problems of others, why not Canterbury too?

In 1568 the Dutch and Flemish congregation in Sandwich was suddenly augmented by a huge influx of French-speaking Walloons from Normandy and French Flanders who formed themselves into a separate congregation in addition to the existing Dutch congregation. Little is known about it, but what is certain is that the arrival of these people in Sandwich practically doubled the number of strangers there and placed an almost intolerable strain on the town's resources. Instead of comprising one sixth of the population, they were now a third. Nor was this the only problem. Together with the Dutch strangers they indulged in piracy on Spanish ships in the Channel and caused so much trouble that the Crown decided to reduce their numbers. In consequence, the French congregation was moved in a body to join a very much smaller French congregation from Winchelsea which was already established in Canterbury.[6]

For the most part, this group of people from Sandwich came from Armentières, Cambrai, Lille, St Amand, Tournai and Valenciennes, though there was a smaller number from Picardy, French Flanders, Artois, Arras and Amiens which included some of those who had previously been settled in Sandwich from London in 1561. They were all French-speaking but the French that they spoke was a variant French *patois* which must have sounded strange to Canterbury ears judging from some of the curious renderings of some names in the Canterbury parish registers. Jean de la Beque very soon became Dealbeake, and a few names were anglicised: John du Bois became John Wood; Charpentier became Carpenter; de Bourges, Burgess; de la Croix, Cross; de Lespau, Shoulder. These are only a few examples and it must be admitted that in comparison with Maidstone in West Kent there was very little actual changing of names, only mishearings and translations.[7]

Queen Elizabeth I visited Canterbury and Sandwich in 1573 and perhaps the idea of establishing a large colony in Canterbury was finally settled during her visit to the city at that time. The problems of Canterbury cannot have been unknown to the queen. One of her Privy Councillors, Nicholas Wootton was Dean of Canterbury until his death in 1567 and he had been instrumental in bringing about trade negotiations favourable to England between Elizabeth I and Margaret, Duchess of Parma, Philip II's regent in the Low Countries in 1564.[8] However it was arranged, the strangers arrived in Canterbury in June 1575. They were a tiny minority of those who had suffered for their beliefs. They had chosen exile in an alien country and an alien culture. Life cannot have been easy but they apparently settled down fairly well. They came with royal permission and entered into an agreement with the Mayor, Aldermen and Commonalty of Canterbury. They asked for free exercise of their religion, a place of worship and a place to bury their dead; for free habitation in the city only for those who could produce testimony of good character; for leave for their own schoolmaster to teach their own children and others who wished to learn French; and finally leave to make Florence serges, Orleans serges, Frotz, silk, Mouquade, Mauntes, Bayes and Stofes Mouquades.[9]

The Dean and Chapter of Canterbury gave them St Alphege church in Canterbury which was in their gift and its burial ground, though this is not specifically stated. The minute reads:

> Item yt ys agreed the Wallons Strangers shall be licensed as much as in us the Deane and chapter lyeth to have thuse of theire comen prayer and Sermons in the paryshe Churche of St Elphes in Canterbury in such sorte at suche tyme as the parysheners there be not hyndred or disturbed of theyre commen prayer.[10]

The strangers were also allowed all the other things for which they had asked with one exception: they were not permitted to trade retail in the city because it was feared that they would steal the markets of the English merchants, and therefore would be barred from becoming freemen. In consequence they could have no vote in the city and no say in its administration.

The church of St Alphege was in fact almost in the centre of the area where the strangers were first settled. Many of them were offered houses in this parish in the St Alphege lane, Blackfriars, King Street, Abbots Close, Knotts Lane area, which were still there until the early 1960s when they were demolished under a Compulsory Purchase Order. Others were settled in St Peters, Holy Cross and All Saints parishes, and a few in St Mary Northgate Parish. Generally speaking this was the poorer area of the city where there were many small houses built with narrow frontages to the street.

St Alphege church soon proved too small or perhaps inconvenient. At least thirteen known Walloons were christened in the church and two buried in the churchyard between June 1575 and March 1576. But few in the years following.[11] During the summer of 1576 arrangements were made, probably by the Crown, for the strangers to use the western crypt of the cathedral as their church. Exactly when this was decided and by whom has always been a matter of doubt. Bunce states that it was in the mayoralty of Peter Kelsham but gives an earlier date.[12] Somner gives no date.[13] Peter Kelsham was Mayor in both 1568 and 1575–6. It therefore seems reasonable to accept that Bunce meant the later date as this fits in with the lack of baptismal entries in the St Alphege parish register. As there is no record in either the City Burghmote minutes or the Dean and Chapter minutes of the move to the crypt, it seems likely that permission was given by the Crown. The crypt was in any case used only as a coal and wood store and no longer for services. At first it was intended that the strangers should pay towards the maintenance of the crypt, but after arguing with the Dean and Chapter for six months, the congregation was allowed to use it just as they were later allowed to use the Black Prince's chantry chapel in 1897, for as Canon Francis Holland said then, 'It is better this way. If they have no rights, they can maintain none'.[14] The elders of the congregation were allowed to use St Gabriel's chapel as a vestry and as a meeting place for the Consistory, and the deacons the Black Prince's chantry chapel as their vestry.

From the first the congregation was a separate unit in the city. All discipline, moral and ecclesiastical was administered by their religious leaders, the Consistory, composed of the two ministers, the elders and the deacons of the congregation. In 1582, however, the elders declined to retain the quasi-magisterial functions thrust upon them. Until then they had dealt with all matters brought before them: marriage contracts, probate, settling quarrels and legal matters as well as lapses in moral behaviour, and they found it too difficult. In fact it is abundantly clear that they could not cope. Therefore a body of twelve men was chosen from among the strangers to oversee the newcomers and disorderly householders and servants; to see that all observed the ordinances of the city magistrates; to maintain the company of strangers in good repute; settle legal matters; maintain the rights of the congregation and workers; prove wills and generally represent the congregation and act as a liaison between them and the city authority. The twelve were chosen on 21 October 1582 and presented to the Mayor.[15] They were four of the Consistory, two drapers, two woolcombers, three master *passementiers* and one tailor. These were the 'Politic Men'. They were sworn into office by the Mayor and constituted a court which was generally respected. If an offender refused to submit to their judgement, the Politic Men could appeal to the Mayor to arrest him or her and order public confession. Each year one third of the Politic Men resigned and others were elected and sworn in their place. Their names were enrolled on the dorse of the Sessions Roll for that year with those of the scrutators and other officials.[16]

The Politic Men were peculiar to Canterbury and Norwich and were an immensely successful innovation in that they kept the city and the congregation in immediate contact. When Noe Grave and Simon Beharel were ordered to be evicted from the city on a charge of bankruptcy and robbery, a note was sent to the Consistory by the Politic Men to inform them.[17] And on numerous other occasions they were useful to both sides in all sorts of ways.

The deacons were the most important element in the survival of the congregation intact. There were twelve of them divided into four groups of three. Each group was responsible for one of the four quarters into which the city was divided for the administrative purposes of the French Church: north, south, east and west or Sandwich, Dover, Rye and London. It is not at all clear from the deacons' accounts or the minutes where the boundaries of these quarters ran, but it would appear that each group of deacons was looking after a similar number of members of the congregation.[18] In times of plague the deacons were the only visitors allowed in their own quarter; nor were they allowed to stray outside. The ministers were forbidden to visit throughout the city at such a time for fear they would catch the plague and be lost to the congregation, or spread the plague. Deacons were more expendable but even so were strictly confined to their own quarters. Principally the deacons had two main functions: the collection and distribution of alms and clothes, and visiting the sick; and the collection of information about slack discipline. Each month every single member of the congregation, man, woman or child, was expected to contribute to the poor fund for the relief of persons poorer than themselves. Alms were distributed weekly or monthly as the need was, and clothes once a year, usually in October. Their accounts are amazingly detailed and give a marvellous picture of life in the poorer parts of the city.[19]

In 1582 the city authorities began to be seriously worried about the increasing number of strangers in their midst, for they were increasing both by birth and by new arrivals.[20] They complained that houses were overcrowded and a cause of the continued spread of the plague which raged in the city at the time. It is true that very many of the strangers did die of the plague in Canterbury; their wills and administrators' accounts all tell their own sad story; and the plague-relief papers among the city records confirm it, listing strangers helped when disaster hit their households. Many of them were extremely poor, but they could hardly be blamed for the spread of a disease which favoured neither rich nor poor, especially since no one understood how it spread. Nevertheless the authorities attempted to stem the inflow and decided to send away all those who had come, not for conscience's sake, but to escape the war.[21] They asked the Consistory to make enquiries for them and even proposed a new settlement in Dover. Nothing however came of this until much later, and very little appears to have been accomplished in reducing the numbers. Only later plagues were to decimate the population of the city and congregation alike.

There is no official estimate of the number of strangers who came to Canterbury. Somner says there were only eighteen families but he was almost certainly referring to those who came from Winchelsea. In 1640 he wrote that the crypt was like a hive.

> The West part whereof, being spatious and lightsome, for many yeares hath beene the Strangers Church. A congregation for the most part of distressed exiles, growne so great and yet daily multiplying, that the place in short time is likely to prove a hive too little to containe such a swarme. So great an alteration is there since the time the first tribe came hither, the number of them then consisting of but eighteene families or thereabouts.[22]

If it is assumed that the population of Sandwich was somewhere around 4500, then there would have been at least 750 strangers which would have been a reasonable number for Canterbury to accept in view of its offer of one hundred houses. A count made in 1582 showed that there were 1679 or more members of the congregation. An examination of the number of baptisms of foreign children in all the city parishes for the period 1591–1600 gives a fair indication of the size of the congregation at this time.[23] (See Table 4.1) It is true that this takes no account of the numbers who returned home or the relatives who joined those already here, but perhaps these last two categories cancel one another out.

The population of Canterbury at this time was around 9000, so it can easily be realised how very obvious these people were in the city.

Throughout the period 1577–1639 baptisms were recorded in the registers of the congregation and in the city parish registers. To give one example only, Joseph, son of Lewis Tevelinge was baptised in the French Church in the crypt on 10 December 1587 and this fact is recorded in the parish register of All Saints, Canterbury where the family lived.[24] The greatest numbers were concentrated in the

Table 4.1 Baptisms of foreign children in the city parishes, 1591–1600

Year	Baptisms	Congregation
1591	120	2760
1592	144	3312
1593	131	3013
1594	132	3036
1595	133	3059
1596	106	2438
1597	90	2068
1598	72	1656
1599	100	2300
1600	107	2461

parishes of St Alphege, Holy Cross, St Margaret, St Mary Northgate, St Mary Bredman, St Mildred and St Peter with a few scattered elsewhere throughout the other eight parishes. By far the greatest number during this period were living in St Mary Northgate. The Subsidy Rolls for Canterbury for the years 1598 and 1599 show the wards where they lived but not the individual parishes, and they do show a far larger concentration in Northgate ward than elsewhere.[25]

Subsidy Rolls are admittedly difficult to use. A brief examination of the 1599 Canterbury roll would at first sight suggest that there were in fact more aliens than natives living in the city. However, if one assumes that some Canterbury natives had property elsewhere on which they paid the subsidy rather than their city properties, or that some aliens paid the subsidies that natives should have paid, this might account for the discrepancies. Some aliens seem to have escaped the Subsidy altogether if the figures in Table 4.2 are accurate.

An examination of the Deacons' accounts for the period 1631–47 would suggest similar figures (see Table 4.3). These are taken from the Extraordinary Accounts made by the deacons either for poor relief or for special purposes, when every person in each household, even small children, was expected to contribute something, however small. The figures given are for the four administrative quarters of the city, London, Rye, Dover and Sandwich.[26] They show constantly shifting figures with some large increases and some large decreases. The low 1638 figures can be accounted for by the outbreak of plague in 1637 and 1638, and the low 1647 figures perhaps by increased toleration in France fostered by the Commonwealth government.

Table 4.2 Figures for aliens and natives in Canterbury Wards, 1599

Ward	Natives	Aliens	Aliens, including wives and children
Westgate	42	42	75
Northgate	36	107	188
Burgate (with St Martin)	34	14	26
Newingate	57	12	14
Ridingate	11	6	11
Worthgate	39	96	143
Totals	219	277	457

Table 4.3 Collections for poor relief in Canterbury, 1631–1647

Collection	London	Rye	Dover	Sandwich	Total
09 May 1631	196	188	177	212	773
11 June 1632	233	234	226	226	919
20 October 1634	227	247	160	189	823
23 April 1638	139	119	94	142	494
16 May 1642	181	151	144	162	638
28 February 1643/4	64	85	40	64	253
— October 1644	66	70	26	58	220
27 October 1646	158	198	127	217	700
27 September 1647	74	–	45	36	155
22 October 1647	45	59	38	46	188

This general pattern is borne out by the figures given for *passants*, persons passing through Canterbury, which included large numbers which were returning home after years of exile in the city (see Table 4.4). These people are a prominent feature of the deacons' accounts in the period 1630/1–1647/8.

In their accounts of the *passants*, the deacons also give names and numbers for persons travelling through Canterbury to and from the continent of Europe to Holland, France, Antwerp, Dover, Sandwich, Rochester and London. *Passants* tended to travel in fairly large groups and were given money by the deacons to assist them. In March 1631/2 Paul Erfo, his wife, Nicholas de Sainct, his wife and thirteen other persons, women and children on their way to London were given

Table 4.4 Passants 1630/1–1647/8

Year	Jan.	Feb.	Mar.	Apr.	May	Jun.	Jul.	Aug.	Sep.	Oct.	Nov.	Dec.	Total
1630/1	–	–	41	30	18	7	21	12	22	45	15	19	230
1631/2	18	16	51	13	19	18	28	38	31	28	26	21	307
1632/3	22	15	26	34	35	36	42	31	27	27	49	16	360
1633/4	18	22	59	45	33	55	58	23	31	20	22	11	397
1634/5	16	10	20	21	28	17	9	8	40	16	20	10	215
1635/6	14	16	21	55	43	18	7	18	10	9	9	26	246
1636/7	19	21	14	15	13	18	19	18	22	3	10	12	184
1637/8	24	24	16	29	24	10	15	18	4	23	9	6	202
1638/9	9	41	29	24	22	8	12	22	33	19	19	31	269
1639/40	16	5	11	11	14	22	7	7	49	23	11	26	202
1640/1	18	20	15	16	61	40	18	44	48	36	22	55	393
1641/2	22	19	35	16	23	33	22	14	11	16	13	18	242
1642/3	10	30	17	18	9	8	6	2	2	6	1	6	115
1643/4	4	6	4	2	8	2	12	2	5	9	4	6	64
1644/5	13	8	8	3	7	11	12	6	7	10	6	5	96
1645/6	2	7	20	14	5	10	2	12	4	8	20	10	114
1646/7	9	2	9	6	11	4	2	3	9	20	16	10	101
1647/8	18	12	8	4	10	8	4	8	5	9	5	5	96

5*s*; in September Pia Louche went back to Holland with her children to rejoin her husband. She had 11*s*. In April 1635 Jaques de Wuider, his wife and three children on their way to St Christophe, landed at St Pierre where one of the children died. They were given 4*s* and lent a further 6*s* to go back to France. In addition to these, there were large numbers of French and Flemish sailors passing through who received help: eleven French sailors in April 1633; three said to have been captured by the Turks in January 1637; twelve in February 1638, sixteen in March and eight in April of that same year; nine in April and another twelve in October 1646; and two Flemish sailors who had lost their boat, going to Dover in July 1652. All these people were helped on their way with anything from 9*d* to 10*s*; men, women, children, poor students, ministers travelling back and forth, friars minor who had renounced Catholicism in 1631 and joined the church at Dieppe; and others out of work who were lent money until they found work.[27]

Wills provide another source of numbers and tell us the great variety of people who came to Canterbury. In 1577 the Canterbury Consistory asked for and obtained the same jurisdiction in the matter of wills as the Sandwich congregation had. Between 1577–82 no fewer than one hundred wills were proved by the Consistory and only four in the Canterbury church courts. After 1582, when the congregation was ordered to conform to English law and prove their wills in the Canterbury church courts, many of them did so, almost to the exclusion of the local people. Between 1582 and 1703 at least 356 wills have survived for known Walloons. It is true that for the most part, the marriage contract or *partage* of property set up before a notary or the clerk of the Politic Men, was of greater importance; but after the third generation, and increasing denization, and when families began to acquire properties in Canterbury and elsewhere, this ceased to be so. Cross says that most of the people who came to Canterbury came from about 250 separate families.[28] The largest number were silk-weavers, weavers and wool-combers, and in addition there were ministers, merchants, surgeons and physicians, silk-dyers, schoolmasters, reed-makers, glovers, wheelwrights, painters and tailors.[29] In all, some 4000 persons can be accounted for in these wills.

The wills are most interesting. Many of them are nuncupative; many are in French with literal English translations; and some mention property and family in the country of origin.

When Philippe Delme, the minister of the French Church visited Roger Salome to make his will in 1624, he found him 'being fall downe sick' as if it had happened very suddenly. He asked him three questions: did he leave all his goods to his wife for her life, and after her death to be divided equally among her kindred and his? Did he give his wife leave to give to the poor and the Walloon Church in Canterbury? And did he make his wife and John de Bever his executors? To all three questions Roger answered 'Yea' in the presence of two of his workmen, Israel Caron and Gilles le Clercq.[30]

Elizabeth le Blan alias White, who died in about 1598, never learned to speak English and her nuncupative will was 'by her uttered and declared … in the Walloon tongue or speech'. The translator has translated every name into English as well as every word: le Blan *alias* White, du Boys *alias* Wood, de Lespau *alias* Shoulder.[31]

Adrian van Os was a Canterbury silk-weaver who had escaped to England leaving the greater part of his family behind. In his will, dated 1620, he left £6 to his brother Peter and his two sisters Margaret and Catherine still in Antwerp.[32]

All these people left money to the ministers of the Walloon Church and the poor of the congregation, and their legacies often form a distinctive addition to the deacons' accounts.

Although the strangers were not allowed to own or purchase property in the city, they could rent it and they did purchase leases. They also purchased property elsewhere. Rents in Canterbury were fairly high in the late sixteenth century. Lucien Runer, for instance, rented a very small house in St Alphege from Nicholas Sympson, one of the prebendaries of Christ Church cathedral, for which he paid £8 a year in 1592.[33] As well as rents, the strangers were also liable for all city rates and taxes, although they tried hard on many occasions to win exemption. By their agreement entered into with the city on 15 March 1576, they were to be liable for all city taxes and duties, particularly those relating to the defence of the city: that is murage and watch. According to the city accounts for 1588, the Canterbury men drilled and marched to the roll of Walloon drums on Barham Downs in preparation for the war with Spain.[34]

Generally speaking, relations with the local population were good. There was none of the aggravation found in London where Londoners were frequently admonished for calling the strangers rude names in the streets. Instead there were pinpricks. Canterbury people were officious. They deliberately spelt strangers' names wrongly or mispronounced them; they were jealous of their apparent wealth and ability to work hard; occasionally they reported strangers for doing things they knew were allowed, to see what would happen, and perhaps also to see what their appreciation of their rights was. There are several petitions to the city Burghmote Court complaining of this sort of thing. Parents of a crippled child had regularly traded in the market with toleration, but when she was orphaned in about 1640, the market officer expelled her. He was reprimanded and she reinstated.[35] However, in contrast, in about 1648 John le Lew *alias* Wolfe was fined for producing cloth narrower than the permitted widths because he was taking an unfair advantage of others of his compatriots.[36] Anthony Palfar was also fined in about 1657 'for throweinge down of sope sudds' and complained at his harsh treatment, claiming it was because the court had been provoked 'by the unhandsome carriage of diverse of the French Congregation in the Citty'. He had no redress.[37]

Despite the general ruling that strangers would only be allowed to trade wholesale to Canterbury and other merchants, from 1577, a large number of strangers were allowed to 'open windows' in the city, that is they paid for the privilege of opening shops. They could not be free of the city, but in many instances were granted toleration from year to year for a small payment.[38]

In the years before 1600 the strangers paid no parish poor rate, but they do seem to have been liable for rates to the parish officials. Lucien Runer was liable for 4d a quarter towards the wages of the parish clerk of St Alphege, who presented him in the Church Court because he refused to pay 6d which was demanded. It was generally agreed among the witnesses at the court that only 4d was due, but all, with one exception (the wily parish clerk), said that they had never spoken to Mr Runer, and the churchwardens did not seem to know much about the matter at all.[39]

Archbishop Laud's attempts to force the members of the Canterbury French Church of the second and third generations to go to their parish churches was resisted vigorously by the members, but it had one very real effect: after 1638 the parish churches in Canterbury expected the Walloons to pay towards the relief of the English poor as well as their own. An attempt by St Peter's church was resisted in 1628 by John de Bever, but the churchwardens of St Mary Northgate successfully prosecuted many of the community there for non-payment in 1639.[40] Equally the clergy demanded tithes. James Bissell, rector of St Mary Bredman pursued Thomas de Rue in the church courts for months for non-payment, and won.[41] After 1655, with the backing of the Crown, the city ordered that the strangers should be liable for parish poor rates as the English were, though their grumbles about the matter still rumbled on.[42]

In the organisation of their work, the strangers had good relations with the city authority and the local community. Their market hall was established at Blackfriars in what is now known as the Dominican Priory, in about 1576. There all goods were examined and sealed before sale. The duty for sealing was 2*d* a piece. Even so, some attempted to withhold the money. John Ware, a silk-dyer, was examined at the 1606 Quarter Sessions for withholding £7 seal money on three pieces of silk rash belonging to Peter Cuteane, wool-comber, which were sent to him to be dyed black. In his defence he said that he had not undone the silk to avoid damaging it, and therefore technically he had not yet received it. He was ordered to bring the pieces before the court when they had been dyed.[43]

Receipts for 1576 were £6 18*s* 6*d* which represented 830 pieces of worsted and worsted variants made. Between 1577 and 1587 the average was 630 pieces, but from 1600 the number of pieces began to fall. In 1600 only 333 were sealed; in 1601, 353; in 1602, 205 and 1603, 238.

As well as the seal duty, the strangers also paid loom money at 3*d* for a normal sized loom and twice as much for a Dutch loom. In the ten years, 1583–93, the average number of looms was 800, although the number fluctuated a good deal and fell later. In 1610 silk-weavers James de New, James le Keux, Mardoche Renard, Abraham Monnier and Pierre le Noble petitioned the City Burghmote to allow them to pay a yearly stipend instead of loom money. The idea does not appear to have been accepted but with hindsight, it might have been better if the city had so agreed.[44]

But if the strangers had good relations with the city in this respect, they frequently fell foul of the London weavers who complained that the strangers were stealing their trade by working too hard; not producing the correct widths of material; and worst of all, contravening the apprenticeship regulations which denied to anyone the right to produce such goods unless he had served a seven-year apprenticeship. This no stranger could do because Canterbury people could teach them nothing. Indeed strangers taught them.

Because they were so worried and harassed by spies and informers from London, the Canterbury strangers formed themselves into a trade union, the Drapers' Union, for their own mutual defence. Nevertheless, the London weavers continued their persecution and in 1638 persuaded the king, for a huge bribe, to make the Weavers' Company of London responsible for weavers throughout the country. As might be imagined, this caused nothing but strife and endless litigation, and was one of the principal causes of the decline of the Canterbury cloth industry. Even the reversion of the decision on the monopoly failed to help, and many Canterbury weavers went bankrupt or migrated to London.[45]

The ultimate decline of this major industry makes one wonder whether the enterprise of accepting a company of strangers did come up to the city's expectations. The answer is undoubtedly yes. Canterbury benefitted to a very real extent in that by the eighteenth century it had become a most prosperous place. Nor did it suffer from having the strangers within its walls. Each year the city authority issued a statement to the Crown that the Walloon congregaton 'not onely maintaine their owne poore at their owne charge without permitting any of them to begg... but also sett many hundreds of the English poor on work'. The system worked. There was no question that the strangers would come on the parish rates if they maintained their own poor so efficiently, and helped the city by providing work for its own poor and others. They brought finance too. Many of the strangers became wealthy and influential citizens. And so the city continually pressed that the Walloon congregation remain separate, and opposed Archbishop Laud's ideas of integration with vigour. And although the congregation dwindled rapidly towards the end of the eighteenth century, there are still many names in the city to remind us of a successful and laudable experiment.

Notes

1. W. Boys, *Collections for a History of Sandwich* (Canterbury, 1786–92) p. 740.
2. Ibid, pp. 740–2.
3. Canterbury City Burghmote Minute book, 1567, p. 21v.
4. Wallóon Church records.
5. F. W. Cross, *History of the Walloon and Huguenot church at Canterbury*, Huguenot Society of London, Quarto Series, vol. XV (London 1898) p. 22.
6. Ibid, pp. 21, 22.
7. See Maidstone parish registers for this period and Register Transcripts.
8. H. J. Todd, *Some Account of the Deans of Canterbury* (Canterbury, 1793) p. 20.
9. Cross, *History of the Walloon and Huguenot Church*, p. 15.
10. Dean and Chapter Act Book 1575, p. 86v.

11. St Alphege parish register, no. 1.
12. C. R. Bunce, *Notes from the City Archives*, (London, 1791). See also Cross, *History of the Walloon and Huguenot Church*, p. 39.
13. W. Somner, *Antiquities of Canterbury* (Canterbury, 1640) pp. 175, 176.
14. Dean and Chapter Minute book, 1897.
15. Walloon Church *Actes II*, p. 23.
16. City Quarter Sessions Roll 1606 is a good example of this.
17. Walloon Church *Actes*, 1597.
18. Walloon Church Deacons' accounts C1, C2.
19. Ibid.
20. Canterbury City Burghmote Minute book, 1582, p. 44v.
21. Ibid.
22. Somner, *Antiquities*, p. 175.
23. The figures for the size of the congregation were supplied to the City by the Consistory.
24. All Saints, Canterbury, parish register.
25. Canterbury City Subsidy Rolls B/C/S III, 1–36, 1598–1601.
26. See Deacons' accounts.
27. Ibid.
28. Cross, *History of the Walloon and Huguenot Church*, p. 25.
29. It has generally been said that the first influx of strangers in Canterbury were not silk-weavers but worsted-weavers. The explanation is that silk-weavers were being employed to weave worsted and included silk in some types of cloth.
30. Canterbury probate records, original will, 1624.
31. Ibid, original will, 1598.
32. Ibid, original will, 1620.
33. Canterbury Court Book X.11.2, pp. 293, 294.
34. See Canterbury Muster Rolls where foreign names appear with great frequency. City Account book, 1598.
35. Canterbury City petitions.
36. Ibid.
37. Ibid.
38. Toleration fines in Canterbury City accounts.
39. X.11.2, see note 33.
40. Canterbury Court Books: presentations 1628, 1639.
41. Ibid, 1610.
42. Walloon Church records, court cases and opinions.
43. Canterbury City Quarter Sessions records, 1606.
44. Canterbury City Petititons.
45. See note 42.

5 Jacob David:
A Huguenot London Merchant of the late Seventeenth Century and his Circle

Henry G. Roseveare

London has always harboured a cosmopolitan merchant community. Throughout the Middle Ages the city had been the beneficiary of successive visitations and immigrations of Lombards, Flemings, Hanseatics, Venetians, Gascons.[1] The late sixteenth century had added a distinct influx of French and Walloon refugees and the 1650s had brought the return of the Jews.[2] By Charles II's reign most trading nations were well represented, both by naturalised immigrants and resident agents domiciled in and around the city and its Thames-side wharves.

There was nothing unique about London in this respect. Few great trading towns of Europe (or, indeed, the East) were without their colonies of 'strangers' and naturalised foreigners. By the mid-seventeenth century about 12 per cent of Moscow's merchants were of alien origin – mostly Dutch and German and the odd Englishman left over from the expulsion of the Russia Company in 1649.[3] In Narva there were Swedish, German, Finnish, Estonian, Russian and English churches to serve the needs of its several merchant colonies,[4] and Dutch, English and German were heard as much as Swedish in the streets of Stockholm or Gothenburg.[5] Hamburg's merchant community was quite remarkably mixed. Of more than 1000 merchant-burghers inducted in the course of the century, between 50 and 60 per cent were immigrants – Dutch and Flemish, Portuguese and English, who sustained the city's strong links with Iberia and the Mediterranean, as well as with London, Amsterdam and Rouen.[6] In Cadiz, of the 4800 foreign merchant-residents, more than half were Italians and a third were French but there was still room for several hundred English, German, Dutch, Russian and Polish traders.[7] Genoa, Leghorn,

Naples, Venice, Constantinople, Smyrna and Aleppo all had their foreign-merchant colonies, and an elaborate network of Dutch, English and French consulates protected their interests on both sides of the Mediterranean.[8]

The compulsions of world trade ensured this large and growing dispersal of business connections, and the late-seventeenth century is a particularly significant stage in the process for it is an epoch which saw the fruits of earlier colonial exertions begin to pay off and extend the range of commodity demand in western and central Europe. Apolaustic males, from Kinsale to Kiev, were insisting on the consolations of tobacco; an insatiable sweet-tooth was summoning the sugars of Brazil and the Caribbean, the raisins of Malaga and the currants of Zante. The peppers of Malabar, Java and Sumatra were competing with the ginger-roots of Barbados and Jamaica to spice the food of European households.[9] And these luxuries were getting cheaper all the time. By 1660 sugar prices had fallen nearly 75 per cent in twenty-five years, tobacco by 85 per cent.[10] Pepper prices nose-dived in the 1660s and were only preserved by rationing supply.[11] More pertinent to the economic life of western Europe was the less dramatic but valuable fall in raw-material prices for the textile industries of England, France and the Netherlands as cottons and vegetable dyes, like indigo, came into wider production in the West Indies and Americas.

It was pre-eminently the Dutch who were the intermediaries in this expansion of world trade, but after mid-century the balance of commercial power was beginning to shift slowly against them as a protectionist England and Colbertian France digested the lessons of Holland's business supremacy. After more than fifty years of depression and crisis in European economies, the seventh and eighth decades of the century saw stirrings of growth and change. There were new opportunities to be taken and fortunes to be made both in Rouen and in London.[12]

Among those who seized these opportunities and prospered in seventeenth-century London was the Lethieullier family – Protestant immigrants whose forebear, Jan Le Thieullier, had been martyred in Valenciennes in 1567 or 1568.[13] His grandson, John Lethieullier I (1591–1679), had been settled in England since 1605 and by the 1650s he presided over a prosperous trading house and a family of thriving sons.

It is his eldest son, John II (1633–1719) who is a central figure in much that follows. Respected by Pepys as 'a pretty, civil, understanding merchant' he had a wife whom Pepys positively adored – 'my fat brown beauty', 'a very noble lady'.[14] John had married her in 1658, and it was a rich match for her father was Sir William Hooker, a future Lord Mayor of London.[15] 1658 was also significant for the marriage of John's sister, Leonora, to a more recent immigrant called Charles Marescoe. Born about 1633 he had come from Lille in 1649 – a Protestant certainly, but not necessarily a refugee.[16] His brother Peter came with him and while Peter set up in what was probably the family-business, as a silk-weaver, Charles served his apprenticeship as a merchant, keeping the books and answering the letters of a London-based Dutch merchant called Jaques Boeve (*alias* James Bovey). Boeve conducted a diversified trade, not merely with the Netherlands but with the Baltic, and it was this Baltic connection which Marescoe cultivated when he set up independent trade in 1654, initially partnered by a John Buck from Hamburg. It must have been a successful business for Marescoe to be able to attract the alliance of the wealthy Lethieulliers by 1658 and indeed, by 1664, Marescoe was worth at least £13 000.

The survival of his ledgers from this date allows us to see him at work, exporting to Hamburg, Amsterdam, Lille, Rouen and Cadiz and importing largely from Stockholm and Gothenburg. Since the 1650s he had been lucky enough to acquire the London agency for some of Sweden's major merchant-industrialists, manufacturers and exporters of iron, copper, steel and latten, and for the great monopoly Tar Company which supplied most of the pitch and tar requirements of western Europe. When Pepys tells us, on 23 July 1665, that the Council spent most of a Sunday on 'Marisco's Tar-business' we can only imagine what it was, for neither the records of the Council, nor of Pepys, nor of Marescoe, tells us precisely. But Marescoe in 1665, at the start of a strenuous Anglo-Dutch conflict, had shrewdly equipped himself with the raw materials of war – iron, copper, pitch and tar. More poured in for him on neutral Swedish shipping. Marescoe was thus ideally placed to make a fortune at the British navy's expense and he did so, reaping huge profits which meant that by 1667 he had more than doubled his capital and was worth over £30 000.

Marescoe was now a substantial citizen, firmly rooted in the commercial life of London. He had secured naturalisation under the Protectorate, in 1657; he prudently re-enacted this under the monarchy in 1660. In 1662 he had been nominated by the Lord Mayor to take the freedom of the city by redemption[17] and he became a liveryman of the prestigious Clothworkers Company. He rented a house in Fenchurch Street until its destruction in the Great Fire, after which he shared accommodation with John Lethieullier and his family. His own family was growing. A daughter, Leonora, had been born in 1659 and she was followed by Jane in 1661, Elizabeth in 1663, Mary in 1665 and Anne in 1666. His own brother and sisters were also settling down, Peter in Spitalfields, where he was joined by their parents, Jacques and Jeanne. Sister Anthoinette was married to David le Griel, sister Marie to David Cocqueau, both naturalised immigrants from Dieppe.[18] All were members of the French Church, Threadneedle Street, where most of their numerous progeny were baptised,[19] and Marescoe's petty-cash books show him to have been a regular contributor to the Church's poor and clergy. (The wife of a Samuel Marisco, who received poor relief from the Church in 1667,[20] was evidently not his kin.) However, this was not the only church to which he was attached. His parish church was St Dunstan in the East, where some of his daughters were baptised,[21] and in 1666, after the loss of his house, he became a parishioner of Low Leyton in Essex where he rented a country refuge for his wife and children and those of John Lethieullier. It was here, in 1668, that his remaining sister Elizabeth was married to his junior partner, Peter Joye.

Joye (1636–1721) has left a bigger mark than Marescoe in the annals of English commerce.[22] As a substantial Admiralty contractor in later years he grew very wealthy and was a leading member of the Eastland Company and Royal African Company. He too was of immigrant origin, probably Flemish, and was baptised into the Dutch Church, Austin Friars. This is another church to which Marescoe had affiliations and to which he made occasional gifts. Indeed, Marescoe, who could write good English and was perfectly at home with French, preferred to keep all his business records in Dutch, and the whole orientation of his trade was towards the vast Dutch network of commercial contacts stationed between Riga and Venice. Until 1665 France played little part in his affairs, but during the Second Anglo-Dutch War, under Swedish promptings, he was introduced to a number of trading houses in Rouen. Some of these too were of alien origin, such as Hermann Wetken from Hamburg, François de Coninck from Antwerp and his wife Catherine Crommelin who belonged to a wealthy manufacturing dynasty from the Netherlands. Even Thomas Legendre, the wealthiest merchant of Rouen (and perhaps of France), has been said to be of Dutch origin.[23] Certainly their affiliations were all Protestant, as were those of Marescoe's most genuinely French correspondent in Rouen, Robert Oursel. They belonged to a Huguenot community which has sometimes been numbered as large as

10 000 but more recently has been assessed on demographic evidence at barely 4000.[24]

One can sense the closely-knit, defensive posture of this community in Oursel's inquiry to Marescoe in September 1669 about the morals and religion of a young Frenchman then working in London who was to be affianced to a local Protestant family. 'Sy vous scavez la raison po'quoy il n'est plus antien de l'église francoise, obligez-moy de m'en faire participant.'[25]

It was in the same spirit of prudence and piety that, in July 1668, Oursel himself had offered a character reference. Marescoe had evidently asked him to recommend a suitable French-speaking clerk and Oursel put forward the name of Jacob David. He was young but experienced, the son of a Darnetal clothier but skilled in merchant-bookkeeping and 'quite free of the usual vices of youthful debauchery'.[26]

This innocent and well-meant recommendation was to have profound consequences, not for Oursel or Charles Marescoe, but for the Marescoe family, the Lethieulliers and, one might say, for the City of London and its French Protestant community.

But in 1668 this could not be foreseen. From the autumn of that year David entered the Marescoe household and counting-house at £30 p.a. and began to put his mark on the firm's bookkeeping. It was a neat, even elegant, mark, considerably superior to that of the other young clerk in Marescoe's service, Moses Coulon. Coulon, also of the French Protestant congregation, had an irredeemably untidy scrawl and it was left to him to keep the rough notebooks and cash-books of the counting-house. Jacob David, on the other hand, was quickly entrusted with the journals and ledgers, the very summit of the bookkeeping system formerly kept by Marescoe, in which mistakes and alterations were simply not permissible. There can be no doubt that David was hard-worked. Even with the help of his partner, Peter Joye, and the two clerks, Marescoe must have been hard put to keep pace with the huge volume of business he now generated. In 1668 he received imported goods on forty-three ships and loaded exports on to ninety-four involving an enormous amount of paperwork and comings and goings to pack, load, land and store and clear through customs. At the same time the firm was receiving about thirty letters a week in four or five languages which all required answers in duplicate.

The volume and value of business declined somewhat in 1669, for the post-war boom had come to an end and many overseas markets were glutted. Hamburg had enough sugar, Rouen enough tin and

Seville enough cloth to last them some time. But there were still forty-one ships to receive and seventy to despatch, and the partnership continued to thrive.

Marescoe was now well able to afford to live in a style appropriate to his stature. Recognised by the English government as the official agent for Swedish imports, and having won an important legal dispute about these imports with the City of London, he determined to put down his marker in bricks and mortar and build himself a mansion near the river. In 1669 he began to build on a site he had purchased between Thames Street and Tower Street, not far from Custom House quay, and he built not one house but several, four of which he quickly leased. At the centre of the group was a mansion house which, when completed, was to pay tax on twenty-three hearths.

A son, Charles, had been born to the Marescoes in May 1668 but died a year later. Another son, James, was born early in 1670 and it was to this child that Marescoe bequeathed all his recently-acquired real property when, in September 1670, he made a will.[27] The illness which prompted this precaution was a fever lasting nine days. At the end of it Charles Marescoe was dead.

In facing this sudden loss the widow Leonora had good and capable support. Her brother John was close at hand, as were Peter Marescoe and Peter Joye, all overseers of the will. But there was another important, interested party – the City of London. As a citizen leaving children in infancy, Marescoe (or his estate) was subject to the 'custom of London' which meant that the Court of Aldermen, through its Orphans Court sub-committee, had jurisdiction.[28] One-third of the estate might go absolutely to the widow and the testator could dispose of one-third as he wished, but the other one-third was absolutely the children's and must remain under the administration of the City until they came of age or married. The estate would have to be audited and registered before the City's Common Sergeant before administration could begin.

It took some time to establish the final figures and two reports were filed before all debts were in, but at the end of the day one can say that Marescoe died worth about £40 000 excluding his real estate, of which about £3300 was in cash and over £32 000 adventured in trade. He had shares in five ships and some East India Company stock as well as a small hoard of gold and silver coins valued at £200. His personal effects are eloquent of a decent simplicity – three dark suits, two coats, two cloaks, two waistcoats, six shirts, six drawers, a dozen pocket-handkerchieves – the whole lot valued at £10.[29] But he left £150 to the

French Church, Threadneedle Street and £5 apiece to its ministers. Christ's Hospital received £50 and the poor of Low Leyton and St Margaret Pattens were remembered. He gave £25 each to Moses Coulon and Jacob David, and there were may other small bequests to kinsmen, godchildren, servants and friends.

The widow Leonora quickly helped herself to £18 850, which turned out to be nearly £6000 too much. Divided into thirds the net estate due to her was £13 001 0s 11d – the remaining £26 000 being invested in the Chamber of the City of London on behalf of the children. She was made to disgorge the balance, though not before she had earned some interest on it, and she kept her hand tightly on the East India Company shares.

This could have been the end of the matter, and so it was for some years. At worst, eyebrows may have been raised at the widow's new style of living. Confined to £10 a month housekeeping during her husband's lifetime she now began to spend considerably more. Her account books (kept in French) baldly record *'fraits de mesnage'* at the rate of £100 per month! The unfinished mansion began to receive ornate and costly alterations. There were tapestries, silver, cabinet-work, jewels ... She bought herself a diamond bracelet and spent £210 on a miniature portrait of her late husband surrounded by more diamonds. The children did not impede her. James died in 1671, Elizabeth and Mary in 1673. The remaining daughters were packed off to boarding school at Hackney for a total of £100 p.a. which came out of the interest on their estate, as did much of the cost of their father's funeral – a lavish £630 – and the expenses of completing the mansion – another £2760.

However, Leonora did not give herself wholly to pleasures. She determined to continue her husband's business as best she could with the existing team, retaining Joye as her partner with a £4000 share, putting up £4000 herself and taking in Coulon and David at £1000 each. She also continued trading on her own account in collaboration with her brother John, who was a rising man in the Merchant Adventurers, the Levant Company and the East India Company. On this basis she could hope to cover some of the costs she was incurring.

But 1671 was a year of some depression in European commerce, and with only one-third of her husband's resources she could not easily meet the demands for credit and deferred terms which were made both by her import-suppliers and export-purchasers. Inevitably, customers were lost. The Tar Company turned elsewhere, as did some of the great Swedish industrialists. The Third Anglo-Dutch War, which broke out in 1672, found the firm without the substantial stocks of 1664–5, which was just as well, for there was nothing like the same surge of demand. Between 1670 and 1673 her net gains were barely £720 p.a. compared with the £3900 p.a. reaped in her husband's last years, and her assets were threatened by the 'Stop of the Exchequer' of January 1672 which had the effect of freezing her £1500 on deposit with the goldsmith–banker, Isaac Meynell.

Whether it was her decision or Joye's that their partnership should break up is not clear, but at the close of 1673 it was wound up and Joye went his way towards independent prosperity. He was immediately replaced by Jacob David, and perhaps this could have been foreseen, for when the partnership of October 1670 was set up David's £1000 share had been lent him by Leonora – the first indication that he may have been held in her special esteem. Certainly he had no great means and his recent dividends in no way equipped him to be Leonora's equal partner. Only a marriage could make sense of the relationship, but for the moment there was no marriage.

Instead it was the 16-year-old daughter, Leonora II, who was partnered in marriage in February 1675 to Thomas Frederick, son of Alderman Sir John Frederick, a former sheriff and Member of Parliament for the City.[30] It was a rich and ostentatious wedding. Her portion was £11 000 and the Fredericks endowed them with £6500 in cash and rentals of £300 p.a. The wedding-feast at Drapers' Hall was a lavish affair, costing a delighted Mrs Marescoe £500.[31] Nor did she stop there. Having lavished presents on bride and bridegroom she insisted that the couple should come and live in the mansion with free bed and board for themselves and their servants. This they did, for several months, until Leonora and Jacob announced their own nuptials in October.

The young Leonora Frederick was deeply shocked and indiscreetly said so, remonstrating with her mother. No doubt, as a young heiress newly allied with the merchant aristocracy, she felt herself diminished by her mother's alliance to a penniless man she had always regarded as a domestic servant. Perhaps she detested David? Whatever the case, a furious and vindictive row broke out between mother and daughter, and amid the mother's accusations of rank ingratitude the Fredericks were bundled out of the house and pursued with large bills – £200 for their wedding feast, £300 for their board, and £575 9s for the bride's trousseau! They took refuge in Islington.

Jacob and Leonora were duly married and continued trading with the wife's capital of some £15 000. Charles II had made his peace with the Dutch in February 1674 and while most of Europe remained at war neutral England enjoyed a free run of European commerce from the Baltic to the Levant. It was a time of booming commercial prosperity and the Davids, with their influential customers in Stockholm, Hamburg, Amsterdam, Rouen and Seville, had the chance of huge gains. David was commissioned to supply the Swedish Queen Mother's household livery; he despatched salt and wine to Stockholm and received large amounts of iron and copper in return. He enlarged the firm's trade with France, sending goods to Rouen, La Rochelle and Bordeaux. He tried to break into the jealously-guarded trade of the Levant Company, soliciting imports from Aleppo, Smyrna and Constantinople. In 1677 he secured (through no great effort of his own) the coveted contract to sell the Swedish Tar Company's pitch and tar throughout England. At a time when the English navy was just beginning a massive rebuilding programme for thirty new ships this was a golden windfall.

Inevitably it provoked jealousy, but it also generated official concern. The English Resident in Stockholm reported a number of disturbing features of the situation – that English vessels were being excluded from carrying the pitch and tar, that the contract was a furtive one and that 'Mr Davis' was in fact a Dutch stooge, front-man for a Dutch-financed operation which could at will cut the lifeline of this vital strategic commodity.[32] He was not aware (although the English government must have been) that 'Mr Davis' was in fact a Frenchman, endenizened in 1675 but not yet naturalised.[33]

There is not the slightest evidence that David or his Swedish and Dutch suppliers had any sinister intention towards the English economy or navy. On the contrary, it was the Tar Company's market strategy to use David and the two large Thames-side warehouses he had hired to hold stocks for the Dutch market as well as the English, so it was the former that was at risk. But the situation in which David was placed in 1677–9 is one in which it is easier to understand the suspicion and hostility which was beginning to surround him.

Young Thomas Frederick was the principal source of that hostility and he had every justification. He had received little over £8000 of his wife's portion and when he asked David for an elucidation of the accounts in February 1676 he was angrily repulsed.[34] There seemed to be little he could do but simmer until 1678, when he received a friendly hint from the deposed Peter Joye.[35] His advice was that Frederick should find out what had become of the East India Company shares which had once formed part of the Marescoe estate.

Marescoe had bought the shares shrewdly when they stood below par and by his death held £2250 in paid-up stock. Valued at par this had been transferred to the widow as part of her £13 000. It was to be revealed later that the City's normal practice was to have such stock sold and the proceeds pooled for the beneficiaries, but by an oversight this had not occurred. Indeed, by an even stranger oversight the shares had been inventoried not as an asset but as a 'good debt' owed by the East India Company. It was, the widow later admitted, 'a great mistake of him or them that writt and made up said inventory' but being a woman and ignorant of financial matters she denied any deliberate intent to deceive.[36]

However, her actions tend to belie this story. In 1672, presumably in order to mask their origin and validate her ownership she 'sold' the shares to her brother John who then immediately 'sold' them back to her (although without registering the transfer in the East India Company records). In 1675, after the quarrel with Frederick, she transferred them to the trusteeship of her brothers, Sir John (as he now was) and Samuel. By October 1677 the shares were worth £5512 and had yielded £2925 in dividends since 1670.

Frederick's discovery of these transactions opened up another avenue for legal action to add to his existing case against the mismanagement of his wife's patrimony. Large, unwarranted sums had been debited to the children's estate and yet the widow was living high in the mansion for a peppercorn rent. Frederick felt he had a case to lay before the City's Orphans Court, and it was not difficult to get a hearing for his father was a member. Thus in 1678 the Davids were at last called to render account and tried to do so, but their report was found insufficient as was a second in February 1679. Frederick was given leave to sue the Davids and the City Chamberlain was joined to the suit as fellow-plaintiff on behalf of the other children, who were still minors.[37]

The Davids responded with a mixture of cunning and defiance. They judged it would shorten the odds against them if the other two daughters could be married off and through the services of a professional marriage-broker they negotiated the disposal of Jane, aged 18, to John Lewknor, the under-age Member of Parliament for Sussex.[38] He was a deferential and needy young man who, for £7100 down, willingly signed a general release discharging the Davids of further responsibility for Jane's estate. That left Anne, and in 1681 the

Davids tried to repeat the strategem of 1679. They selected a boyhood friend of Jacob, called David Gansel of Rouen. He was, it seems, fat and 40 and quite clearly a fool, for his letters betray a weak fumbling and totally incompetent character which was ideally suited to Jacob's needs. Enticing him to England with Anne's prospective fortune, appealing for his help to safeguard her from kidnap, Jacob finally offered him an extra £1000 down to marry the girl on only one condition – that he sign a post-dated release, discharging the Davids from any further claims. This he trustingly did, for he could read no English.[39]

I can find no record of the marriage of Gansel and 15-year-old Anne, which is hardly surprising for it was a clandestine one, undertaken without the permission of the Orphans Court. Can it be true, as was later alleged, that David presided at the nuptials and himself read a sermon!? Whatever the case, the marriage could not remain secret for long and by the end of July 1681 David and Gansel were under arrest in Newgate, pursued by the rancour of the Fredericks and the outrage of a francophobe public.[40]

So far, Frederick's Chancery case against the Davids had been going slowly. Employing some of the best lawyers of the day, Jacob had thrown an endless series of delays in the path of a full hearing and it was not until October 1682 that a ruling could be given on the side-issue of the East India Company shares. It found 'that there had been a secret contrivance which is a badge of fraud in the defendants, to deprive the testator's estate of the said stock'.[41] The Davids were ordered to make good the plaintiffs' share in the stock and its dividends.

But that was far from the end. Altogether, the case of 'Frederick *v* David' was to last eleven years and involve no fewer than 105 hearings before the Court. It is impossible to narrate here all the excuses and evasions which impeded its course, but David had been quickly released from Newgate in 1681 and had carried on business as if nothing was amiss, joining the Eastland Company in 1682 and carrying on his large trade with Sweden.[42] In February 1684 the Court found the Davids provisionally liable for over £11 000 in concealed profits but a year later they had paid nothing. Ultimately, on 4 August 1685 a writ of execution was served upon them and, after a brief period under arrest, they fled to Amsterdam on 9 October, still defying Chancery and the Fredericks. In their absence the final reckoning was given by Lord Chancellor Jeffreys on 22 April 1687. He found the Davids liable for nearly £20 000 and plaintiffs' costs, put at

£1885 8*s* 5*d*, were awarded against them. Even Gansel, who had suffered so much, was allotted his share.[43]

What is the significance of this unedifying story for the Huguenots of London? It is difficult to believe that it had none. After all, Jacob David had been a deacon of the French Church, Threadneedle Street, between 1676 and 1678 and he was an elder in the years 1684–6. He played a leading part in the reception of the refugees in 1681 and was involved in their later migration to America in 1685.[44] He made generous gifts to the Church in 1680–1 and the Church in turn had £150 on deposit with him at 6 per cent since 1676. He was clearly an eminent, active and trusted member of the French Protestant community in which he had many relatives and friends. Among his business associates were the whole Houblon family and he negotiated insurance policies with Abraham, Isaac, John and Peter. Among his correspondents were Hillaire Reneu, Hermann Olmius, Charles Trinquand and Humphrey Willet, men whose names must figure in the Huguenot heritage.[45] Among those who gave evidence in the preliminaries to the trial were George Papillon, Moses Coulon and the whole Lethieullier clan, including the venerable John I.

In Rouen he had trusting admirers, among them a future émigré family, the Beuzelins. Young François Beuzelin, son of the merchant Benjamin (an elder of the Rouen consistory)[46] had been a welcome visitor to London, and in the darkening atmosphere of 1679 he wrote touchingly of his love for the city – 'for I receive more support there than in any other place, I am near my friends and one breathes there an air of liberty which one cannot find anywhere else'. But older men watched the English scene with some anxiety. Robert Oursel had welcomed the marriage of William of Orange and the Princess Mary in 1677 but in 1679 he and his friends were dismayed by the anti-Catholic fury of the Popish plot and lamented the propaganda value of English Roman Catholic refugees arriving in Dieppe.

An unpleasant fate of exile or abjuration awaited several of these correspondents. Hermann Wetken abjured but his wife would not and was immured in a convent. The great Thomas Legendre abjured, as did the Vroulings, another important merchant family of Dutch origin. The Beuzelins fled, first to Hamburg, as did Robert Oursel's eldest son.[47] Much of David's clientele in Rouen must have been broken up by the end of 1685, and compared with the travails that they endured those of David must have appeared insignificant. One cannot judge for no letters from them survive after 1680.

But the letters of one of David's most interesting friends do.[48] The Rev. John Strype, the great antiquarian and historian of the Church, was the minister of Low Leyton, and the friendship of this amiable and distinguished scholar does something to redeem one's opinion of the Davids. Like the French Church he had entrusted Jacob with his savings of £250 at 6 per cent and there is no evidence that the trust was ever abused. Through Jacob and Leonora's letters to him one can briefly trace their later lives. At first all was well. Settled in Amsterdam they were joined by their 12-year-old daughter Isabella and an 8-year-old son who within months were happily speaking Dutch and learning to skate. Old and new friends gathered around them, trying to appease Leonora's bitterness at her daughter and son-in-law. Jacob described her pacing the house, consumed with resentment, 'nothing but skin and bon[e]'. But by 1689 she had more substantial griefs. The children died of smallpox and within a short time the broken-hearted father followed them. Leonora lived on, arthritic and house-bound. Thanking God 'I have enough to spare, but not to spend prodigally' she consulted Strype about her plans for a fitting monument at Low Leyton to her first husband 'dear Mr Marescoe' and long-dead children from that marriage.[49] In the living ones she could take little satisfaction. Jane Lewknor had disgraced herself by a very public adultery and in 1685, after eloping with her lover (the Member of Parliament for Stockbridge) she was duly divorced and her children illegitimised. Anne Gansel's husband, after years of torment in the hands of Chancery, exhibited an alarming streak of extravagance in building a fine mansion at Low Leyton.[50] The Gansels were to found a short-lived county family which produced a Lieutenant-General William Gansel in the third generation but died out in debt.

As for Thomas Frederick, he grew wealthier and became Deputy Governor of the East India Company but died with little love for his children from whom he diverted £9000 to London hospitals on grounds of their disaffection. But his wife was not ashamed of her Marescoe blood. As a widow after 1721 she commissioned a *famille verte* porcelain service with the armorial bearings of Frederick impaling Marescoe, with the Marescoe arms repeated twice.[51] Her pride in family was to rise still higher in 1726 for in that year her daughter Jane, already widowed, married James Murray, Duke of Atholl.[52] The Marescoe-Lethieullier line had thus followed the almost-ideal pattern of upward social mobility, though shot through with scandal and ill-feeling. In that respect it was probably not unique in the Huguenot heritage, and despite the discreditable circumstances of its

transmission we must be grateful for Jacob David's legacy, the vast body
of correspondence and commercial documents which illuminates the
trade of western Europe.[53]

Notes

1. A. Beardwood, *Alien Merchants in England, 1350–1377* (Cambridge: Massachusetts, 1931); S. Thrupp, *The Merchant Class of Medieval London, 1300–1500* (Chicago, 1949); G. A. Williams, *Medieval London, From Commune to Capital* (London, 1963); T. H. Lloyd, *Alien Merchants in England in the High Middle Ages* (Brighton and New York, 1982).
2. C. Roth, *A History of the Jews in England* (Oxford, 1964); A. S. Diamond, 'The Community of the Resettlement, 1656–84: A Social Survey', and M. Woolf, 'Foreign Trade of London Jews in the Seventeenth Century', in *Transactions of the Jewish Historical Society of England* 24 (1974–5) pp. 38–58.
3. P. Bushkovitch, *The Merchants of Moscow, 1580–1650* (Cambridge, 1980) pp. 58–69.
4. S.-E. Åström, *From Cloth to Iron: The Anglo-Baltic Trade in the Late Seventeenth Century*, Part 1 (Helsingfors, 1963) p. 125.
5. Per Sondén, 'Broderna Momma-Reenstierna', *Historisk Tidskrift* (1911) p. 145.
6. H. Reincke, *Hamburg: ein Kurzer Abriss der Stadt geschichte von den Anfängen bis zur Gegenwart* (Bremen, 1925) p. 184; M. Reissmann, *Die hamburgische Kaufmannschaft des 17.Jahrhunderts in sozialgeschichtlicher Sicht* (Hamburg, 1975) p. 214.
7. L. Garcia Fuentes, *El comercio español con America, 1650–1700* (Seville, 1980) p. 46.
8. K. Heeringa (ed.) *Bronnen tot de Geschiedenis van den Levantschen Handel II, 1660–1726*, Rijks Geschiedkundige Publicatien 34, (The Hague: 1917); P. Fraser, *The Intelligence of the Secretaries of State, 1660–1688* (Cambridge, 1956); P. Masson, *Histoire du commerce française au xviie siècle* (Paris, 1897) pp. 445–57.
9. E. E. Rich and C. H. Wilson, *The Cambridge Economic History of Europe: IV: The Economy of Expanding Europe in the Sixteenth and Seventeenth Centuries* (Cambridge, 1975); R. Davis, *The Rise of the Atlantic Economies* (London, 1973); K. G. Davies, *The North Atlantic World in the Seventeenth Century* (Minneapolis and London, 1974); K. Glamann, *Dutch–Asiatic Trade, 1620–1740* (Copenhagen and The Hague, 1958); K. N. Chaudhuri, *The Trading World of Asia and the English East India Company, 1660–1760* (Cambridge, 1978).
10. K. G. Davies, *North Atlantic World*, pp. 178, 188; Jacob Price, 'The Tobacco Adventure to Russia', *Transactions of the American Philosophical Society* new series, 51, Part 1 (Philadelphia, 1961) pp. 5–9.

11. K. N. Chaudhuri, *The Trading World*, pp. 318–19.
12. Jean-Pierre Bardet, *Rouen aux xviie et xviiie siècles: Les mutations d'un espace social* (Paris, 1983) pp. 188–96; R. Grassby, 'The Personal Wealth of the Business Community in Seventeenth Century England', *Economic History Review*, 2nd series, XXIII (1970); Grassby, 'English Merchant Capitalism in the Late Seventeenth Century', *Past and Present*, 46 (1970).
13. L. B. Ellis, 'The Lethieullier Family', *Proceedings of the Huguenot Society of London*, XIX, 2 (1954) pp. 60–3.
14. R. C. Latham and W. Matthews (eds) *The Diary of Samuel Pepys*, VI, (London, 1972) pp. 316, 328, 338.
15. For Lethieullier's career, and that of Sir William Hooker, see J. R. Woodhead, *The Rulers of London 1660–1689*, London and Middlesex Archaeological Society (London, 1965) pp. 92, 107.
16. W. A. Shaw, *Letters of Denization and Acts of Naturalization for Aliens in England and Ireland, 1603–1700* (Lymington, 1911) pp. 71, 78, Huguenot Society of London Quarto Series, vol. XVIII. For further details of Marescoe (and Jacob David) see H. G. Roseveare, *Markets and Merchants in the Late Seventeenth Century: The Marescoe–David Letters, 1668–1680*, Records of Social and Economic History Series, The British Academy (1987). The documents on which this is largely based – Public Record Office, Chancery Masters Exhibits, C. 114/63–78 – are currently under arrangement and withdrawn for conservation, so further references will be by date only.
17. City of London Record Office, Repertory 69 f.14b.
18. W. J. C. Moens (ed.) *Registers of the French Church, Threadneedle Street, London* vol. II. (Lymington, 1899) pp. 41, 155, Huguenot Society Quarto Series vol. XIII; Shaw, *Letters of Denization* p. 78.
19. Moens, *Registers*, pp. 155, 157, 163, 167, 169, 171, 180, 181, 186, 195, 204.
20. Records of the French Church, Threadneedle Street; Poor Relief Book (1661–1715) DB.MS 51, 11 Aug. 1667: see Huguenot Society Quarto Series vol. L, p. 46.
21. R. H. D'Elboux (ed.) *The Registers of St Dunstan in the East 1653–1691*, Publications of the Harleian Society, LXXXIV, LXXXV (London, 1954, 1955) pp. 8, 10.
22. K. G. Davies, *The Royal African Company* (London, 1957) pp. 67, 171–2; Åström, *From Cloth to Iron*, pp. 123, 160, 164, 165, 236; Woodhead, *Rulers of London*, p. 100.
23. J. Bianquis, *La révocation de l'édit de Nantes à Rouen*, with *Notes sur les Protestants de Rouen* by Emile Lesens (Rouen, 1885) p. 87; J. Mathorez, *Les étrangers en France sous l'ancien régime*, II (Paris, 1921) p. 161; Philippe Mieg, 'Les De-Coninck au Havre et à Rouen', *Bulletin de l'histoire du Protestantisme Français*, 5th Series (1921) pp. 97–115, 154–74, 252–67; Herbert Luthy, *La Banque protestante en France*, I (Paris, 1959) pp. 70. n.24.
24. J.-P. Bardet, *Rouen*, pp. 217–8.
25. Robert Oursel to Charles Marescoe, 17 September, 11 October 1669. The man was Laurent Martell.

26. Oursel to Marescoe, 11 July, 1668. 'Il a esté chez moy viron deux ans, pendant lequel temps m'a servy avecq toute fidellité ... il s'est perfectionné a tenir les livres et faire ce qu'un marchand doibt observir au fait du commerce. Je n'ay point apprins qu'il soit addonné a aucun vice de debauche de jeunesse, mais il se rend fort assidu aux affaires.'

27. PRO, PROB.11/333 No. 114.

28. Charles Carlton, *The Court of Orphans* (Leicester, 1974). Carlton's references to 'Jacob Davies' and 'Charles Morriscee' pp. 44, 71, being based on the prejudiced version in the subsequent court cases, are erroneous in almost every detail through no fault of the author.

29. PRO, C.10/199/30, Bills and Answers, 26 February 1681 (with inventory).

30. Woodhead, *Rulers of London*, p. 73; B. D. Henning (ed.) *The History of Parliament: The Commons, 1660–1690* (London, 1983) II, pp. 363–5.

31. The original butchers' and greengrocers' bills survive and reveal a feast containing pork, veal, Westphalia hams, haggis, calves tongues, oysters, pickled smelts, as well as tarts, syllabubs, ices, blancmanges and jellies, in a hall strewn with sweet herbs and adorned with twelve dozen nosegays.

32. Coventry MSS. Longleat, vol. 66 f.488 (Sir Edward Wood to the Secretary of State, 22 July 1677).

33. David secured letters of denization in October 1675 (*Calendar of State Papers, Domestic Series, 1675–76*, p. 585) and set on foot a bill of naturalisation but the long prorogation of 1675–7 deferred its completion until April 1677 – *Historical Manuscripts Commission, 9th Report*, Appendix, House of Lords MSS, pp. 87a, 95a.

34. PRO, C.24/1060 Part 2; evidence of John Whitehead, 3 January 1682 in 'Frederick *v*. David'.

35. Ibid, evidence of Peter Joye, 13 January 1682.

36. PRO, C.10/330/38 'Bills and Answers' – Answer of Jacob David and Leonora David, 18 March 1682.

37. To anticipate Frederick, Jacob David appealed first, but unsuccessfully, to Chancery for relief – PRO, C.10/137/38 (August 1679). For Frederick *v*. David see C.10/138/99; for Lord Mayor, etc. *v*. David see C.10/330/38; also C.10/199/30. Frederick *v*. David is also documented in the City of London Record Office, Small Suits, Box 1, no. 43.

38. B. D. Henning, *The Commons, 1660–1690*, II, p. 743. The draft marriage contract survives among the Marescoe–David papers.

39. PRO, C.10/225/54 – Further answer of David Gansel, 9 December 1686.

40. PRO, ADM.77/1 f.194v (newsletters to Sir Francis Radclyffe, 28 July, 1681). I am indebted to Dr Robin Gwynn for this reference.

41. PRO, C.33/259 f.53.

42. R. W. K. Hinton, *The Eastland Trade and the Common Weal in the Seventeenth Century* (Cambridge, 1959) p. 224; Åström, *From Cloth to Iron*, p. 235. David was also made free of the East India Company by redemption, 5 December 1679.

43. PRO, C.33/267 ff.642–4.

88   *Jacob David: Huguenot London Merchant*

44. Dr Robin D. Gwynn to the author, 29 January 1974.
45. Robin Gwynn, *Huguenot Heritage: The History and Contribution of the Huguenots in Britain* (London, 1985) pp. 67, 152–3.
46. J. Bianquis, *La révocation de l'édit de Nantes à Rouen*, p. 9.
47. Bianquis, pp. 9, 20, 53, 87; Mathorez, *Les étrangers en France*, II, pp. 161, 289; P. Mieg, 'Les De Coninck', p. 100.
48. Cambridge University Library, Strype MSS.
49. A. Hills, 'The Marescoe Slab in Leyton Church', *Essex Review* LI (1942) p. 221.
50. T. Wright, *The History and Topography of the County of Essex* (London, 1831) vol. II, p. 497; W. R. Powell (ed.) *The Victoria County History of Essex*, VI (1973) pp. 179, 186; G. O. Rickword, 'The Story of a Short-Lived County Family: Gansel of Leyton Grange and East Donyland Hall, Essex', *Essex Review* LIII (1944) pp. 81–5. (The information in 'The Marescoe Mansion', *Essex Review* LIII (1944) p. 69 is largely erroneous.)
51. A. Hills, 'Lethieullier Family China', *Essex Review* L (1941) pp. 204–8.
52. G. E. C[okayne] *The Complete Peerage* (London, 1910) vol. I. p. 319.
53. The Marescoe–David correspondence numbers some 10 500 letters, from which I have selected and translated 480 for publication in *Markets and Merchants*.

6 London Huguenot Silver

Hugh Tait

For the purposes of this survey, the following definition has been adopted: silver plate made in London by French-speaking Protestant silversmiths, who had decided to leave France or the Southern Netherlands (now Belgium and northern France) during the various periods of religious persecution in the sixteenth and seventeenth centuries. It has been decided to include with the French Protestants, those who were listed as 'Walloons'; they spoke a related dialect and, to the average Englishman, were virtually indistinguishable from the French Protestants. Indeed, around 1570 the French-speaking church that existed alongside the Dutch one at Sandwich (Kent), for example, was predominantly Walloon and in 1591 the minister of the Walloon/French church of London, Jean Castel, reported that the greatest part of his congregation came not from France but from 'Hannonii, Artesii, Flandri, Gallicani, that is, sprung out of the countries which obey the Spaniard' – in today's terms, the Franco-Flemish area approximating to that of modern Belgium.[1] This account will attempt to assess their contribution to the formulation of new fashions and tastes among the English patrons and to the adoption of new techniques by the London craftsmen. The latter are always referred to as 'goldsmiths' because, although they mainly worked in silver, they had become Freemen of the Worshipful Company of Goldsmiths and were thus able to have their silver plate assayed and marked at Goldsmiths' Hall, that is 'hallmarked'.

Various frauds perpetrated by goldsmiths and silversmiths in England in the early thirteenth century had led to the earliest recorded attempt to regulate the standard for gold and silver wares in this country, for an order was passed in 1238 by King Henry III requiring London's mayor and aldermen to choose six goldsmiths of the City to superintend the craft and lay down the standards of fineness for gold and silver, the latter to be no lower than the coinage of the realm. From this simple beginning there had developed, with the passing of statutes in the fourteenth and fifteenth centuries, a powerful medieval guild or livery company to control the craft of the goldsmith and silversmith in London.[2] Indeed, by the Statute of 1477 the Goldsmiths' Company was responsible for the 'Keeper of the Touch' and became liable for penalties for his misdoings, especially marking substandard wares. As a result, the Company appointed the first full-time assayer and agreed to pay him a salary of £20 a year. Furthermore, under this Statute, all alien and stranger goldsmiths within the City of London and two miles beyond were subject to the Wardens of the Goldsmiths' Company. Consequently, there was no longer any need to admit foreign craftsmen into the Company in order to control them. The Company tended to admit only those craftsmen in London who had served their long apprenticeships and had, therefore, all the requisite backing from their 'masters', all of whom would be Freemen of the Company and some might have been elected Liverymen of the Company. As a system, it had its virtues but over the long term such a closed shop system could have its faults.

Already in the reign of Henry VIII (1509–47), an instance of this closed-shop attitude can be glimpsed from the tantalisingly incomplete documentary accounts concerning the exclusion of a talented goldsmith, Hans von Antwerpen (John of Antwerp), by the Goldsmiths' Company of London. By piecing together the fragmentary evidence, enough of his life has been established to show that he had come to England from Antwerp as early as 1511, and, therefore, not as a refugee from religious persecution.[3] He had married an Englishwoman, had a large family and, indeed, the last known reference to him occurs in July 1550, when another son was born to him and baptised at the parish church of St Nicholas Acon, in Lombard Street, the church where goldsmiths had traditionally congregated. In 1528, some seventeen years after he had come to England, his workshop was evidently in a flourishing state because, in that year, four of his apprentices – all with Flemish-sounding names – were admitted to the Goldsmiths' Company, though he himself had not been admitted. According to the Company's records (Book D, p. 249 and p. 262) the four were Lucas Enover, Remyge Youge, Jasper Mylde, and Barthu Myller. However, in the following year, he and three Dutchmen were evidently in such trouble with the Company for refashioning old plate and returning it to the owners without first submitting it to the Hall for marking that they were required to provide sureties against any repetition of this offence or else suffer the closing down of their workshops. In 1536 Hans was sent to prison for employing in his workshop a foreigner, Andrew Pomert, without the necessary written authority (Book F, p. 42) but suddenly within ten months the Wardens of the Goldsmiths' Company had withdrawn their objections to this alien who had been working in their midst for more than twenty-five years and on 27 September 1537 he was admitted as a freeman of the Company. The Wardens' dramatic change of heart was due to the direct intervention of the powerful Thomas Cromwell, Henry VIII's Lord Privy Seal, who had signed a letter of recommendation dated 9 April 1537, requesting the admission of John of Antwerp. It seems that John had become a very close friend of the court painter, Hans Holbein the Younger, who between 1534 and 1536 was able to obtain court patronage for his goldsmith friend; by 1536, at the latest, Hans von Antwerpen was receiving commissions from Thomas Cromwell and in March 1537, his name appears in the Privy Purse Expenses of Henry VIII's daughter, Mary.[4] Faced with Thomas Cromwell's demand, the Goldsmith's Company no longer dared to refuse this foreign goldsmith admission to the Freedom.

This particular case from the 1530s serves to illustrate the Company's unwelcoming and unrelenting attitude towards alien craftsmen, especially if they were men of substance and quality. This closed-shop reaction was to be meted out consistently by the Company over the next 200 years to the more outstanding foreign goldsmiths and there is no indication that it made any difference if they had come to England for reasons of religious persecution or simply to earn a better livelihood under English patronage than they could hope to earn in their native cities. In the thirty-seven years of Henry VIII's reign, the number of foreigners living in London was steadily growing, far more being Flemish, Dutch or German-speaking than French, and early in Henry's rule, anti-alien feeling was brutally punished when, for example, fifteen Londoners were hung, drawn and quartered for their part in the 'Evil May Day' riot of 1517. If other foreign goldsmiths, active in London before Henry VIII died in 1547, were, like Hans von Antwerpen, made unwelcome at Goldsmiths' Hall, they were probably not French-speaking Protestants but mainly Flemish craftsmen, probably Walloons or Dutch-speaking goldsmiths.

However, it is important to observe the difficulties experienced by the subsequent waves of Huguenot silversmiths in the context of this traditional closed-shop attitude of the English craft guilds. Again and again, the same pattern seems to recur: the more gifted and influential the alien goldsmith, the more unwelcoming his reception at Goldsmiths' Hall and the more frequently court patronage and royal intervention was needed to safeguard his freedom to prosper in London. The country from which the alien goldsmith had come and the reason for leaving it seem not to have had much bearing on the

Company's closed-shop attitude, which sprang from a desire to protect the prosperity and privileged security of its members. Consequently, the London Goldsmiths' Company was always vociferously opposed to aliens when times were bad for their craft and when the threat from a group of aliens was calculated to contain serious consequences for their livelihoods.

The names of most makers before 1697 cannot be identified from the makers' marks stamped on pieces of English silver plate surviving from the sixteenth and seventeenth centuries because the London Assay Office was burnt down in 1681 and virtually all the previous records of working goldsmiths were destroyed in that disastrous fire. Consequently, it is extremely difficult to establish if a piece of silver plate bearing London hallmarks dating from those two centuries bears a maker's mark of a native English goldsmith or a maker's mark of an *immigré* or alien goldsmith. The difficulty is further complicated by the widespread practice of alien goldsmiths, who had not been admitted to the Freedom of the Company, to submit their products for assaying through a London goldsmith who was willing to collaborate with them; such pieces bear the mark not of their true maker, but of the London goldsmith who took them to the Hall to be assayed and marked. Finally, the problem is compounded by the fact that until 1696 there was no strict requirement for a London goldsmith to submit his plate for assay at the Hall if it had been specifically commissioned by a patron from him; it was only necessary for the plate *made for stock* to be assayed and hallmarked – and rarely would a goldsmith's stock have contained any of the really ambitious and important items. Specifically commissioned plate (not hallmarked) had to be sent to the Hall and marked if, and when, it was returned to be sold as part of stock; as a result, before 1697 a piece could bear a date-letter that post-dated the year of its manufacture, possibly by a number of years.[5]

Consequently, the identification of London sixteenth-century plate as the work of *immigré* goldsmiths, let alone French-speaking Protestant craftsmen, is virtually impossible, though a strongly un-English character or a peculiarly Continental technique may sometimes be detected and, in combination with other fragments of evidence, may cause a few extant pieces of plate to be attributed to *immigré* goldsmiths. From Henry VIII's reign, there are almost none, though it has been argued that one of the two famous silver-gilt Rochester Cathedral tazze (Plate 1, figures 2–3) may have been the work of a foreign craftsman using a large maker's mark with the device of an open crown, such as was used by certain goldsmiths on the Continent.[6]

It is suggested that the companion tazza, which is clearly struck with the London hallmarks for 1528 and a different maker's mark, was made as a close copy and, in 1532, was provided with a beautiful cover of matching design by yet another London goldsmith, for it bears a full set of London hallmarks for 1532 and another maker's mark. Certainly, the tazza with the crown mark no longer bears any hallmarks that can be read with certainty; they are too indistinct for definite identification. As the only other recorded tazza of this distinctive form is to be found in a drawing by Hans Holbein the Younger (Plate 1, figure 1), there are grounds for suggesting that it is the work of a foreign craftsman.

Similarly, the so-called girdle prayerbook of Queen Elizabeth I (now in the British Museum)[7] which was actually made in London for the English court at the beginning of the 1540s, has gold enamelled covers, the front of which is almost certainly by a foreign goldsmith from the Southern Netherlands, probably active in Antwerp. In the mid-sixteenth century, the city of Antwerp was the most prosperous and flourishing centre of fashion, with more than 124 goldsmiths and cutters of diamonds recorded there in 1557. The front of the girdle prayerbook is set with a gold relief of the Brazen Serpent that corresponds almost exactly with that used by the leading Antwerp goldsmith, Hans Mamacher, as a small part of his large elaborate silver-gilt bookcover, completed by 1543 for the Abbey of Tongerlo (now in Belgium). Not only has the Antwerp relief been copied in the London workshop but the front of the girdle prayerbook is enamelled in a far more accomplished and technically more difficult manner. Again, the presence of a foreign craftsman, probably from the Southern Netherlands, offers the most convincing explanation.

During the six years of the reign of Edward VI (1547–53), the ruling forces in England were increasingly Protestant and by 1550 both the Dutch and French churches of London had been established by Letters Patent to cope with the growing numbers of aliens, though how many of them were trained goldsmiths is not recorded. Under Mary I (1553–8), even after her marriage to Philip II of Spain in 1554, these foreign craftsmen and merchants were not required to leave the country if they had already been granted letters of denization or were 'known' merchants. Few fine pieces of English silver plate survive from the middle decades of the sixteenth century and yet there are two examples which have, with some justification, been attributed to alien goldsmiths working in London. Bearing different maker's marks, both were made in 1554, have clearly stamped London hallmarks and have well-attested pedigrees. The Bowes Cup (in the Goldsmiths' Hall)[8] was given to the Worshipful Company of Goldsmiths in 1561 by Sir Martin Bowes, a former Lord Mayor of London and Prime Warden of the Company. It is designed to incorporate polished and carved rock-crystal and both in its Mannerist style of ornamental detail and in its meticulous execution it is far in advance of what the London goldsmiths are known to have been producing at this time. Likewise, the silver-gilt Wyndham Ewer of 1554 (Plate II)[9] is executed in the full-blooded Mannerist style – a late phase of the Renaissance style that was at the height of fashion at the leading courts in Italy, France and Germany. Not only the surface ornament but the sophisticated form of the ewer, with its half-satyr, half-sphinx handle, is wholly *avant-garde* and accords closely with the tastes of the Fontainebleau court school and the derivative ateliers in Antwerp and the Southern Netherlands. Only one other Mannerist silver ewer of earlier date is recorded; it is the Aspremont-Lynden Ewer, made in Antwerp in 1544 (in the Waddesdon Bequest, British Museum).[10] It is perhaps executed with greater virtuosity but in general the Wyndham Ewer shares many of its principal characteristics. It would, therefore, be very surprising if so strangely un-English a piece of London plate had not been made by one of the foreign goldsmiths residing in England at that time.

Although Queen Elizabeth I (1558–1603) aligned herself with the French Protestants, making England an attractive refuge for the *immigré* craftsmen, the 1573 Return of Aliens, compiled the year after the Massacre of St Bartholomew in France and the outbreak of the second revolt against the Spanish in the Southern Netherlands, gives a total of no more than 7143 members of the foreign churches of London and the environs. Furthermore, the Return of 1573 indicates that 2541 of that total had come for reasons of employment rather than religion. There were some thirty-nine goldsmiths and silversmiths recorded in the metropolis in the 1593 Return of strangers.[11]

It becomes increasingly difficult to gauge how much influence these different groups of alien goldsmiths had on Elizabethan and early Jacobean London, because not only has much of the best plate been destroyed but the identity of these aliens and their products defies almost all attempts at recognition. Two very obvious and well-documented exceptions can be cited to illustrate the force of high-quality alien skills, the extent of which can only be guessed at today. First, there is the Gleane Cup,[12] a wholly un-English looking silver-gilt covered cup richly embossed in relief with scenes from the story of

Abigail and King David. It was given in 1633 to the church of St Peter Mancroft in Norwich, Norfolk, by Sir Peter Gleane, a former mayor and MP for Norwich. The London hallmarks on the cup had been previously read as '1625' but it is now established that the cup bears the date-letter for 1565. Though the maker's mark remains indecipherable, the maker's talents are outstanding and his work can stand comparison with the work of those foreign craftsmen who were specialising in this type of embossed figural work for patrons at the leading courts of Europe.

Second, there is the unparalled magnificence of the famous Rutland Ewer and Basin composed of agate and finely chased silver-gilt plate fully hallmarked; London, 1577[13]. Agate was not readily available in England and this magnificent ewer of Mannerist design is made of four cylinders of polished agate, of differing diameters, fitted together with finely worked silver mounts. The basin is most elaborately embossed with marine motifs and is set with thirteen bosses of polished agate. The writhing movement of the merman handle and the fine chasing of the four free-standing brackets framing the body of the ewer are executed to the highest standards prevailing at the major courts of Europe. The Duke of Rutland's Ewer and Basin, so very significantly finer in quality than the average London goldsmiths' work in Elizabeth I's reign, has some of the characteristics of Mannerism most favoured by the French court but its individuality sets it apart and the maker's mark – three trefoils within a trefoil – remains an enigma.

The foreign-looking silver-plate made in London during the Jacobean period tends to exhibit a mainly Dutch or Germanic quality, as in the case of the tall Booth Cup (in St John's College, Cambridge)[14] which is skilfully embossed with figures of classical warriors, gods and goddesses, and yet bears a complete set of London hallmarks for 1616 on both the cover and the body of the cup. Similarly, the small group of Jacobean plate ornamented with filigree and granulation can be attributed to the maker using a curious monogram mark, which may be read as 'TvL'.[15] This mark appears on two tall covered cups, both bearing London hallmarks for 1611, and both decorated with filigree and granulation – techniques much used by jewellers throughout Europe but never adopted by the English goldsmiths when making silver-plate. It would seem, therefore, that a short-lived London-based workshop belonging to a foreign craftsmen, perhaps of Netherlandish origin, was responsible for making these varied objects of excellent design and proportion.

With the creation of the independent Dutch United Provinces – in effect first recognised by the Spanish king in 1609 when a twelve-year truce was agreed – and with the return to more secure and better conditions in France after the Edict of Nantes in 1598, there was little need for French-speaking or Walloon Protestants to cross the Channel. As a result, these alien communities in England shrank as their members became assimilated into English towns and others started returning to France, where, especially after 1630 under Colbert's economic policies, the prospects were increasingly attractive. Nevertheless, in January, 1621/2, the Goldsmiths' Company of London had submitted to the Solicitor-General a petition and a list of some 180 aliens and strangers, whose activities still gave them grounds for concern.[15a] By 1625 when Charles I began his reign the amount of foreign plate being imported appears to have greatly declined, and, although the Company was by then functioning in a most efficient manner, there is no record that there was any ill-feeling expressed towards the Dutchman from Utrecht, Christian van Vianen, who in 1630 entered the King's service and in 1634 was awarded the enviable task of supplying a splendid set of plate for St George's Chapel, Windsor, for the account of the Order of the Garter. He was never admitted to the Company, although he lived in Westminster and, quite successfully, supplied outstanding pieces of plate to prominent members of the nobility until the Civil War forced him to return to Utrecht in the 1640s.[16]

However, after the restoration of the monarchy in 1660, Charles II appointed a foreigner 'in van Vianen's place' to be 'silversmith in Ordinary to His Majesty for chastwork within his Maties Closett and Bedchamber, and also the Closett and Bedchamber of the Queen'. The French-speaking goldsmith he appointed in 1661 was Jean-Gérard Cockus,[17] the son of a cordwainer of Liège, and by 1679, some eighteen years later, Cockus, along with another foreign goldsmith, was driven to submit a petition to the King complaining that he was being molested by the Goldsmiths' Company and that his work was being denied assaying and marking at the Hall because he was employing foreign craftsmen who, he maintained, were necessary for the techniques which he used. The precise outcome of his petition is not known but he appears to have continued in London as active as before, until 1697 when he was buried at St James, Piccadilly. As Jean-Gérard Cockus never registered a mark at the Hall, it must be assumed that he had an arrangement with some of the London goldsmiths to stamp their mark on his work, though his special commissions, like the famous and costly silver bed that he made for Nell Gwynn in 1674, would not have needed any hallmarking. After James II came to the throne in 1685, he was engaged in fitting out the new Royal Chapels at Whitehall, Windsor, Edinburgh and Dublin so that they could be adapted for Catholic worship and in the Royal Accounts Jean-Gérard Cockus was named (with the goldsmith, Charles Shelley) as the maker of the new sets of altar-plate but no piece of plate survives that can be identified as his work with any degree of certainty. There is no evidence to show whether Cockus was a Protestant when he left Liège nor to whom he had been apprenticed to learn the craft. It is not known if the foreigners he employed in his London workshop were French-speaking Protestants but, by 1679 when he had appealed to King Charles II for protection from the Company, a new and cruelly oppressive interpretation of the Edict of Nantes was being implemented in parts of France, thereby preventing trained Huguenots from entering guilds and exercising their skills. It may be supposed, therefore, that this French-speaking goldsmith from Liège might have offered employment to some of those French Protestant goldsmiths who were beginning to flee from France but if Cockus was also instrumental in getting an otherwise unknown Frenchman, Jean Henri Demoor, on to the Lord Chamberlain's list in 1678 as 'silversmith in ordinary', then his part in that story has not been recorded.

The Goldsmiths' Company had protested to the King as early as 1664 when two foreigners – Wolfgang Howzer, born in Zurich, and Jacob Bodendick, 'native of Limburg in Germany' – presented letters from the King instructing the Wardens to assay and mark their wares. The King acknowledged the reasons for the Company's reluctant agreement, adding that both men would only employ native subjects 'and not Strangers in their manufacture'.[18] This royal assurance was designed to allay the fears of the Company, whose members knew from experience that the workshops of prosperous alien goldsmiths were usually manned by foreign craftsmen and, according to the Company in 1664, for lack of orders many London goldsmiths did not have one-third of a day's work. Soon after, Sir Robert Viner, the Royal Goldsmith, became a prominent figure at Goldsmiths' Hall and, although he did not withdraw royal patronage from the foreigners, he seems to have avoided employing fresh immigrants. However, the delicate balance could no longer be maintained when the flood of Huguenot goldsmiths began to arrive in the late 1670s and early 1680s because of the *dragonnades* and other brutal forms of harassment and injustice inflicted on some Protestant communities in France.

The widespread anxiety at Goldsmiths' Hall is first recorded in the Minute Books of the Company in July 1678, when the Court of the Company heard from Sir John Shuter that the Lord Mayor desired:

> to acquaint the Company that there was a bill depending in Parliament for the licencing of Protestant Strangers to come from parts beyond the seas and here to exercise manual occupations without any let or molestation which if granted would very much tend to the prejudice of the natives of this kingdom and in especial to the artificers of this Company, as he conceived. And therefore advised that this Court would cause some enquiry to be made ... and declared it a business of great concern to the Artificers of this Company and to be opposed by this Court on behalf of the Members in general.[19]

As this proposed Bill had not become law by 1681 and Parliament took no new steps to pass a Bill of Naturalisation, the matter was brought to the attention of the King, and on 28 July 1681 Charles II declared his intention to grant 'Letters of Denization under the Great Seal without any charge whatsoever', and also a number of other concessions and privileges which related to the requests set out in the Memorial, or petition for aid, which had been submitted to the King in Council on 21 July. These requests included equality (with the native-born) in the exercise of their trades and handicrafts, concessions that might be 'an help and an ease' towards their transport by sea and land, together with sympathetic treatment by customs officials when they arrived. The Letters Patent were finally ready and the King signed them on 10 September 1681.[20]

On 20 October 1681, Pierre Harache, rightly regarded as the foremost figure among this new wave of Huguenot goldsmiths, was granted customs-free delivery of plate brought by him from France (see Cal. Treasury Books 1681–5, p. 279).[21] On 26 June 1682, his name, with that of his wife, Anne, appears on the Denization Papers and on 21 July, the Court of the Goldsmiths' Company received an Order of the Lord Mayor and Council of Aldermen of the City of London requiring that 'Peter Harache shall be admitted into the freedom of the City by Redemption into the Company of Goldsmiths'. An accompanying certificate testified that:

> Peter Harache, lately come from France for to avoid persecution and live quietly is not only a Protestant but by his Majesty's bounty is made a free denizen, that he may settle here freely with his family in

token whereof we have given him this certificate [signed by five persons including the Minister of the French Church of the Savoy].[22]

On payment of a fee of £10, Pierre Harache was made a freeman – the first of this new influx.

Within a week, a second order came from the Lord Mayor and Aldermen in respect of another Huguenot goldsmith, Jean Louis, about whom nothing is known – not even his maker's mark or an existing piece of plate or a record of one being made.[23] This request was stoutly resisted by the Goldsmiths' Company and led to the drawing up of formal petitions complaining of the ill-effects on the livelihoods of the members as a result of the admission of the alien goldsmiths into London. After a series of delays and, finally, a formal meeting with the Bishop of London at Fulham Palace, the Wardens completely failed to convince the Lord Mayor or the Bishop of the validity of their case and so, some fourteen months later, Jean Louis was admitted to the freedom on payment of £10 on 11 November 1683. However, the Company's united resistance seems to have given the Lord Mayor and others reason to pause; there is a lull for several years but as no further Huguenot goldsmiths seem to have taken out denization papers, at least until December 1687, the true position in London in the 1680s is difficult to assess. Most probably, the 1682–3 petitions of the Company were guilty of exaggeration about the 'great numbers of alien goldsmiths' in London, but it is curious that, with the worsening situation in France both before and after the Revocation of the Edict of Nantes in October 1685, there is no evidence in the Goldsmiths' Company records of renewed and regular requests for admission from Huguenots. Certainly, the Company viewed the threat to their prosperity with great alarm and the Apprentices Register for 1682, for example, reveals the strength of this feeling because the name of Domenico Arighi has been deleted and, in the margin, the annotation reads: 'Not admitted because son of alien'.[24]

Pierre Harache was a very talented goldsmith and perhaps deserved the good fortune that attended him from his swift passage through customs in October 1681, to his freedom of the Company in July 1682. Not surprisingly, he was a highly respected member of the community, living at the corner of Suffolk Street, near Charing Cross, in a house that was big enough to hold substantial meetings of members of the congregation of his church in Jewin Street, where he is first recorded in 1687. He was one of three elders originally deputed to establish the chapel of St James's Square (opened 1689) and later at Swallow Street (from 1694). He was concerned with the negotiations for the Chapel and its fitting out and, finally, he prepared a full account of the expenditure on the setting up of the church. He was still an elder in March 1694. His signature fortunately, is preserved and is different from that of another 'Pierre Harache', who was received as elder of Leicester Fields church on 25 June 1693, when he signed the *Actes*.[25] This Pierre Harache II was probably a son; he was free of the Goldsmiths' Company in 1698. Unfortunately, the similarity of their marks, entered at Goldsmiths' Hall, has caused much confusion in identifying some of their work, but no such uncertainty concerns the ewer and basin, made by Pierre Harache Senior for the 1st Duke of Devonshire and punched with the London hallmarks that, uniquely, were only in use for two months, between 27 March and 29 May 1697, (Plate III).[26] This magnificent ewer and basin, most sensitively engraved (perhaps by Simon Gribelin) with the ducal armorial bearings, remained at Chatsworth until 1958, when it was sold at Christie's. The basin measures 26 inches in diameter and the ewer is 12 inches high; the combined weight is 251oz 15dwt. This Devonshire set is the earliest ewer and basin of this pattern and is, undoubtedly, one of Harache's most successful and pleasing. It was repeated, perhaps by Pierre II, with slight variations to the strapwork designs on the ewers; there are two sets at Althorp, both made in 1701 as part of the ceremonial plate presented by King William III to Marlborough, when he was appointed Ambassador Extraordinary to the States General at The Hague and Commander-in-Chief of the English forces in Holland.[27] The Althorp pair, on average, weigh about 15oz more but are identical in size and form. Even slightly heavier is the only other known set, the ewer and basin made in 1702 for the Duke of Portland. One single ewer of this 'helmet fashion' (as the Lord Chamberlain's *Jewel Office Plate Book* PRO LC 9.46 describes the form in 1701) has survived in the Vintners' Company, having been sold in 1843 from the Duke of Sussex's collection; it is also hallmarked 1697. Two other single ewers of this design by Harache have been recorded: the Earl of Ancaster's is dated 1700, Sir Paul Methuen's example is dated 1703 and in design is the closest to the Chatsworth ewer especially in its strapwork ornament.

In the same year, 1697, Harache made one of the most elegant large oval wine-coolers (22 inches long) with handles similar to those on the ewers. This beautiful piece of plate was later presented to the Barber-Surgeons' Company by Queen Anne (died 1714) and, once again, the patronage enjoyed by Pierre Harache was the highest in the realm.[28] The records kept by John Hervey, 1st Earl of Bristol, indicate that he patronised Pierre Harache, along with three other leading Huguenot goldsmiths in London.[29] It would seem that William III commissioned work from the gifted maker because in the Cumberland plate, formerly part of the English royal plate, there is recorded a Pierre Harache gold salver of 1691 engraved with the King's cipher.

Regrettably, Harache's date of birth, death and place of origin have never been discovered, though some writers categorically state that he came from Rouen.[30] Sadly, nothing is known of his training – whether in Paris in the workshop of a greater master or in some provincial centre. Perhaps a metropolitan background is indicated by both his mastery of proportion and elegant design and the fact that he brought to London a 'gold cruit, with the French King's Arms cast on it, weight about 30oz'. This description appeared in *The London Gazette*, 3–7 November 1687, when a notice was published offering a £5 reward if it was returned to 'Mr Peter Harache, a French goldsmith, at the corner of Suffolk Street, near Charing Cross'.

The importance of Pierre Harache, senior, to the story of the Huguenot goldsmiths settling in London after the upheavals following the Revocation of the Edict of Nantes in 1685 can hardly be exaggerated but, alas, too little is known of his day-to-day role in helping his fellow craftsmen and countrymen. Without exception the surviving plate from his hand is of such quality that it not only appealed to the richest patrons but must quickly have had an electrifying effect on his English contemporaries in Goldsmiths' Hall. His personality, however, evidently contributed to his successful career in London and in 1687, he was elected to the Livery of the Company. When, a few years later, thieves broke into his house through his bedroom window and the silver communion cup belonging to his church was taken, he offered to replace it, but this gesture was unanimously refused because he had suffered losses in the robbery. Though inconclusive, there emerges an impression of a much respected, hard-working and very well-organised family man, whose skills were difficult to match among the London goldsmiths of his day.

He excelled in fine cast work, especially in the round; his pierced appliqué strapwork (cut from sheet silver and applied with solder) is delicately and imaginatively executed. These techniques, together with his use of a heavier gauge of silver and far higher relief work, were innovations that quickly captured the attention of the court and the aristocracy. The helmet ewer, once introduced, remained a favourite with the English.

Many of the best qualities of the work of Pierre Harache can be seen again in the silver plate of Simon Pantin, another important Huguenot who settled in London. An exceptional and large two-handled covered cup of 1705 (Plate IV, figure 2)[31] bears his mark, first registered at Goldsmiths' Hall on 23 June 1701, when he was described as a 'largeworker' and his address was St Martin's Lane. He had been made a freeman of the Company three weeks earlier, on 4 June 1701. However, great uncertainty surrounds his earlier history and previously published accounts leave the question unresolved. A hitherto unnoticed reference to this Huguenot *immigré* does, however, occur in the list of French Protestant refugees receiving relief through the Threadneedle Street Church in London;[32] from 4 July 1682 until 16 March 1683/4, Simon Pantin, goldsmith, with wife and two children, received a total of 54 grants amounting to £17 11s 0d; in one instance, the grant was 2s 'for a pair of child's shoes'. Unlike Pierre Harache, this goldsmith had not managed to bring any of his property, even the bare necessities of life for his family's well-being. Consequently, it is not surprising if it took Simon Pantin many years to succeed and to gain admission to the Goldsmiths' Company in contrast with the nine months it had taken Pierre Harache. His name, with his St Martin's Lane address, appears in the Lists in 1709 – the result of the Act of General Naturalisation finally being passed by Parliament; and so, again, he appears to have been forced to wait until he could take advantage of that brief period when he was allowed to obtain naturalisation without the usual expensive and painstaking procedures. During the last two decades of the seventeenth century, while he was building up his business, he probably had his wares marked at the Hall by some London goldsmith, with whom he had an arrangement, and attention is drawn to one of Simon Pantin's earliest kettles with its silver lampstand, made in 1706 (The Wilding Bequest).[33] His mark appears in four places, twice partially obliterated by the overstamping of another maker's mark, that of John Bache, a contemporary London goldsmith. The practice of overstamping is variously explained and in this case there is no certainty. Happily, he was elected to the Livery of the Company in October 1712, and lived until 1728. It must be assumed, therefore, that he was probably a young married man when he arrived in England and sought relief at the Threadneedle Street Church on 4 July 1682.

Previous accounts have given his place of origin as Rouen but as yet there is no evidence to confirm this view and, indeed, it may be caused by another, and slightly, later record concerning a Huguenot goldsmith of the same surname.[34] An 'orfev'' of Rouen, Esaie Pantin, with his wife and daughters, made *reconnaissance* at the French Protestant church of Hungerford Market (later Castle Street) on 22 October 1699, and an 'Esaie Pantin, goldsmith of St James' is recorded in 1709 (according to Ambrose Heal's study of London trade cards).[35] However, as there is no maker's mark for Esaie Pantin registered at Goldsmiths' Hall, this goldsmith from Rouen cannot have become a silver-plateworker active in London. He may, however, have been related in some way to the 'Esaie Pontin, *natif de Rouen*', who was married on 30 October 1658, at the French church in Threadneedle Street, London, to 'Elizabeth Maubert, *natif de Rouen*'; his occupation is not recorded.

Simon Pantin is stated to have served his apprenticeship with Pierre Harache before becoming a freeman of the Company in June 1701, but no record of the apprenticeship agreement exists.[36] Simon Pantin's two-handled covered cup, fully hall-marked for 1705, is the best kind of evidence available at this time to support the idea. Its similarity in excellent proportions, clean line, and a well-disciplined use of fine appliqué strapwork indicates a close connection between these two Huguenots – but not, perhaps, necessarily a master–apprentice relationship.[37]

This distinctive type of massive two-handled covered cup was also favoured by a far more important and successful contemporary Huguenot goldsmith, David Willaume,[38] as can be seen in the 1709 example (Plate V, figure 1).[39] He had come to England from Metz, where he had been born on 7 June 1658; his father, Adam, lived at the Pont des Morts and was a goldsmith. Metz, one of those frontier towns not unaccustomed to changing its nationality and allegiance, was far removed from the sophisticated fashions of Paris but David Willaume, upon his arrival in London, quickly gained the patronage of the most wealthy. He appears to have been residing at the Windsor Castle in Charing Cross as early as 1686 (according to Ambrose Heal)[40] and certainly his name appears in denization papers taken out on 16 December 1687. In less than three years, he had found a bride: he was married on 19 October 1690, at the French Chapel of La Patente, in Spitalfields, to Marie, the daughter of Samuel Mettayer who was the Minister there. Three years later her brother, Louis, was apprenticed to learn the goldsmiths' trade and his master, not unexpectedly, was

David Willaume, because on 27 January 1693, David had been made
a freeman of the Company by order of the Lord Mayor and Court of
Aldermen of the City of London. Seven years later his first apprentice,
Louis Mettayer, became a freeman of the Company, prospered and
married Anne Hobbema '*veuve, dem. chez* Mr Harache, *orpheuvre*,
Suffolk Street...'.[41]

This strong impression of a small, well-knit community of like-min-
ded Protestant *immigré* goldsmiths helping each other is yet again to
be seen when David Willaume's daughter, Anne (born in 1691), was
married in 1717 to a Huguenot goldsmith, David Tanqueray,[42] who
had been apprenticed to David Willaume in 1708. Once again, the
excellent training that the master, David Willaume, gave to his
apprentice led to a successful career, with commissions from rich
patrons, like the Duke of Devonshire.

Shortly after his own marriage, David Willaume 'assisted' at the
marriage of his sister-in-law to the famous Huguenot engraver, Simon
Gribelin. Not infrequently, the engraved ornament and heraldic
decoration on the best Huguenot silver plate seems to be the unsigned
work of this gifted artist, whose father had been an engineer in Blois.

After 1697, David Willaume lived in Pall Mall where he enjoyed
court patronage, and in October 1698 he was, most understandably,
elected to the Livery of the Goldsmiths' Company. His prosperous and
expanding workshop was carried on by his son, David, after he retired
in the late 1720s, but by 1720 he had developed banking, as a
profitable sideline, at his premises in St James's Street. On the profits,
he was able to purchase the manor of Tingrith in Bedfordshire, not far
from Woburn Abbey, the seat of the Duke of Bedford, where there is
still preserved a bill for £31 19s 0d (written in French) for silver items
supplied by this *immigré* goldsmith in 1707 (see *The Quiet Conquest*,
catalogue no. 335). It is doubtful if he would have accumulated such
wealth if he had been able to stay in Metz and practise his religion
without interference.

Like the giant-sized – and rather clumsy – two-handled covered cup
at Trinity Hall, Cambridge,[43] which David Willaume made for Philip,
Lord Stanhope, to present to his College in 1714, the Wilding Bequest
example, dated 1709, has a heavy, ponderous quality that contrasts
with the refined elegance of Pierre Harache's work. It is, perhaps, the
résult of the strong Germanic influence of his youthful background
and training in Metz but without doubt, Willaume's weighty monu-
mentality appealed to a powerful section of his English clientele and,
at its best, his style can be very impressive. David Willaume's 1709

covered cup was a version copied with only minor variations by later *immigré* goldsmiths, like Nicholas Clausen (in 1719)[44] and Paul de Lamerie in 1725.[45] (Plate V, figure 2).

It is often stated that the Huguenot goldsmiths introduced into England, as a new form, the two-handled cup and cover, but this theory has now been disproved.[46] As early as 1685, if not before, the typical English landed gentry, of modest scale and moderate wealth, were instructing London goldsmiths, like Benjamin Pyne, to make plain but large two-handled covered cups (15 inches high and 9 inches in diameter) with the £30 legacies they had just received under the terms of a family Will. It was evidently common practice in England by that date and the two extant examples – the 1685 Croft cups (Plate IV, figure 1) are sombre commemorative pieces of plate, executed in the current simple English style, with slightly old-fashioned cone-shaped 'steeple' and baluster finials on the covers and heavy cast 'rat tail' handles. The Huguenot goldsmiths, like David Willaume, were apparently grafting new trimmings – albeit beautifully executed and ingeniously designed – on to a long-established and much respected form of ceremonial plate, the two-handled cup and cover. Their English competitors strove hard to rival the work of these Huguenots as can frequently be seen but few examples demonstrate the point more effectively than Thomas Farren's silver-gilt cup and cover complete with its salver, that he made in 1715 for the Great Hall of the South Sea Company, near the junction of Threadneedle Street and Bishopsgate, at the cost of £63 13*s* 0*d* (Museum of London).[47]

Occasionally, the Huguenot goldsmith seems to have produced a piece of plate of unique design and form, the like of which cannot be paralleled in the work of English goldsmiths – nor even on the Continent among the tiny fraction that escaped the melting-pot to finance the wars of Louis XIV and later rulers. On one occasion, David Willaume created a unique pair of 'vases' (Plate IX).[48] They are not really vases but standing cups with covers; however, they were briefly described as vases in 1769 when Lady Betty Germain's collection was dispersed after her death: 'Two magnificent ivory VASES, beautifully decorated with bacchanalians of boys, elegantly carved, and rich silver-gilt stands and covers'. The ivory 'sleeves' or cylinders, fitting over the tall silver bodies of the two cups, are finely carved by an unidentified artist, perhaps François Langhemans, whose work can be seen in the church of St Gudule in Brussels. The carving is certainly the work of a Flemish artist, most probably executed during the last quarter of the seventeenth century in the Southern Netherlands and brought over to England, where in 1711 David Willaume was given the task of providing suitably grand silver-gilt 'vases' to show them off to the best advantage. He did not make a pair of tankards, as he might be expected to have done in Germany for a princely patron. He has created an original form – most impressively baroque, richly ornate and yet severely disciplined and well-proportioned.

Regrettably there is no evidence to show if David Willaume's solution is his own invention or whether his patron, as yet untraced, brought along an artist to sketch a design that would incorporate the ivories. The patron may have been Lady Betty Germain's husband, Sir John. He was a renowned soldier, greatly esteemed by King William III, with whom he campaigned both in Ireland and in Flanders against the French. In 1711, when Willaume completed his task, Sir John and Lady Betty had been married five years and on his death in 1718 she inherited the whole of his estates, including the vast property he had received from his first wife, the divorced Duchess of Norfolk, in whose possession the ivory carvings might have been kept as curiosities. The quality of the intricate surface decoration, including the sphinx-like masks on the covers and the satyr-like masks on the stems, is of the highest order, indicative of the exceptional calibre of this Huguenot from Metz.

In 1687, the same year that David Willaume's name appeared in the Letters of Denization, another Huguenot goldsmith was listed. He was Daniel Garnier, perhaps from Caen,[49] who three years later than David Willaume was made a freeman of the Company by order of the Lord Mayor and Aldermen; he was, however, elected to the Livery in the same year as Willaume, 1698. He seems quickly to have gained the patronage of George Booth, 2nd Earl of Warrington, who was slowly re-equipping his country seat at Dunham Massey;[50] at least, one set of casters in the house bore only the maker's mark used by Daniel Garnier before 1697. The Earl consistently bought and commissioned plate from Huguenot craftsmen for some fifty years – and his large-scale investment in fine plate, mainly after 1729, was intended to impress. He was a man of fervent Low Church piety and furnished his private chapel in 1706 with plate purchased from Isaac Liger, a Huguenot *immigré*; it has remained at Dunham Massey to the present day. His library contains numerous books on theology and his notebooks record the donations he made to charities for refugee French Protestants, sometimes as much as £150 in one year. He bought Spitalfields silks and damasks but it is the extent of his patronage of Huguenot goldsmiths that provides a unique and richly documented source for this aspect of the story, especially between 1729 and his death in 1758.

Comparatively few Protestant refugees crossed the Channel in the early part of King James II's reign (1685–8) because he was a Catholic and deeply committed to Catholicism. In 1687, after James II had proclaimed his Declaration of Indulgence promising his subjects liberty of conscience and free exercise of religion, the main influx of refugees began and the number of immigré goldsmiths grows steadily. From Rouen comes Samuel Margas whose name appears on 20 March 1687 among the Reconnaissances of the French Church of the Savoy and whose son, Jacob, later apprenticed to an English goldsmith, Thomas Jenkins, became a gifted maker and one of the Subordinate Goldsmiths to the King.[51] From Blois comes Jean Chartier,[52] whose name appears on 17 May 1688, in the Reconnaissances of the French Church of the Savoy; he married Suzanne Garnier and had a son baptised at Leicester Fields in December 1697, the year he obtained his denization papers. The next year he became a freeman of the Company and one of his rare pieces is the coffee pot of 1700 (Plate VIII, figure 1).[53] Its simple and harmonius design is both highly functional and in complete contrast to the prevailing taste of so many of the London goldsmiths. Influenced by works of this calibre, the tableware of the London goldsmiths of the early eighteenth century steadily improves.

The year of the Glorious Revolution, 1688, saw the flight of James II and the installation of Mary Stuart and William of Orange; their coronation took place in the following year on 11 April. Coming in their train from Holland were several goldsmiths, one of whom was Pierre Platel (1664–1719).[54] His family had fled from Lorraine to Flanders in 1685, back to their home town of Lille, and Pierre arrived in England with his brother, Claude. Pierre Platel's name, like those of Jean Chartier and Louis Cuny,[55] appears in denization papers dated 8 May 1697. Two years later, Platel became a freeman of the Company by order of the Court of Aldermen and within two weeks he had registered his mark at the Hall. Fortunately, there survives from that first year one beautiful example of his work: a covered cup with harp-shaped handles. It reveals another approach to the design of this very fashionable item of plate and it is interesting to compare it with Louis Cuny's unusual version, incorporating the English love of fluted decoration. Both pieces are in the Wilding Bequest (Plate VI, figures 1 and 2)[56] and, strangely, Louis Cuny's example was also made in the first year immediately after his mark had been registered at the Hall in

1703. Pierre Platel's finest and most sophisticated piece is the gold ewer and basin that he made for the 1st Duke of Devonshire in 1701.[57] Platel's range of domestic plate is very varied and in addition to the more obvious forms of tableware, he made several forms, like *ecuelles* (Plate VIII, figure 2) that were new to the English.[58] His influence was undoubtedly considerable but perhaps it had its greatest impact through the work of one of his more gifted apprentices, Paul de Lamerie,[59] who was born in Holland and brought to England as a baby, 11 months old, in 1689, (Plate V, figure 2).

This survey is not intended to extend beyond an account of those Huguenots who were practising goldsmiths when they left their native cities to settle in London. Paul de Lamerie's generation had been born in England and, though it was the custom to apprentice them to Huguenots, they were growing up in London, alongside English craftsmen, and to some extent they were adapting to their English environment. Their teachers, the old Huguenot masters, were in the main successful in handing on their secrets and their special skills: Simon Pantin to his pupil, Augustine Courtauld (apprenticed 1701), Louis Cuny to both his son (apprenticed 1710) and to John Hugh Le Sage (apprenticed 1708), Jacob Margas to Peter Archambo (apprenticed 1710), and Jean Chartier to Pezé Pilleau (apprenticed 1710). This continuity was their great contribution to the story of the craft in eighteenth-century London but it also brought with it a dangerous tendency towards repetition, both in the use of casting moulds and of decorative designs.[60] Phillip Rollos, I, for example, trained his son, Phillip, so successfully that there has been endless confusion over the correct identification of some of their most outstanding achievements (Plate VII, figures 1 and 2).[61] Others could be cited but, unquestionably, the two talented exceptions were Paul Crespin (apprenticed to the totally unknown Jean Pons in 1713)[62] and Paul de Lamerie. Apprenticed at the age of 15 to Pierre Platel, Paul de Lamerie acquired the soundest of schoolings in his craft and with this training allied to his creative genius, he went on to become one of the greatest exponents of the art of silversmithing in a totally different style – the idiom of the English Rococo.

Bibliographical notes

Four much-quoted works have been given the following abbreviated form:

Evans, 1931: Joan Evans, 'Huguenot Goldsmiths in England and Ireland', *Proceedings of the Huguenot Society of London*, vol. XIV (London, 1931–2) pp. 496–554.

Hayward, 1959: J. F. Hayward, *Huguenot Silver in England 1688–1727* (London, 1959).

Tait, 1972a: Hugh Tait, 'Huguenot Silver made in London (c. 1690–1723): The Peter Wilding Bequest to the British Museum', *The Connoisseur*, Part I (August 1972) pp. 267–77.

Tait, 1972b: Part II (September 1972) pp. 25–36.

Grimwade, 1976: Arthur G. Grimwade, *London Goldsmiths, 1697–1837* (London, 1976) revised 1982.

Notes

1. Robin D. Gwynn, *Huguenot Heritage* (London: 1985), p. 33.
2. *Touching Gold and Silver*, an exhibition catalogue, Goldsmiths' Hall (London, 1978) pp. 14–17.
3. J. F. Hayward, *Virtuoso Goldsmiths, 1540–1620* (London, 1976) pp. 112–13.
4. L. Cust, 'John of Antwerp, Goldsmith, and Hans Holbein', *The Burlington Magazine* (1906) vol. VIII pp. 356–60.
5. C. Oman, *Caroline Silver, 1625–1688* (London, 1970) p. 7, where attention is also drawn to the rule that prohibited a piece of imported foreign silver being exposed for sale before it had been marked by a London goldsmith, sent to the Hall to be assayed, and been fully hallmarked.
6. G. E. P. How and J. P. How, *English and Scottish Spoons ... and Pre-Elizabethan Hallmarks on English Plate*, (1957) vol. III p. 111; also C. J. Jackson, *History of English Plate* (London, 1911) p. 164, figures 182–3; illustrated in Hayward, *Goldsmiths*, figures 297–8.
7. H. Tait, 'Historiated Tudor Jewellery', *The Antiquaries Journal*, XLII, plate 2 (1962) pp. 232–5, plate XLI, a–b; H. Tait *Jewellery through 7000 Years* (British Museum, 1976) no 286, colour plate 24; H. Tait, in *Princely Magnificence* (Victoria and Albert Museum, 1980) pp. 48–50, no. 11; H. Tait, 'The Tablett: An Important Class of Renaissance Jewellery at the Court of Henry VIII', *Jewellery Studies*, ii (London, 1986).
8. Jackson, *English Plate*, pp. 172–3, plate facing p. 173.
9. G. E. P. How, *Notes on Antique Silver* (London, 1949) p. 7, plate 4; H. Tait, 'The Wyndham Ewer and Basin', *Proceedings of the Silver Society*, III (London, forthcoming).
10. H. Tait, *The Waddesdon Bequest: The Legacy of Baron Ferdinand Rothschild to the British Museum* (London, 1981) p. 63, figures 41–2.
11. SP 12/84 f. 433, quoted R. E. G. Kirk and E. F. Kirk, *Returns of Aliens*, Huguenot Society of London, Quarto Series, vol. X, part 2, p. 156; I. Scouloudi, *Returns of Strangers in the Metropolis, 1593, 1627, 1635, 1639*, Huguenot Society of London, Quarto Series, vol. LVII, pp. 234, 236, 366.

12. Hayward, *Goldsmiths*, p. 401, plate 653; the earliest French example, the St Michael Cup (c. 1530–40) was presented by Charles IX in 1570 to the Archduke Ferdinand, and is preserved in Vienna.
13. Jackson, *English Plate*, p. 193 with plate facing.
14. Hayward, *Goldsmiths*, p. 402, plates 665–7.
15. H. Tait, 'The Use of Filigree and Granulation on Jacobean Plate', *The Proceedings of the Silver Society* (London, 1983) vol. III, no. 3, pp. 66–70.
15a. The author is indebted to Robart Barker for this reference.
16. Oman, *Caroline Silver*, p. 27.
17. J. Yernaux, 'Jean-Gérard Cockus, orfèvre liègeois à la cour d'Angleterre', *Revue Belge d'Archéologie et d'Historie de l'Art* (1940) vol. X. pp. 67–70; D. McRoberts and C. Oman, 'Plate made by King James II and VII for the Chapel royal of Holyroodhouse in 1686', *The Antiquaries Journal*, vol. XLVIII, part 2, pp. 285–95, plates LXXX–LXXXV; Oman, *Caroline Silver*, p. 26.
18. Oman, *Caroline Silver*, p. 33.
19. Hayward (1959) p. 15.
20. A. P. Hands and I. Scouloudi, *French Protestant Refugees Relieved through the Threadneedle Street Church, London, 1681–1687*, Huguenot Society of London Quarto Series, vol XLIX (London, 1971) pp. 2–4.
21. The author is indebted to Dr R. D. Gwynn for this reference.
22. Hayward (1959) p. 17; for a detailed analysis of the evidence relating to Pierre I and Pierre II, see Grimwade (1976) pp. 533–5.
23. Hayward (1959) pp. 17–18; He seems unrelated to the 'Jean Louis *le jeune* with wife and young child', who was given aid through the Threadneedle Street Church in London, 1682–4 (see *Huguenot Society of London, Quarto Series*, vol. XLIX (1971) p. 132).
24. Evans, 1931, p. 506, n. 5.
25. The author is grateful to Dr R. D. Gwynn for culling these details from MSS preserved in the Huguenot Library, University College, London (Burn Donation 8 and 25).
26. Tait (1972a) pp. 268–9, figures 2–3, including the basin *en suite*.
27. A. G. Grimwade, 'Silver at Althorp', *The Connoisseur* (October, 1962) pp. 1–3, figure 3.
28. Hayward (1959) p. 36, plate 21.
29. Hayward (1959) Appendix, pp. 81–4.
30. *The Quiet Conquest, The Huguenots 1688–1985*, Museum of London exhibition catalogue, compiled by Tessa Murdoch (1985) p. 230, no 329; Hayward (1959) p. 9.
31. Tait (1972b) p. 27, figure 1.
32. Published in *French Protestant refugees relieved through the Threadneedle Street Church, London, 1681–1687*, Huguenot Society of London Quarto Series, vol. XLIX (1971) p. 150.
33. Tait (1972b) p. 27, note 5, figure 2.
34. *The Quiet Conquest*, p. 236, no. 339; Grimwade (1976) p. 613.
35. Sir A. Heal, *The London Goldsmiths, 1200–1800* (Cambridge, 1935).
36. Evans (1931) p. 548; Grimwade (1976) p. 613.
37. The Wilding Bequest provides a unique opportunity for making comparative studies of this kind. Mr Peter Wilding died in 1969, leaving his

remarkable collection of more than fifty pieces of Huguenot silver plate to the British Museum. They are the work of fourteen goldsmiths; all made before 1724, they belong to the important transitional period.

38. Evans (1931) p. 554; Grimwade, 1976, p. 704.
39. Hayward (1959) p. 33, plate 7.
40. Heal, *London Goldsmiths*.
41. Savoy Church Register, Huguenot Society of London Quarto Series, Vol. XXVI.
42. Evans (1931) p. 553; Grimwade (1976) p. 676–7.
43. *Cambridge Plate*, an exhibition catalogue, compiled by R. A. Crighton, Fitzwilliam Museum, Cambridge (1975) p. 42, no. 247.
44. Tait (1972b) p. 35, figure 17.
45. Hayward (1959) pp. 32–3, plate 8.
46. H. Tait, 'The Advent of the Two-handled Cup: The Croft Cups', *The Proceedings of the Silver Society* (London, 1982) vol. 11, nos 11–13, pp. 202–10, figures 328–39.
47. Rosemary Weinstein, 'The South Sea Company Plate', *Antique Collector*, (October, 1983) pp. 70–3, illustrated.
48. Tait (1972a) pp. 270–4, figures 5–8.
49. Evans (1931) p. 538; Grimwade (1976) p. 519, where he puts forward an alternative origin to that published by Joan Evans.
50. J. F. Hayward, 'The Earl of Warrington's Plate', *Apollo* (July 1978) pp. 32–9, figures 1–15.
51. Evans (1931) p. 545; Grimwade (1976) pp. 590–1, where attention is drawn to a misinterpretation by Joan Evans and the resulting confusion; Samuel Margas, junior, is now established as the brother of Jacob Margas to whom he was apprenticed in 1708. Heal's statement (1935) that he was not the brother of Jacob but the son, can be disregarded.
52. Evans (1931) p. 510 and p. 531; Grimwade (1976) p. 462.
53. Tait (1972a) pp. 274–5, figure 9.
54. Evans (1931) pp. 511 and 549; Grimwade (1976) p. 627.
55. Evans (1931) p. 512 and p. 549; Grimwade (1976) p. 482.
56. Tait (1972a) p. 276, figures 10, 12.
57. Hayward (1959) p. 44, colour frontispiece; *Treasures from Chatsworth*, exhibition catalogue (International Exhibitions Foundation, 1979) p. 77, no. 156, illustrated.
58. Hayward (1959) p. 55, plate 69.
59. Grimwade (1979) p. 488.
60. One of the most convincing instances of this slavish repetition came to light very recently when there was sold by auction by Christie's of Geneva at the Hotel Richemond on 15 May 1985 a pair of ice-pails by David Willaume with the London hallmarks of 1700. They were hitherto unpublished and an unknown form in his *oeuvre*. They are, however, identical to the well-known pair of ice-pails by Louis Mettayer and hallmarked, London 1713, which were part of the official plate of Sir Thomas Hanmer, Bart, Speaker of the House of Commons from 1714 to 1715; they passed to his nephew, Sir William Bunbury, Bart. and are now preserved in the Eton College collection (see *The*

Quiet Conquest, catalogue no. 338). Apart from the different engraved heraldic devices, the two pairs are truly identical, the castings having been made from the same moulds.

61. Grimwade (1976) pp. 645–6, where the misinterpretations of Jackson, Heal and Hayward are, for the first time, corrected and an attempt is made to reattribute some of the major items to Phillip Rollos II, the son, who became a freeman in 1705 and, like his father, a Subordinate Goldsmith to the Crown.

62. Evans (1931) pp. 510–11, 532; Grimwade (1976) pp. 478–9, where an *Index of Apprentice Books* (Society of Genealogists) is quoted as the source for Crespin's apprenticeship to the unknown Jean Pons in 1713. My attention has been drawn by Dr R. Gwynn to a contemporary reference, which may be relevant and may lead to further information coming to light: at the French church, Castle Street, between June and September 1701, a Jean Pons of Furnel in Agenois made *reconnaissance* and signed the *Actes* (in the Huguenot Library, University College, London, Burn Donation, 2, p. 41).

Editor's note

Fully detailed captions to Plates I–IX inclusive will be found in the List of Plates on p. vii–ix.

The London hallmarking year in this period was from May to the next May; in the captions the year given is always the earlier of the two because it is slightly longer.

7 Huguenot Upholsterers and Cabinet-makers in the Circle of Daniel Marot

Gervase Jackson-Stops

The importance of the Huguenots in shaping the whole development of the decorative arts in England between 1695 and 1714 – from the Revocation of the Edict of Nantes to the Hanovarian Succession – is indisputable. On the one hand we have the long lists of carvers, joiners, cabinet-makers, upholsterers, weavers and mercers recorded as immigrants, and attending the French churches in London – lists compiled from the papers so painstakingly published by the Huguenot Society over many years. On the other we have the wonderfully ornate state beds and couches, looking-glasses, tables and stands, picture-frames, fire-screens and chandeliers of the period – all in the French taste, and all finding close parallels in the engravings of Daniel Marot, William III's Huguenot architect and *dessinateur*. But while Marot is obviously at the centre of a whole web of Huguenot craftsmen – more than anyone responsible for introducing the full-blown Louis Quatorze style to England and Holland – it is all too rare to be able to put the names of such craftsmen to specific items. Either there are tantalising bills, or there are maddeningly anonymous objects. How one would like to see the 'douze chaises à la manière de la chine' supplied by Marie Parisels to the 1st Duke of Montagu in 1709,[1] or the 'two scrutores [or *escritoires*] inlaid with flowers' bought by William III from the cabinet-maker John Guilliband, 'for our dearest Consort the Queen's service at Whitehall' in 1692.[2] How much, too, would one like to know the identity of the upholsterer responsible for the Melville Bed, now in the Victoria and Albert Museum, that impossible 'Princess and the Pea' confection – or the maker of the pier table, pier glass and candle stands inlaid with pewter and brass in a corridor at Grimsthorpe Castle, perhaps among the finest surviving pieces of English boulle. Only a few, very tentative, answers to such questions can be provided so far. But my hope is that in showing something of the richness and variety of Huguenot craftmanship in this field, interest in

113

the extent of their achievement may increase, and more work be undertaken in this comparatively neglected field.

French influence on English furniture was strong well before 1685. Cosimo III of Tuscany, visiting this country in 1669, commented that:

> there does not pass a day in which the artizans do not indulge themselves in going to the public-houses, which are exceedingly numerous, neglecting their work however urgent it may be; hence it is, that the French make fortunes in London, for being more attentive to their business, they sell their manufactures at a lower price than the English[3]

It was of course difficult for foreigners before the Revocation to avoid the restrictions imposed by the City's guild system, but the important loophole here was the Great Wardrobe. A document of 1671 among the Sackville papers talks of the 'power ... given to the Keeper of the Great Wardrobe to let the houses, shops, tenements, cellars, etc., thereunto belonging to any artificer or tradesman native or foreign, and [these are] ... exempted from paying all taxes and duties'.[4] Thus a Frenchman like John Casbert could become chief upholsterer to the Royal Household as early as 1660, not just supplying furniture himself but, for instance, 'altering and fitting a Crimson Damask bed bought of a Frenchman with supplyes of severall necessaryes thereunto' for the large sum of £73 6s 6d in the following year.[5] There is evidence that Ralph Montagu, as Master of the Wardrobe to William III, actually used his position to try to create an English Gobelins, where Charles de la Fosse and Daniel Marot could have rivalled the positions of their erstwhile masters Le Brun and Berain.

Casbert's bed 'bought of a Frenchman' could well have been a direct import from Paris for in 1672–3 a well-known upholsterer Jean Peyrard made two trips to London with no fewer than six beds supplied for Charles II, while Simon Delobel, maker of the King's Bed at Versailles, brought several more which were laid out to be 'viewed by their Majesties in the Banqueting House' at Whitehall in 1685.[6] On balance it now seems likely that the great state bed in the King's Room at Knole, with hangings of gold and silver thread, lined with cherry-coloured satin, is actually French. If it is one of those brought by Peyrard in 1673 it could indeed be the marriage-bed of the future James II and Mary of Modena and this would explain the coronet on the backboard – more like a royal duke's than a king's – the cupids with bows and quivers on the chairs, the putti with billing doves on the cross-stretchers, and the hearts with crossed arrows on the sides.[7]

Both the King's Bed and the bed in the Venetian Ambassador's Room at Knole were acquired by the 6th Earl of Dorset as perquisites early in the reign of William III. The latter bears James II's monogram, this time with a royal crown and lion and unicorn – and can almost certainly be identified with a bed 'of green and gold figured velvet with scarlet and white silk fringe', ordered with two armchairs and six stools for use at Whitehall Palace in August 1688, only a few months before the Glorious Revolution. The upholsterer would almost certainly have been Jean Paudevin (otherwise known as Poitevin, Baudrine, Potrin, or by a dozen other spellings) who succeeded Casbert as chief upholsterer to the Royal Household in 1677, while the carving is certainly by Thomas Roberts.[8] His caryatid chair frames seem consciously to imitate the earlier seat furniture in the King's Room, although the scrolling arms and so-called 'horsebone' ornaments on the stretchers are very different in feeling, and more Dutch than French in origin.

Daniel Marot was of course the guiding spirit behind the great state beds of the 1690s, many of them made by another Huguenot, Francis Lapiere. Like Jean Paudevin he had his premises in Pall Mall, conveniently near the Lord Chamberlain's office at St James's, and of course outside the City limits. It may even be that he succeeded to Paudevin's business, for after the winter of 1688 when the latter supplied a magnificent 'crimson mohair bed lined with green satin' with its accompanying furniture to the Duke of Hamilton for Hamilton Palace, costing the huge sum of £326,[9] his name disappears from the Royal Household accounts and is replaced by that of Lapiere.

One of the finest of all surviving baroque beds, in another great Scottish house, Blair Castle (Plate X, Figure 1) may be attributed to Francis Lapiere not only on grounds of style, but because it came from the royal palace of Holyroodhouse, where it is said to have stood in the apartments of the Duke of Hamilton's son-in-law, the Marquess of Tullibardine. It shows striking similarities with the bed in the frontispiece of Daniel Marot's *Second Livre d'Appartements*, pub-lished about 1701 (Plate X, Figure 2), and a direct link between the two men has been established in recent years by the discovery of Lapiere's bill at Boughton, dated 1706. This describes in detail a 'Bed of striped Tapestry needlework, lined with satin' for which the Duke of Montagu paid £151 2s 0d, including two small but highly significant items: 'paid to Marot for drawing the cornishes £1 15s 0d/ paid for drawing the Cupps £1 5s 0d'.[10] So grand is the Blair Castle bed that one would not be surprised if it were likewise made by Lapiere for William

III after a design by Marot, and given to the Marquess of Tullibardine as a perquisite from the palace after the king's death in 1701. It would have been a comparatively simple matter to change the monogram on the headboard (surmounted by a marquess's coronet) at that date, two years before he was created 1st Duke of Atholl.

Other courtiers may well have patronised Lapiere, among them the 2nd Viscount Scudamore, builder of Holme Lacy in Herefordshire, whose crimson damask state bed (almost entirely re-covered) is now at Beningbrough Hall – and William Blathwayt, whose state bed has been generously loaned back to Dyrham Park by the Lady Lever Art Gallery. Blathwayt, who was William III's Secretary at War, had his own apartments at the palace of Het Loo in Holland and would thus have been familiar with Daniel Marot's sumptuous interiors there. No wonder that he employed a Huguenot architect, Samuel Hauduroy, on the rebuilding of Dyrham, and furnished it with Delft tulip vases, as well as a state bed and its accompanying chairs and window cornices, in a thoroughly Marotesque style. Covered with the original crimson and yellow velvet, and with an interior of sprigged satin, the bed has the elaborate broken cornice and prominent 'cups' or vases typical of Marot's designs – like a drawing in his hand found in the archives at Siena,[11] which also shows a gilded case curtain rod, like that described in the 1710 inventory of Dyrham, and recently reinstated. English state beds of the 1690s were on the whole more elaborate than their French counterparts, and there is evidence that they were developed by Marot from the very feminine hangings of ladies' dressing rooms, such as those prepared for Madame de Maintenon at the Trianon de Porcelaine.[12] The contemporary daybeds seen in engravings by Allard and others are very similar in outline to Marot's angel-tester beds – with canopies hung from the ceiling so as to dispense with the need for end-posts. These in turn have close parallels with the tester of the great state bed which Francis Lapiere made for the 1st Duke of Devonshire at Chatsworth in 1697, and which miraculously survives as a canopy in the long gallery at Hardwick. With its original seat furniture, this cost the staggering sum of £470, and is the most expensive I have yet found – probably worth more at that time than all the rest of the contents of the house put together.[13] Interestingly the frame alone cost only £15. The *mouchoirs*, not unlike the long cravats of the period, give the canopy a particularly three-dimensional effect.

Like the Duke of Devonshire, the 1st Earl of Melville was a staunch Williamite, actually exiled in Holland between 1685 and 1688. The headboard of the famous Melville bed in the Victoria and Albert

Museum with the monogram GCM at the centre – for George and Catherine – is again so close to Marot's engravings that one is tempted to make an attribution to Lapiere, the upholsterer with whom he probably had closest ties.[14]

The state bed at Drayton in Northamptonshire (Plate XI) has the much simpler, more architectural, outline of French state beds at this period, though the backboard is elaborately close-covered with yellow taffeta in the Marot style. It was made for the Duchess of Norfolk just after her marriage to Sir John Germain, reputedly an illegitimate half-brother of William III, in 1700 – and some recently discovered bills reveal that the embroidered curtains were the work of two (probably Huguenot) needlewomen named Rebekah Dufee and Elizabeth Vickson, while the upholsterer was another Huguenot, named Guillotin.[15] The Drayton bill gives his address as Castle Street (off Air Street, Soho), but an earlier newspaper advertisement of 1691 reveals that, like Lapiere, he then had premises in Pall Mall.[16] The very different hanging of the embroidered bed at Houghton, apparently based on designs for japanning like those of Stalker and Parker, must date from the 1720s for they bear Sir Robert Walpole's Order of the Garter. But the backboard and tester are still Marotesque in style, and also suggest the hand of a Huguenot upholsterer – though it remains sadly undocumented.

With the famous Hornby Castle suite, now at Temple Newsam (Plate XII, Figure 2) we are on slightly firmer ground, for among the Duke of Leeds' papers recording the furnishing of Kiveton in Yorkshire (designed by William Talman) is an entry for 9 November 1703 'pay'd Gilbert, ye joyner by my Lady Duches's order 2/-'.[17] This craftsman is very likely to have been Philip Guibert who in 1697–8 equipped Windsor Castle and Kensington Palace with pieces that sound very similar – for instance 'a couch of carved walnutree, the headboard carved with his M'ties cyphers and ornaments belonging to it' costing £6, and 'a fine black soffa of a new fashion, filled up with fine hair, and its cushion filled up with downe, the frieze and cheeks all molded and fringed'.[18] The Hornby Castle suite still preserves its original upholstery of red and green cut-velvet, with a wonderfully elaborate fringe. Although previously thought to be Genoese, it is possible that this material is also among the first cut-velvets to be made in England by Huguenot weavers.

The only comparable day-bed complete with its accompanying furniture is at Penshurst Place in Kent, and this is still rarer in having parts of its original 'paned' wall-hangings *en suite* (Plate XII, Figure

1).[19] Probably commissioned by the 5th Earl of Leicester for his London house between 1702, when he succeeded, and 1705, when he died, they must have been designed for dressing-rooms or closets something like the one shown in a Marot engraving thought to represent one of Mary II's apartments in the Winter Gallery at Hampton Court – small but very richly decorated. Paned hangings – so called after their rectangular 'panes' or panels – can be seen in other Marot engravings and a few examples survive, notably in the Queen's Dressing Room at Ham and the Duchess of Norfolk's Closet at Drayton.

The 1st Lord Onslow's state bed at Clandon Park, again very much in the Lapiere style, has floral embroidered hangings that may also be of Huguenot origin. It is also rare in having an armchair as well as a set of six single chairs *en suite*, reminiscent of the armchair in the Penshurst set. Instead of sitting closely in front of a fireplace as one might imagine, this was probably a 'chair of state', placed formally in front of the bed when its occupant was receiving a ceremonial visit from his host or from other guests. Marot's engravings of upholstered chairs are again close to English examples of the 1690s and 1700s, like the example from Rushbrooke in Suffolk, accompanying a state bed that is now marooned in the basement stores of the Metropolitan Museum in New York.[20] As a postscript to the world of upholstery a valance from some bed-hangings recently discovered at Dunham Massey in Cheshire (Plate XIII, Figure 1) is evidently part of a 'velvet bed' valued at the large sum of £250 in an inventory of 1694.[21] With its amazingly extravagant fringe using vellum strips bound with silver thread, it is very different in feeling to the close-covering of the carved and moulded testers of Lapiere's known work. The scalloped shape of the top is reminiscent of the upper valances on the the King's Bed at Knole, and I cannot help thinking it may also be French rather than the work of a Huguenot upholsterer working in London.

The 1st Earl of Warrington, who acquired the Dunham bed, also patronised the mysterious Mr Boujet, said by Vertue to be the designer of Montagu House in London. Two drawings apparently signed by Boujet seem connected with the remodelling of the great hall at Dunham in the early 1690s, and a series of carved benches in the house are very much in the same Marotesque vocabulary.[22] Lord Warrington was another passionate supporter of William III's cause, and the Infant Hercules strangling the lion in the central cartouche of one of these benches (Plate XIII, Figure 2) must be a direct reference to one of William's favourite allegorical *persona* dating from the time of his minority, when he was declared 'Child of state' by the States General. Montagu House, Boughton and Petworth have so many features derived from the designs of Daniel Marot that the continuing enigma of his relations with Boujet are intensely frustrating: a Huguenot jigsaw that still needs to be completed. It is frustrating too that the carver of the Dunham benches is not known, for he would doubtless also have produced some of the large sets of carved 'back-stools' as they were called, with ornament close to Marot's engravings, like those in the Long Gallery at Haddon or those now in the great hall at Dyrham. A carver like John le Sage, who turns up at Lamport, Ickworth, Kensington and Hampton Court in the 1680s and 1690s[23] or Robert Derignée or Deringer, who was working in London by 1688 but whose name occurs previously in the *Comptes des Bâtiments* working at Clagny and Versailles between 1679 and 1683,[24] would be the sort of candidates.

One very specialised type of Huguenot furniture is the painted looking-glass, of which examples survive at the Victoria and Albert Museum, at Melbourne in Derbyshire (Plate XIV, Figure 1) and at Dalkeith Palace near Edinburgh. All are probably the work of the flower-painter, Jean-Baptiste Monnoyer, who worked extensively at Boughton and Montagu House.[25] Vertue records the 'Looking Glass at Kensington House', probably the one in the Victoria and Albert Museum, as being 'the most curious of all his works...painted for the late Q Mary of Glorious Memory, her Majisty sitting by him almost all the while'.[26]

Like painters, silversmiths should by rights be outside the scope of this chapter, but it is hard to resist including silver furniture like the famous chandelier, dated 1694,[27] at Chatsworth – once again close to Marot designs – and the several pairs of andirons from Knole – none of them marked, yet almost certainly by a Huguenot smith like David Willaume or Philip Rollos.[28]

In the field of carcase furniture, one must return briefly to the 1670s and to Paris. The little bureau at Boughton, almost certainly by Pierre Golle or Gole, traditionally believed to have been given by Louis XIV to Ralph Montagu on one of his many embassies to France has superb marquetry of pewter and brass, with borders of ebony inset with mother-of-pearl.[29] Drawings of the private apartments at Versailles, discovered not long ago by M. Alfred Marie, show the kind of setting for which it must have been designed.[30] Today the bureau shares the Low Pavilion Antechamber at Boughton most appropriately with four outstanding pieces of English boulle furniture – two mirrors and two chests of drawers in so-called *première* and *seconde partie*, superbly engraved and finished. The existence of a very similar chest of drawers in the Royal Collection, documented as the work of Gerrit Jensen,[31] makes it virtually certain that these are also the work of William III's principal cabinet-maker – probably made to celebrate Ralph Montagu's third marriage in 1692.[32] The cresting of one mirror has his monogram and earl's coronet, while the other has a heart pierced by arrows.

Jensen, perhaps of Dutch or Flemish descent, may not himself have been a Huguenot, but his close ties with Pierre Golle are shown by the fact that at his death in 1683 Golle owed *'Sieur Janson, ébéniste à Londres'* 400 *livres* for English glue.[33] Not only was Golle's sister Catherine married to Daniel Marot, but his brother Cornelius was also in England in the 1690s where he is recorded as making certain pieces of furniture for Mary II, also appearing in the accounts of Ralph Montagu's executors in 1708.[34] It may well be that Cornelius Golle and Daniel Marot provided Jensen with drawings, and this is particularly suggested by the tapered pillar support (a favourite Marot motif) found in many other Jensen pieces, for instance a pewter and brass inlaid table and stands at Drayton in Northamptonshire (seen in front of the bed in Plate XI),[35] and a little dressing-table with sliding panels on the top – once at Hamilton Palace and now at Lennoxlove (Plate XV, Figure 1).[36]

Jensen may not have been the only maker of boulle furniture at this period, for an ornate table at Petworth (Plate XV, Figure 2) not unlike Marot's design for a caryatid table at Het Loo – is much cruder in execution than his other known pieces, and the treatment of the frieze almost suggests that the maker bought a French panel of brass-and-tortoiseshell inlay, and simply cut it up to use as a veneer like lacquer or coromandel.[37] A pair of candlestands *en suite* survives at the house, together with a boulle mirror frame recently found in the attics which may make up the set.

Marot's drawing indeed underlines the immense importance attached to the sets of furniture which stood on the piers between the windows of a baroque state room. Caryatid candlestands of very much the same composition can still be found at Boughton, and suggest that he had a personal hand in the decoration of Ralph Montagu's interiors – not just confined to Lapiere's beds and the painted panels from Montagu House, which he is known to have designed. But apart from the silver furniture at Knole, perhaps the most spectacular of such sets is that at Hopetoun House, (Plate XIV, Figure 2) again with caryatid stands, but combined with floral japanning in a more overtly Dutch manner. John Guilbaud, probably the same as the John Guilliband mentioned earlier as providing furniture for Mary II, appears among the Hopetoun accounts, and as 'Japan Cabbinets, large tables and looking Glasses' appear on his trade label, may perhaps have made these marvellously rich pieces.[38]

Another important maker to appear in Ralph Montagu's accounts is Jean Pelletier, who also appears frequently in the royal accounts along with Renée and Thomas Pelletier – probably his widow and son.[39] A large number of the frames for the Monnoyers and other pictures at Boughton can be identified by their measurements in Pelletier's detailed bills, one of the finest being one for a copy of Van Dyck's 'Earl of Strafford' (Plate XVI, Figure 1), whose pilasters are clearly described.[40] The cresting on top of the frame is reminiscent of Pelletier's documented firescreens: one at Hampton Court, matching another at Knole (Plate XVI, Figure 2) which was evidently acquired as a perquisite by the 6th Earl of Dorset. Just how similar these are to contemporary Louis Quatorze firescreens can be seen in contemporary French engravings, like those of Allard.[41] Pelletier's gilt gesso tables at Boughton, very similar to one at Penshurst with a *Vernis Martin* top,[42] are also close to Marot engravings – distinctly *retarda-taire* in manner compared with the work of his successors Belchier, Gumley and Moore, who seem to catch the lighter spirit of the Régence despite their reliance on Berain.

John Belchier's origins still remain obscure, but I think it is at least possible that he came of Huguenot stock, and one would certainly like to claim the magnificent pier glasses at Erddig as examples of Huguenot craftsmanship (Plate XVII, Figure 2). The silvered mirror in the Tapestry Room (Plate XVII, Figure 1) is puzzling in that although his bill survives, it exactly matches some others in the house provided by John Pardoe – otherwise known only from his trade label. Perhaps the two were partners for a time. Perhaps too they had a hand in the superb gilt-gesso work of the Erddig state bed.[43]

Stylistically, however, their work takes us on beyond the Daniel Marot period into the slightly better-charted waters of the Palladian Revolution. If this voyage through the baroque has at times seemed in want of a compass, one can only hope that it will stimulate further work on a fascinating period – in which French influence on the English decorative arts established a supremacy that it was to maintain both in the rococo and the neoclassical periods – the worlds of Isaac Ware and René Duffour, Henry Holland and Paul Duchemin.[44]

Notes

1. MS at Boughton; Account Books of the 1st Duke of Montagu's Executors, vol. 2

2. Public Record Office, Wardrobe Accounts LC9/124, p. 53; the two desks together cost £30.

3. *Travels of Cosimo the Third Grand Duke of Tuscany, through England, during the Reign of Charles the Second* [1669] (London, 1821) p. 398.

4. C. Phillips, *History of the Sackville Family*, 2 vols (London, 1929) p. 446.

5. Public Record Office (as note 2) LC5/39.

6. Ibid, LC9/273, p. 21 and LC5/42, p. 42, and *Calendar of Treasury Books* 1685–9, pp. 1040, 1151, 1153, Out Letters (General), X, pp. 42, 54, XI, pp. 9–10; for Delobel see also Henry Havard, *Dictionnaire de l'Ameublement, III*, pp. 383–4 and Jules Guiffrey, *Comptes des Bâtiments du Roi sous le Règne de Louis XIV*, 1881–1901, I, pp. 1152, 1314, II, p. 342.

7. G. Jackson-Stops, 'Purchases and Perquisites: the 6th Earl of Dorset's Furniture at Knole, II', *Country Life*, (9 June 1977) p. 1622, figures 7 and 9.

8. Ibid, figures 6 and 8.

9. K. Marshall, *The Days of Duchess Anne* (London, 1973) pp. 156–7.

10. First discovered by Mr John Cornforth; see G. Jackson-Stops, 'Daniel Marot and the 1st Duke of Montagu', in *Nederlands Kunsthistorisch Jaarboek* (*festschrift* for Professor Th. H. Lunsingh Scheurleer) (1980) vol. 31, pp. 244–62.

11. R. C. Smith, 'Five Furniture Drawings in Siena', *Furniture History*, vol. 3 (1967) plate 5.

12. P. Thornton, *Seventeenth Century Interior Decoration in England, France and Holland* (London, 1978) p. 166, plates 14 and 15.

13. MS at Chatsworth, 'Mr. Whildon's Account Book', drawn up for the 1st Duke of Devonshire.

14. See especially P. Jessen, *Das Ornamentwerk des Daniel Marot* (Berlin, 1892) p. 155.

15. G. Jackson-Stops, *Drayton House* (1978) p. 18.

16. Sir A. Heal, *The London Furniture Makers, 1660–1840* (London, 1953) p. 72.

17. C. Gilbert, *Furniture at Temple Newsam House and Lotherton Hall* (1978) vol. II, p. 265, figure 322.

18. P. Macquoid and R. Edwards, *Dictionary of English Furniture* (London, 1954) vol. II, p. 251; the minutes of the Upholder's Company reveal that on 14 October 1702 'Philip Guibert, an Upholsterer in St German's Street was Admitted into the Freedome'; in September of the following year he presented the Company with 'a Triangular Silver Salt Gilt, being in lieu of plate upon his admission'; and in 1705–6 he served as Steward (Guildhall Library ms 7141/1).

19. Illustrated in colour in Marcus Binney, 'Penshurst Place – III', *Country Life* (27 April 1972) p. 998, figure 8.

20. L. White 'Two English State Beds at the Metropolitan Museum of Art',

Apollo, Vol. 116 (August 1982) pp. 84–8.

21. J. Hardy and G. Jackson-Stops, 'The 2nd Earl of Warrington and the "Age of Walnut"', *Apollo* (July 1978) pp. 19–20, figures 14 and 15; and G. Jackson-Stops, 'Dunham Massey – I', *Country Life*, (4 June 1981) p. 1563, figure 7.

22. Hardy and Jackson-Stops, 'The 2nd Earl of Warrington' figures 5–8.

23. Mss at Public Record Office, Works 5/50; Sir A. Heal, *The London Furniture Makers* p. 103, and information from the late Sir Gyles Isham, Bt.

24. *Dictionary of English Furniture*, vol. II, p. 203, and mss in the Public Record Office (e.g. LC9/128, p. 22); see also *Wren Society*, vol. XVI, p. 62, and *Comptes des Bâtiments*, vol. I, pp. 1076, 1289, 1326, and vol. II, pp. 22, 62, 68, 88, 160, 324.

25. E. Croft-Murray, *Decorative Painting in England, 1537–1837* (London, 1962) vol. I pp. 255–6.

26. George Vertue, *Notebooks*, in Walpole Society, vol. XXX, 1955 (Index) p. 180. 'One large looking glass in several pieces painted with flowers and gilt frame' was listed in the Queen's Closet at one end of the long gallery at Kensington Palace in an inventory of 1699, and this may be that now in the Victoria and Albert Museum (W.36–1934), which has five panels; see also R. Edwards in *Country Life* (26 October 1935).

27. F. Thompson, *A History of Chatsworth* (London, 1949) p. 158, plate 69.

28. C. J. Phillips, *A History of the Sackville Family* (London, 1929) vol. 2, appendix V.

29. Th. H. Lunsingh Scheurleer, 'Pierre Gole, ébéniste du roi', *Burlington Magazine* (June 1980) pp. 380–94.

30. P. Thornton, *Seventeenth Century Interior Decoration in England, France and Holland* (1979) pp. 200–2, plate 22.

31. R. W. Symonds, 'Gerrit Jensen, Cabinet Maker to the Royal Household', *Connoisseur*, (1935) vol. 95 pp. 272–3, plates V and VI.

32. The Duke married Elizabeth, daughter of the 2nd Duke of Newcastle, and widow of the 2nd Duke of Albermarle, in September of that year; H. A. Doubleday and Lord Howard de Walden (eds) *The Complete Peerage* (1936) vol. IX, p. 107.

33. Lunsingh Scheurleer, *Pierre Gole* p. 394.

34. Jackson-Stops, *Nederlands Kunsthistorisch Jaarboek*, p. 255.

35. G. Jackson-Stops (ed.) *The Treasure Houses of Britain*, National Gallery of Art (Washington, DC, 1985) no. 98, p. 168.

36. Clive Aslet, 'Lennoxlove', *Country Life* (15 August 1985) p. 448.

37. G. Jackson-Stops, 'Furniture at Petworth', *Apollo* (May 1977) p. 360, figure 7.

38. Mss at Hopetoun House.

39. R. Edwards and M. Jourdain, *Georgian Cabinet-Makers* (1955) p. 35.

40. Mss at Boughton: Lord Charles Scott's notebooks, 19, pp. 63–4, and 1st Duke of Montagu's executors' accounts.

41. Thornton, *Seventeenth Century Interior Decoration*, plate 245.

42. See Binney, 'Penshurst Place – III' figure 10.

43. Martin Drury, 'Early 18th Century Furniture at Erddig', *Apollo* (July 1978) pp. 50–2, figures 3 and 11.

44. Heal, *The London Furniture Makers*, trade labels reproduced as plates
     on pp. 46 and 51.

Editor's note

Fully detailed captions to Plates X–XVII inclusive will be found in the
List of Plates on pp. ix–xi.

8 Huguenots in the English Silk Industry in the Eighteenth Century

Natalie Rothstein

Many years ago Peter Thornton and I attempted to demonstrate the significance of the contribution made by the Huguenot element to the production of the silks for which the original designs existed in the Victoria and Albert Museum.[1] Much further information has come to light since, many records, many silks, much more about particular families in the industry. At the beginning of the present year, therefore, it seemed now urgent to put this information in some context. How many Huguenots were there, who were they, where did they come from and where did they go, what did they do and what, if anything, was their special contribution to the industry? There are several ways in which this could be done but my existing knowledge about individuals suggested that a reasonably accurate assessment could be made by counting the Huguenots in the Weavers' Company of London at ten-year intervals (see Table 8.1) and then comparing certain specimen periods with the insurance policies taken out by weavers at the time. I have so far looked at two periods, 1703–10, when fire insurance was still a novelty, and 1765–74. A similar comparison will be made later this year with the seven to ten years around 1733 and 1793. It could be argued that rate books would give a more complete picture but there is no way of determining who is a weaver (and this is not a demographic study). Moreover, the ratepayer may be the landlord and not all the rate books for the relevant areas of London have survived.

Several qualifying points must be made: first, while the names have been listed by me it has often been an arbitrary decision whether someone is a Huguenot or not and I can only apologise for any inaccuracies. Second, on the principle that those listed by the Clerk at least started the year alive all those marked 'dead' have been included.

Table 8.1 Huguenots in the Weavers' Company of London

Date	Total all weavers	Huguenots	Total of Assistants and officers	H	%	Total of Livery	H	%	Total percentage of Huguenots
1703/4	5919	1046	25	1	4.00	149	3	2.00	17.6
1713/4	5613	1157	23	1	4.30	195	7	3.58	20.61
1723/4	5954	1216	26	2	7.70	229	10	4.36	20.42
1733/4	5858	1072	27	2	7.40	256	18	7.00	18.2
1743/4	3731	616	25	2	8.00	291	59	20.27	16.5
1751/2	2532	342	24	4	16.60	238	54	22.68	13.5
1763/4	1868	265	24	7	29.10	206	47	22.81	14.18
1773/4	1582	219	26	1	3.80	179	48	26.81	13.84
1783/4	1383	173	28	7	25.00	210	40	19.00	12.5
1793/4	1157	101	28	4	14.28	252	42	16.60	8.7

H stands for Huguenot

At the beginning of the century when Canterbury was still important 17.6 per cent of the Company were Huguenots. The percentage of Huguenots rose until they formed a fifth of the Company in the 1720s. The 1730s were very difficult years for the Company when it was losing its grip upon the trade. It was increasingly short of money and thus unable to pursue the non-freemen and the lapsed freemen. (Some of those eventually caught had managed to escape paying dues for thirty or forty years.)[2] It will be seen that they had lost 2000 in the ten years 1733–43. Until the 1740s the Huguenot element, despite its size, had had negligible power in the company. Hardly any Officers, Assistants, or even members of the Livery had French names. The Company however, had been very active in affairs of general interest to the industry, co-opting 'gentlemen from the trade' for particular committees as it needed them. Three very important exceptions were Colonel and Captain Peter Lekeux (their ranks in the City Trained Bands) and James Leman, designer and manufacturer. Both families came from Canterbury and in Leman's case also from Amsterdam,[3] and both became Assistants on the Court of the Weavers' Company. Leman, indeed, played an active part in the great anti-calico campaign of 1719–21 (Plate XVIII, figures 1–4, 6).[4] In 1740, however, the Company swallowed its prejudices and recruited all the prosperous French weavers it could catch for the Livery, forty-five men, an action reflected in the figures for 1743–4. It was a step of immense significance both for the future of the Company and the industry. Although the total size of the Company continued to decline the French element gained a significant voice – 8 per cent of the Court and 20.27 per cent of the Livery in 1743 (a year when the last attempt at sumptuary legislation was defeated)[5] 1763–73. The decade of greatest crisis in the industry, 1763–1773, opened with 29.1 per cent of the Court and 22.81 per cent of the Livery Frenchmen. Despite the fact that the Company was only a third of its size at the beginning of the century it was the natural, official spokesman for the industry. The journeymen, for the most part non-freemen by this time, came to the Court with £100 for the parliamentary campaign to secure the total prohibition of French silks.[6] This was achieved in 1766,[7] reaffirmed in 1786, and only repealed in 1824 with effect from 1826. The Upper Bailiff, the highest office in the Company, in 1762 was Peter Campart, from Normandy; in 1763 Thomas Abraham Ogier, born in Poitou; in 1764 Peter Lekeux, weaver of flowered silks and the third of his family in the industry (Plate XX, figure 3). In 1765 the Upper Bailiff was English (John Hinde) but the Renter Bailiff, second in command, was Zachariah Agace from Normandy and the Upper Warden Peter Arnaud (Upper Bailiff in 1773). Only in 1766 when the battle was won were all the officers English. As their numbers in the table show the Huguenots in the influential ranks of the Company formed a consistently higher percentage than their numbers in the Company as a whole. Once recruited for the Livery they remained. When, in 1793/4, the Company had shrunk to 1157 people of whom only 8.7 per cent were Huguenots they still formed 16.6 per cent of the Livery. Their addresses and occupations were given on this quarterage list. Thus 79 per cent of the Huguenots on the Livery and only 44 per cent of the English were weavers. It is arguable that it was the Huguenot element, therefore, which prolonged the active life of the Company long after many other companies were becoming formal associations of business men. Their loyalty to it was given additional lustre by their ability as witnesses before Parliament. Sixty-three witnesses appeared before the two select committees of 1765 and 1766, including those appearing before both committees. Fifteen of these were Huguenots, several appearing twice.[8] All the master weavers were members of the Weavers' Company.

Thanks to the help of Mr Stuart Turner and his assistants, all volunteers, who have been extracting the textile trades from the Sun Insurance Company policy registers, coupled with my own work on the Hand in Hand Insurance Company which covers London, it is evident without any doubt, that, apart from a few individuals the Huguenots gravitated to two textile centres only, initially Canterbury, and then London. They did not make serges in Devon, they did not even go to Coventry which made both silks and ribbons, nor Norwich, long associated with such immigrants. Outside London, they did not make the plain linens, fustians, sacking and sailcloth which some must have made in France. A weaver admitted to the Company on the basis of his service in Caen was certainly not making silks.[9] Thus, by counting the Huguenots in the London industry we do arrive at totals which are not unrealistic.

There is the problem of non-freemen. There were tax and political advantages for the English to join their company (which they were supposed to do anyway) enough, judging from their insurance policies, to attract two coffee-house keepers and an innkeeper in the earlier period. Others may not have been practising weavers since they lived too far away from the centres of the industry. The Huguenots had to join to practise their profession and, despite some grumbling, probably felt too insecure in the first twenty years of the eighteenth century to flout its rules. 119 weavers – 11.37 per cent of the total – insured their property with the Hand in Hand between 1703 and 1710. Twenty English and five Huguenots were outside the Company. The latter were Christian Dangre of Pelham Street, Peter Hemard of Cox Square who probably were indeed weavers. I have also included John Larchevesque 'gentlemen' because most of his family were certainly weavers in Canterbury and London although he may have retired. John Lekeux, listed on one of the Company's searches and living in Stuart Street in the Old Artillery Ground in the heart of the silk-weaving district, was described as a 'merchant' when he subsequently became bankrupt. John Le Scallet may have begun life as a weaver but kept a coffee-house. Thirteen Huguenots with fire insurance belonged to the Company including Peter Leman (James Leman's father), Peter Lekeux and Peter Marescoe (plates XVIII, XIX, XX) named as one of the founders of the industry in the nineteenth century.[10] The number of weavers insuring their property had risen to 233 in the period from 1765 to 1774; of these people ninety-three, or 39.9 per cent, were members of the Weavers' Company. Twenty-six Huguenots insuring their property were members of the Company and fifty-four (including at least one who had lapsed) were not.[11] Thus just over a third of the policy-holders were Huguenots. The majority of policy-holders were concentrated in Spitalfields, Moorfields, Bishopsgate and Bethnal Green. There were nine in Southwark, all English and all outside the Company. Twenty-six in other parts of London, eight at retirement addresses, three making ribbons in the City and, interestingly, one London gauze-weaver with an address in Paisley. One widow of a Huguenot weaver kept an ale-house and one plush-weaver was established in Westminster. Fire insurance was obviously sensible and it is perhaps surprising that more weavers, both English and Huguenot did not have it. Some of the early immigrants were denizened and only the richest went to the expense of naturalisation in order to pass on property but this was hardly true in the 1770s.

The Huguenots traced so far had come from three main areas of France: Picardy, Bas Poitou, and Normandy – the map in the catalogue of *The Quiet Conquest* shows the communities in France.[12] Some individuals came from elsewhere and the origins of many are unclear since members of the same families in France might be established in different provinces. It has not proved easy to tie up specific individuals, partly because the same Christian names may be used for successive generations and partly because of the complications of intermarriage. The Maze family, for example, married Lamberts in several generations and the Lardants and Lardaus married Deheulles. Some families were established for so long in Canterbury that their French origins are no longer mentioned in the registers of the French Churches in England.[13] One fact is quite certain: only a very few people came from Lyon – where Protestants were not permitted to enter the silk industry.

Why did they enter the silk industry – and stay in this trade in the case of some families for one hundred years or more? Part of the answer may lie in the establishment of the community in Canterbury in the sixteenth century. There was thus a natural centre in which new refugees could find shelter on their way in and out of England. Somner in his *Antiquities of Canterbury*, published in 1640, spoke about the 'Strangers Church. A congregation for the most part of distressed exiles grown so great and daily multiplying that the place in a short time is likely to prove a hive too small to contain such a swarm'.[14] Certainly, many did go on to London and their names are found in the first surviving quarterage list of 1680 as well as in Canterbury. Among the regular contributions to the funds of the Walloon Church in Canterbury in the late seventeenth century are those from London. Opinion had changed by 1719. 'Those who settled here wove all sorts of plain, fine, flowered and wrought silks ... English silks equal if not exceed for fineness and curious workmanship any that are in the world. All of which improvements are owing to these Walloons' but Harris rebuked 'Mr Sumner grumbling at their increase'.[15] By then, however, the Canterbury families were rapidly migrating to London. Some seventy-two Huguenot families associated with the silk industry in Canterbury and in London have been traced so far. By comparing the names with those on the quarterage lists it seems that the majority had moved by 1703 (see Table 8.2).

Many of these had been quite poor in Canterbury in 1699, for example, the elders paid the expenses of an Ouvry child and a dress for a child L'Heureux.[16] Twenty-seven of these families came originally from Normandy. Twelve families described as silk-weavers in Canterbury either died out or failed to make the move. Many of those who did move, like the Duthoits, retained their links with Canterbury until the end of their lives (Plate XXIII, figure 1).[17] By 1777 William Gostling could write of the Huguenot community in Canterbury 'They maintained their own poor and still do ... By the removal of most of their descendants to Spitalfields and the uniting of others with English families they are so reduced that at present there are hardly ten

Table 8.2 Huguenot families on Canterbury quarterage lists, 1703–64

1703/4 (31)		1713/4 (14)	1723/4 (9)	1733/4 (2)	1751 and 1763/4 (2)
Alavoine	Leman	Agace	Campart	Lepine	Flamare (1751)
Battaille	Lekeux	Bourdon	Duthoit	Shoulder	Phene (Livery 1763)
Brument	LeMoine	Despaigne	Deschazaux		
Barine	Lote	Deneu	Jeudwine		
Delahaize	Le Grand	Fremaux	le Hook		
Delamare	Le Count	Hebert	Lieve		
Dubois	Leu	Lanson	Mercier		
Deheulle	Lardan(t)	Le Sadd	Roy		
Danbrine	Larchevaques	Macaré	Voisin		
Ferre	Monceaux	Messman			
Gilles	Manneke	Maillard			
(? Giles)	Morie	Martell			
Guerard	Maze	Ouvry			
Gron/ou	Oudart	Rondeau			
Gastineau	Pilon				
L'Heureux	Vautier				

weavers and about eighty communicants'.[18] Mr Turner's work has revealed several active Huguenot weavers and others in the mid- and later eighteenth century in Canterbury,[19] and taking our work on the two insurance companies together we find that several London weavers insured premises in Canterbury or vice versa.[20] The precise business relationship between the two I am still exploring – I suspect that some of the debtors in the inventories of Canterbury weavers in the late seventeenth century may be London weavers for whom the Canterbury people were sub-contracting, or London mercers. Despite the problems earlier in the seventeenth century,[21] by the turn of the eighteenth century the relationship seems to have been a friendly one. James Leman employed two of the Manneke family possibly cousins rather than brothers, Philip and Benjamin (Plate XVIII, figure 5), as well as a journeyman called Shoulder.

To explain the growth of the silk industry – in all its branches – a wider view needs to be taken. The Huguenots entered every Branch:[22] Plain, Fancy (gauze, etc), Black, Foot-Figured and Flowered, narrow and handkerchiefs as well as becoming dyers, throwsters, and, in due course, silkmen, brokers, satin dressers, waterers of tabby, and designers. No branch was exclusively staffed by Frenchmen. While the process of lustering silks to make alamode and lustering was a French invention there are few other patents in the period. The rise in the demand for silks must be explained by more general economic factors: the difficulties faced by Lyon at the end of the seventeenth century owing to the economic strain of Louis XIV's wars. There is a desperate letter from the Chambre de Commerce in Lyon in 1707 to their intendant in Paris owing to the cessation of all trade. English trade, on the other hand, was increasing with rapid growth in demand, especially from the American Colonies. Not only did this bring a new market but the riches to be gained in such a trade and all that went with it created a demand for consumer goods which benefited such an industry. It is clear that the move to London was very much in the interests of the Canterbury families (their goods in the inventories examined so far are much more modest than those of the later Spitalfields master weavers) and that the expansion of the industry prompted members of Protestant families who had remained in France to come over. The Ogiers from Poitou, a most important family, came over in several groups.[23] Work on the Normandy contingent in 1985 has revealed several interesting facts. The immigrants from the Pays de Caux in Normandy provided a disproportionate number of people whose families became of great importance later. The Pasteur Denis Vatinel reports that for several years there was no Protestant marriage in the district so young people had to come to England to marry – and obviously many stayed.[24] The small town of Luneray which is set in rich agricultural land and which, subsequently, wove fustians (linen and cotton mixtures, as did a number of the neighbouring towns and villages) sent an extraordinary number of such families to England.[25] There are still Protestant Lardants, Ouvrys, L'Heureux in the town who, presumably, preserved the family property by various means.

Although every branch of the silk industry – including the weavers of mixed fabrics – had a proportion of Huguenots, their greatest impact both on contemporaries and since was in the Flowered branch. It must even be argued that there were plenty of Englishmen before, during the height of their involvement, and afterwards in this branch. We have to cite as proof Joseph Dandridge, naturalist and silk designer, who lived from 1664 to 1747 and was a member of the Merchant Taylors' Company. In his teens he worked for James Leman and we have some of his designs.[26] Anna Maria Garthwaite was most emphatically English but of her customers thirty-three were Huguenots and twenty-two including the mercers, English.[27] The nursery for some of this talent may well have been Canterbury. Stephen Duthoit's inventory (he died in 1698) included fifteen montures (the figure harnesses of drawlooms) at 20s each and seven looms at 10s. Apart from raw silk his stock included lutestring, damask, and a material called sultan. These are valued at 3s to 4s 6d for the lutestring, 4s 6d for the damask, and 7s for the sultan, of which he had 1201 yards. His production was thus quite large but these are not the most expensive silks.[28] Peter Le Hook who died in 1690 had four looms and five montures but the total value of his goods was £223 10s 1d, not a very impressive sum.[29] More investigation is needed but if my first impression is correct then at least the new immigrants would have been able to learn their basic techniques in Canterbury. It cannot be over-emphasised that both to design for and to weave on the drawloom, the 'monture' of the inventories, it is necessary to understand it. Silk was expensive, and when James Leman gave 'Ben Manckey' his 'first draught work' he was presumably satisfied with his weaving of plain silks and his progress in understanding the drawloom. Of the designers the origins of Christopher Baudouin (Plate XIX, figures 3 and 4; Plate XX, figures 1 and 2) remain, so far, obscure (though there were Baudouins in Canterbury) and he was the most celebrated.[30] John Vansommer's work for over forty years is now represented by a firescreen and a series of beds at Petworth. Vansommer was a second-generation immigrant and a correspondent of Voltaire.[31] Peter Cheveney said in his evidence to the Select Committee of 1765 that he came from Lyon and he became, briefly, a partner in Vansommer's firm of Ogier, Vansommer and Triquet. (Peter Ogier came from Chassais l'Eglise in Poitou.) Peter Mazell is known only by name,[32] and Peter Abraham de Brissac was a hack designer who provided patterns for both silks and printed cottons, being paid more for the latter. His connections seem also to have been with the Poitevin contingent. We do not know who designed the waistcoat patterns sold by Maze and Steer (Plate XXIII, figure 2), nor, indeed, which Maze was the senior partner. The designers of the silks woven by Batchelor, Ham and Perigal are unknown.

No silks woven from the designs of Leman or Baudouin have yet come to light but we can judge the quality of production by those woven by Huguenot master weavers to the designs of Anna Maria Garthwaite. In addition, there are silks woven by Batchelor, Ham and Perigal and by Maze and Steer. Since it is impossible to identify plain silks the patterned silks are doubly important in this context. Not only were they fashionable (they would not otherwise have sold) but the quality is, indeed, uniformly excellent. Designs woven by Roeloff Grotert, Simon Julins, (Plate XXI, Figure 3) Captain Peter and his son Mr Peter Lekeux (Plate XX, Figures 2, 3; (Plate XXI, Figure 3). Mr Pulley, Mr Sabatier and Mr, probably Daniel, Vautier survive (Plate XXII, Figures 1, 2). It is impossible to know who their journeymen were since no account books or similar information exists. Lekeux's waistcoat of 1747 now in the Metropolitan Museum and shewn in the Rococo exhibition in the Victoria and Albert Museum in 1984 would be outstanding in any context (as were the Lekeux family themselves). Slightly less dramatic are the samples from the Desormaux and Duthoit families (Plate XXIII, figure 1) – but they survive from a period when silk design was not required to be as dramatic.[33] All are technically accomplished, wasting no silk on the back of the textile, for instance, and carrying out their designs faithfully. More of Julins' damasks have survived than the silks of any other weaver (Plate XXI, figure 3) and three of these are in the USA, preserved in former American colonial families. Two are in Boston, Massachusetts, and date from 1751 and 1752, while the third – for which the design was sold in 1743 – is worn by Mrs Charles Willing in a painting by Robert Feke dating from 1746.

If we can accept their efficiency as silk-weavers what else did they achieve? Their most obvious success was their prosperity. Although the contingent from Bas Poitou had probably been among the gentry of their province the Normans, with the exception of the Maillard family who came from the *bonne bourgeoisie rurale*, were not, and they did not make much of a mark in the eighteenth century. Three of the Luneray families produced weavers of flowered silks, since they were customers of Garthwaite, including Vautier, her chief customer. The wills of many Huguenots in the silk industry refer to house property, a country house, money in public funds, books, silver, good furnishings, all accumulated by the third quarter of the eighteenth century. Few Huguenots went bankrupt. Their contribution to the Weavers' Company has already been outlined but they were equally good citizens, serving on Vestry committees to repair the north steps of Christ Church or the cracked tenor bell, while John Sabatier (Plate XXII, figure 2) investigated the possibility of building a workhouse.[34] Seventy-seven firms with Huguenot partners, and fifty-five with English partners, offered men to fight the Young Pretender (1751 and 2038 men respectively). To judge from this list some of the English firms were larger. Huguenot loyalty to their adopted country was equally evident in their charities. They supported the London Hospital in their lifetime and usually left money to the 'five London Hospitals' or some of them, as well as to Huguenot charities. They were interested in education in the broadest sense, from the mathematical instruments and specimens referred to in his will by James Leman, to the school set up by the throwster Peter Nouailles in the early nineteenth century for his workpeople. (Those who learned to read received a Bible as a prize.) They undertook the boring but important duties in the community, from auditing the accounts of Christ Church, Spitalfields, to giving evidence in 1759 on the paving of Norton Folgate (Thomas Abraham Ogier, Zachariah Agace and one English weaver, James Payton).[35] They did not support the more unorthodox charities such as the Foundling Hospital but several joined the Royal Society of Arts.

There are certain features of the English silk industry quite unlike those in France: specialisation not only among the master weavers but by the journeymen was one, but this cannot be attributed to the Huguenot element especially. Nevertheless, Simon Julins was the unique weaver of damasks to advertise in Mortimer's Directory of 1763. The Weavers' Company did not lay down technical requirements such as there were in Lyon but there is no evidence that the English master weavers were any less competent than the French. The analysis I made of the inhabitants of the streets of Spitalfields suggests a division by wealth and to an extent by speciality but not by country of origin.[36] Nevertheless, the immigrants from Canterbury certainly congregated and remained in the streets in the Old Artillery Ground. Immigrants from particular provinces often remained associated until the late eighteenth century but this must not be pressed too far for there were partnerships across provincial and national lines and intermarriage from the seventeenth century onwards. Some families, however, remained exclusively Huguenot until the nineteenth century. After the first ill-feeling had died away (there were still anti-French protests in the Weavers' Company in 1715) Huguenots and English worked together amicably. The role of the French Churches in looking after their poor probably had much to do with the admiration which quickly superseded initial suspicion. We know little about the journeymen but few of the names of those relieved by the Threadneedle Street Church between 1681 and 1687 are those which were to become so familiar later.[37] The exceptions among the silk weavers are Isaac de l'Epine, Nicholas Lefevre, Pierre Paris, Nicholas Bourdon and Abraham de Heule, serge-weaver from Bolbec. While any generalisation can be contradicted by some flagrant exception I have found no evidence to contradict the opinion I had formed in 1960, when I wrote my thesis on the silk industry, that the weavers formed an intensely orthodox community, intelligent, skilled and enlightened within limits but, on the whole, generally anxious to be accepted as 'gentlemen', so often the appellation of those who survived into the later eighteenth century. The silks which have appeared since then show that they were very good at their job. Research upon the Huguenot community suggests that, although always outnumbered by the English, it was they who set the standards remembered with nostalgia in the nineteenth century.

Notes

1. P. Thornton and N. Rothstein. 'The Importance of the Huguenots in the London Silk Industry' *Proceedings of the Huguenot Society of London*, (1958–64) vol. 20, pp. 69–73.
2. Court Books of the Weavers' Company, 12 June 1716, a man became free who had been apprenticed in 1663. Henry Robelon living in Brick Lane, Bethnal Green, bound 1704 to Daniel Oufrey, became free of the Company in January 1753. Ephraim Flamar was summoned 5 September 1748 but refused to be admitted until threatened with

prosecution. He had been bound apprentice in November 1731 to Peter Fondimare.
3. *Témoignage* of Peter Leman at the French Church in Threadneedle Street, January 1673. He was said to be of Amsterdam '*natif de Cantorbery*'. See Huguenot Society Quarto Series XXI, p. 168 W. and S. Minet (eds). Peter Leman was admitted to the Weavers' Company, 20 July 1674 on the basis of his service to his father in Amsterdam. James Leman was apprenticed to his father in February 1702 and free 19 November 1711.
4. There is a list of pamphlets in James Leman's writing concerning this campaign among the papers of the Weavers' Company in the Guildhall Library. The Campaign itself was described by me in *East London Papers*, vol. 7, no 1 (July 1964) pp. 3–21.
5. 27 January 1743. The Upper Bailiff (Captain John Baker, a weaver of flowered silks and a customer of Anna Maria Garthwaite) told the Court of a bill in the House of Commons 'to prohibit the wearing of gold and silver lace thread or wire in apparel, in the event of which several members of this Company are concerned'. The committee formed to fight the measure included James Leman, Peter Lekeux and James Godin (Plate XXIV). 'Gentlemen from the Trade' to be co-opted included Daniel Gobee. There is a draft of their petition among Leman's papers. The measure was defeated.
6. Court Books, 28 March 1764. The Court had been prepared to admonish the journeymen's deputation for being 'a very disorderly and turbulent set of people' – presumably they had to say 'thank you' instead!
7. 6 Geo 111 cap 28.
8.

Jean Jaques Bougeac	1765	Weaver from Nîmes and Lyon
Peter Cheveney	1765	Pattern-drawer, later partner of Ogier, Vansommer and Triquet
Abraham Jeudwine	1765	Velvet weaver, from Canterbury, customer of Garthwaite.
German Lavie	1765 and 1766	Mercer
James Legrew	1765	Weaver
John Lewis (Louis?)	1765	Weaver
James Lesouef	1765	Weaver
Lewis Ogier	1765	Weaver, subsequently emigrated to America
Peter Ogier	1765	Weaver, brother of Lewis and senior partner in Ogier, Vansommer and Triquet
(Thomas) Abraham Ogier	1766	Weaver, brother of Lewis and Peter
Stephen Paris	1765	Weaver, at one time in partnership with a Landon

John Peregol (Peregal)	1765 and 1766	'a weaver of silks from the slightest to the roughest', from Normandy and junior partner in the firm of Batchelor, Ham and Perigal
John Sabatier	1765 and 1766	The family may have come from Lyon. His father had been a member of the Weavers' Company and he was recruited for the Livery in 1740. A customer of Garthwaite's
P. Trequet	1765	Weaver
Charles Triquet	1765	Weaver, junior partner in Ogier, Vansommer and Triquet. One of the Triquets also gave evidence in 1766
Triquet and Bunney	1765	Throwsters

9. Court Books 20 February 1727.
10. J. S. Burn, *The History of the French, Walloon, Dutch and other Foreign Protestant Refugees Settled in England* (London, 1846). The statement was repeated in most later nineteenth century accounts. All were associated together with Monceaux on designs now in the Victoria and Albert Museum (Plate XIX, figures 3 and 4; Plate XX, figures 1 and 2).
11. Ivon le Nain.
12. *The Quiet Conquest: The Huguenots 1685–1985.* Catalogue of the exhibition held at the Museum of London (1985) p. 19.
13. R. Hovenden (ed.) *Registers of the Walloon or Strangers' Church in Canterbury* (1891–8) Huguenot Society Quarto Series, vol. 5. Members of the Lekeux family appear in them from the late sixteenth century onwards.
14. W. Somner, *Antiquities of Canterbury* (1640) p. 175.
15. J. Harris, *The History of Kent* (1719) p. 63.
16. Canterbury City and Diocesan Record Office U 47 C 1–3 Deacons Accounts. Two miscellaneous entries from November and December 1699. I am indebted to Miss Anne Oakley for kindly drawing my attention to these accounts.
17. *Quiet Conquest*, p. 300. The family came from Marq-en-Bareul near Lille. Peter Duthoit, died 1777, had property in both Middlesex and Canterbury (PCC Collier f. 458) John Duthoit, died 1787, left money to his brother Henry, a weaver in Canterbury (PCC Major f. 61). Obadiah Agace, died 1755, left £100 to the Walloon Church of Canterbury as well as £100 to the Charity School run by the French Church in Threadneedle Street.
18. W. Gostling, *A Walk in and about the City of Canterbury*, pp. 217–8, note.
19. Josiah Dernocour, silk weaver, Canterbury, Sun Insurance Co., vol.

207, p. 599 (1771)
Peter de Lasaux, silk weaver, Canterbury, Sun Insurance Co., vol. 209, p. 609 (1771)
Samuel Fremoult, scourer, Canterbury, Sun Insurance Co., vol. 77, p. 97 (1746)
Peter Godiere, silk weaver, Canterbury, Sun Insurance Co., vol. 255, p. 64 (1777) .
John Guerrard, silk weaver and hop planter, Canterbury, Sun Insurance Co., vol. 176, p. 519 (1767)
These are examples, for work is continuing. I am indebted to Stuart Turner, I. M. Garner and Ann Paton for these references.

20. Charles Dalbiac, Stephen Barbut and John Jordan of London insured utensils and stock in a house in Canterbury in the tenure of John Calloway, silk weaver. Sun Insurance Co., vol. 203, p. 331 (1770).
John Landon of London, silk weaver, insured utensils and stock in the dwelling house of James Gant, silk weaver, in Canterbury, Sun Insurance Co., vol. 208, p. 411 (1771)
Abraham Macaré, silk weaver, of Canterbury insured a house in St Ann's, Westminster in 1705 and three more in 1707, Hand in Hand Insurance Co., Guildhall MS 8674/3 f. 451 and 8674/5 f. 239.
Although the Pilons had a branch in London by 1703 Nicholas Pilon, silk weaver, insured a house in Canterbury in 1726. Sun Insurance Co., vol. 22, p. 144.

21. The successful attempt by the Weavers' Company of London to take over the Canterbury weavers in 1638 is outlined by Anne Oakley in her pamphlet, *The French Connection: The Canterbury Walloon Connection* (1985).

22. The branches with capital letters are those recognised by the journeymen in their pay dispute of 1769 when lists of prices (that is, piece-rates) were published.

23. N. K. A. Rothstein, *The Silk Industry in London 1702–1766*, London University MA thesis 1961, pp. 54–5, 198–202.

24. Letter, 19 August 1985 *'J'ai observé qu'entre 1685 et grosso modo 1698 tous les jeunes gens en âge de se marier traversent la Manche pour ne pas se soumettre au marriage catholique. Il n'y a PAS de mariage de protestants en pays de Caux entre 1685 et 1688'*. Official lists of families of 1698–9 show that the only ones to stay in France were those married before the Revocation or very recently by clandestine pastors. Monsieur Vatinel has studied the Protestant community in Normandy for over twenty-five years.

25. Silk weavers with origins in Luneray: Battaille, Larchevesque, Lardant(s), Le Sadd, Ouvry, Peigne, Pilon, Vautier. At least eighty-two families in the London silk industry can be identified from the list of Norman Protestant families compiled by the Pasteur Denis Vatinel and deposited in the Archives Departmentales in Rouen. I am very grateful to Monsieur Daniel Lardans for photocopying this list for me, and for detailed information on the Huguenots in Luneray.

26. An account of his career was given by me in *East London Papers*, vol. 9, no. 2, Winter 1966 'Joseph Dandridge, Naturalist and Silk designer',

pp. 101–18. Mr D. E. Allen and Mr W. S. Bristowe have explored his scientific work.

27. They are listed on p. 292 cat. no. 439 of *The Quiet Conquest*.

28. Maidstone County Record Office PRC 27/35/84, 23 October 1700.

29. Maidstone County Record Office PRC 27/32/141, 1690.

30. Thornton and Rothstein, 'Importance of the Huguenots', pp. 66–9 and 78–83.

31. N. Perry 'John Vansommer of Spitalfields: Huguenot Silk Designer, Correspondent of Voltaire' in *Studies on Voltaire and the Eighteenth Century* LX (Geneva 1968) Institut et Musée Voltaire, Les Délices, pp. 289–310.

32. M. Postlethwayt, *A Dictionary of Trade and Commerce* (1754) article on engraving. He is listed as one of the three designers who introduced the 'principles of painting into the loom', the others were John Vansommer and Anna Maria Garthwaite. His account is the first to mention Lanson, Mariscot and Monceaux and to state that 'the first designer and pattern drawer was M. Boudoin'. He was very flattering about Joseph Dandridge but ignored James Leman.

33. The development of English silk design in the eighteenth century is illustrated in D. King (ed.) *British Textile Design in the V & A Museum*, vols 1 & 2 (Tokyo 1980).

34. The Vestry Committee to consider removing the steps on the north side of Christ Church, Spitalfields consisted of: Mr Snee, Mr Crush, Mr Jervis, Capt Garrett, Mr Lardant, Daniel Pilon, Capt Gilbert, Mr Peter Campart, Mr Samuel Worrall (a local builder), Mr Marsillat, two Mr Lanes, John Ouvry, Peter Abraham Ogier, John Haddow, Peter Duthoit and John Allen. Of the eight Huguenots only Mr Marsillat was not in the industry. Most of the Englishmen were also connected with the textile industries (Vestry Minutes 20 September 1743).

The cracked tenor bell was discussed on 19 November 1746 and the subsequent committee consisted of the Rector, John Peck, Esq. (dyer), Robert Turner Esq. (worsteds), Capt. Baker (flowered silks), Mr Campart (plain silks), Mr Jervis (in Weavers' Company), Mr Thomas Turner (possibly the dyer) and Capt. George Garrett (in Weavers' Company).

15 November 1752, John Sabatier reported on his inspection of workhouses.

35. *House of Commons Journals*, vol. 28, p. 385.

36. Rothstein, thesis, 1961, pp. 13–68.

37. A. P. Hands and I. Scouloudi (eds) *French Protestant Refugees Relieved through the Threadneedle Street Church, London 1681–87*, Huguenot Society of London Quarto Series, vol. XLIX (1971).

Editor's note

Fully detailed captions to Plates XVIII – XXIV inclusive will be found in the List of Plates on pp. xi–xiv.

Figure 1

Figure 2

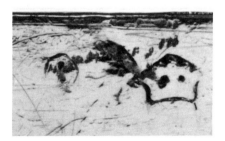

Figure 3

Plate I Figure 1. Design for a tazza by Hans Holbein the Younger
Figure 2. Two silver-gilt tazze from Rochester Cathedral
Figure 3. Detail of unidentifiable marks on the tazza without cover

Plate II The Wyndham Ewer, 1554

Plate III The Devonshire Ewer, 1697: Pierre Harache Senior

Figure 1

Figure 2

Plate IV Figure 1. The 'Croft' Cup, 1685: Benjamin Pyne
Figure 2. Two-handled silver-gilt Cup and Cover, 1705: Simon Pantin

Figure 1

Figure 2

Plate V Figure 1. Two-handled Cup and Cover, 1709: David Willaume
Figure 2. Two-handled Cup and Cover, 1723: Paul de Lamerie

Figure 1

Figure 2

Plate VI Figure 1. Two-handled Cup and Cover, 1699: Pierre Platel
Figure 2. Two-handled Cup and Cover, 1702: Louis Cuny

Figure 1

Figure 2

Plate VII Figure 1. Detail of handle on the Philip Rollos II Wine-cooler
Figure 2. Wine-cooler, 1712: Philip Rollos II

Figure 1

Figure 2

Plate VIII Figure 1. Coffee-pot, 1700: Jean Chartier
Figure 2. *Ecuelle*, 1704: Pierre Platel

Plate IX The Germain Vases, 1711: David Willaume

Figure 1

Figure 2

Plate X Figure 1. The State Bed at Blair Castle, Perthshire
Figure 2. Frontispiece of Daniel Marot's *Second Livre d'Appartements*, published
c. 1701

Plate XI State Bedchamber at Drayton House, Northamptonshire, with bed by Guillotin, hangings by Rebekah Dufee and Elizabeth Vickson, table and candlestands attributed to Gerrit Jensen

Figure 1

Figure 2

Plate XII Figure 1. Queen Elizabeth's Room at Penshurst Place, Kent
Figure 2. Daybed attributed to Philip Guibert, Temple Newsam House, Leeds

Figure 1

Figure 2

Plate XIII Figure 1. Part of a valance from a state bed at Dunham Massey, Cheshire
Figure 2. Carved walnut bench at Dunham Massey, Cheshire

Figure 1

Figure 2

Plate XIV Figure 1. Painted looking-glass, attributed to Jean-Baptiste Monnoyer at
Melbourne Hall, Derbyshire
Figure 2. Looking-glass, table and candlestands, possibly by John Guilbaud, at
Hopetoun House, West Lothian

Figure 1

Figure 2

Plate XV Figure 1. Marquetry dressing table, attributed to Gerrit Jensen, at
Lennoxlove, East Lothian
Figure 2. Carved and gilt table, Petworth House, West Sussex

Figure 2

Figure 1

Figure 1. Picture-frame (over the chimneypiece) by Jean Pelletier, at Boughton House, Northamptonshire

Plate XVI

Figure 2

Figure 1

Plate XVII   Figure 1. Looking-glass and table at Erddig, North Wales. Attributed to John Pardoe
Figure 2. Pier-glass at Erddig, attributed to John Belchier

Figure 1

Figure 2

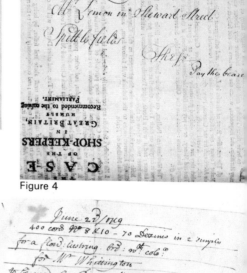

Figure 4

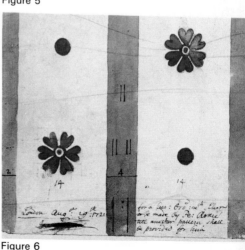

Figure 5

Figure 3

Figure 6

Plate XVIII Figures 1–4. Papers assembled by James Leman
Figure 5. Inscription by James Leman
Figure 6. Detail of a design by James Leman

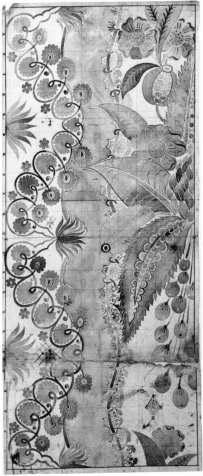

Figure 1

Figure 3

Figure 2

Figure 4

Plate XIX Figure 1. Design by James Leman, 1719
Figure 2. Inscription by James Leman on back of this design
Figure 3. Design by Christopher Baudouin
Figure 4. Inscription on back of Figure 3

Figure 1

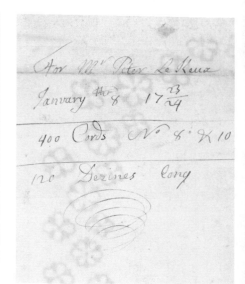

Figure 2

Figure 3

Plate XX Figure 1. Design by
Christopher Baudouin
Figure 2. Inscription on back
of Figure 1
Figure 3. Sleeved waistcoat
designed by Anna Maria
Garthwaite, woven by Peter
Lekeux son of Mr Peter
Lekeux above

Figure 1

Figure 2

Figure 3

Plate XXI Figure 1. Detail from a
pattern book of Batchelor,
Ham and Perigal c. 1755
Figure 2. Detail of a dress,
silk woven by Batchelor,
Ham and Perigal
Figure 3. Detail of silk
designed by Anna Maria
Garthwaite 1752, woven
by Simon Julins
(1687/8–1774)

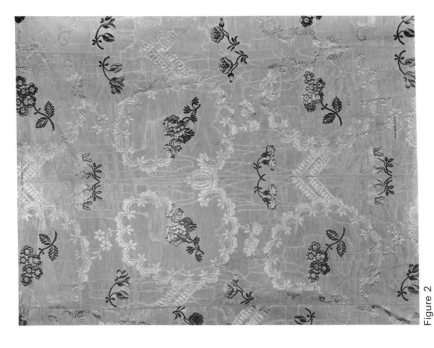

Figure 1

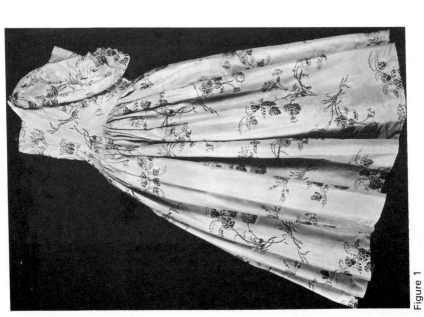

Figure 2

Plate XXII Figure 1. Dress, silk designed by Anna Maria Garthwaite, woven by Mr Vautier, 1747
Figure 2. Silk, watered tabby, designed by Anna Maria Garthwaite, woven by John Sabatier, 1752

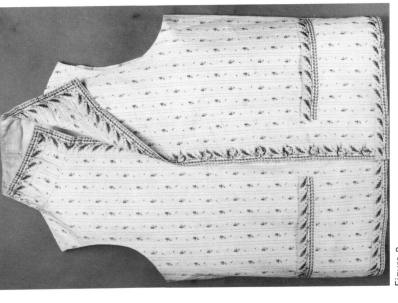

Figure 2

Figure 1

Plate XXIII Figure 1. Sample, c. 1770, probably woven by the Duthoit family
Figure 2. Waistcoat, silk and linen, woven by Maze and Steer, 1788

Plate XXIV Design by Anna Maria Garthwaite 1748, sold to James Godin

Part II
The French Background

9 Great Britain as Envisaged by the Huguenots of the Seventeenth Century

Elisabeth Labrousse

Even when the Edict of Nantes was to some extent fairly administered as in some early periods of the seventeenth century, the French Reformed Churches knew and felt themselves to be, as the saying went, 'under the cross', since the King of France was not of their faith. Obviously this was a considerable handicap for them, even before the French court became openly and bitterly hostile to Protestants. Therefore it is easy to understand why the Huguenots were so prone to comfort themselves by looking for support in the European Protestant camp. At least it was part of their ideology; although in practice the French authorities carefully forbade any official contact between the French Reformed Churches and foreign Protestants.[1] For instance they had prevented the participation of French deputies in the Synod of Dort in 1618, even though delegates had been appointed by the National Synod of Vitré in 1617.

In 1631, the fourth article of the National Synod of Charenton favoured the Lutherans who might travel or reside in France – a ruling which resulted in no gratitude from the Churches of the Augsburg Confession.

But it was above all a kind of 'Calvinist International' which bolstered Huguenot morale, since this constituted their best support outside France. Apart from Geneva, the Swiss Cantons, the Palatinate and the United Provinces, England was their strongest shield. Indeed, as we shall see, the Huguenots were either blind to the peculiarities of the Anglican *via media*, or they grossly under-assessed it, both by wishful thinking and because their knowledge of it was so inadequate. The memory of the help given to Henri IV by Elizabeth I would in itself have been sufficient to account for the sympathy and the trust which the Huguenots felt towards the Church of England. Meanwhile they were blissfully unaware of the fact that the Church of England was far from feeling towards them an unqualified friendliness. However – and at the time this was of paramount importance – there remained the basic solidarity that stemmed from a common and deep hostility to Roman Catholics, or, more precisely – and here the vocabulary of the time is illuminating – to 'popery', an institution deemed to be the fount of all the monstrous aberrations that Protestantism attributed to the Roman communion.

In any case, the seventeenth-century Huguenots' very high opinion of the Church of England was combined with many delusions and blunders. It is quite understandable when one remembers that, in this century, the English language was rarely mastered by foreigners, especially those from Latin countries. In France, Protestant merchants in Bordeaux and in Normandy were exceptional in their knowledge of English; they often exchanged their sons, for a year or two, with their London correspondents, so that each learned a second language.[2] But in general French people's knowledge of England was confined to what they read in the French gazettes. At that time, newspapers were in their infancy and the news they carried was trivial and anecdotal, if not downright inaccurate. Moreover, there was no explanation of the institutional background of the events reported. The paucity of news concerning the English revolution of 1641 that reached even an inquisitive foreigner if his only resources were the papers, is astonishing. Even when such a man corresponded with an exceptionally well-placed friend, as could happen among the intelligentsia, all he got was more scraps of news, still partial and anecdotal.[3]

However, apart from scanty and inaccurate information, the decisive factor was a static view of England, born of an idealised and simplified image of the Elizabethan period – whereas under James I and Charles I big changes had taken place, both in the political arena and in the mentality of the English people. Moreover the Huguenots, unaware of their naive ethnocentrism, were apt to interpret anything they learned of events across the Channel by reference to the values of their own absolutist society. Clarendon too was a victim of preconceived ideas when he assumed that Huguenots were hostile to the cause of Charles I or were firm friends of the Parliamentary party.[4] In fact, the dearest wish of the great majority of French Protestants was to see an end to the English conflict; they misunderstood the issues and their main concern was the threat to the Protestant cause in Europe.

All this entailed a ludicrous misunderstanding. For instance, in the autumn of 1642, Louis Hérault, a pastor from Normandy, was elected as minister for the Walloon Church of Threadneedle Street. He had just arrived in February 1643 when he preached three sermons on John 20,19 – 'Peace be with you'. With more evangelical inspiration than tact or sense of occasion, Hérault admonished his audience to be submissive to King Charles.[5] Of course, he was preaching to a foreign audience, but these French-speaking Londoners had long been resident in England. They had bitterly resented Laud's efforts to suppress the privileges granted to the foreign churches by Edward VI, and they were to a man on the parliamentary side, all the more so because the royalists among them had gone over to the Walloon community in Westminster – later to become the church of the Savoy. Obviously, pastor Hérault would have been wiser if he had taken time to assess the situation in London before rushing hastily into the political arena. However, this Frenchman, committed to the Divine Right of Kings, threw himself lightheartedly into the conflict. It cost him his job as he was quickly obliged to resign and to leave England. After the Restoration, Hérault was called back to London. In 1671, he became a Canon in Canterbury – having taken Anglican orders; he was unpopular with his congregation of Threadneedle Street, but only resigned his post there in 1675.[6]

Shortly before the Revocation of the Edict of Nantes, there was another instance of an uncomprehending intervention in a delicate situation when Hadriaan van Paets and his friend and protégé, Pierre Bayle, enthusiastically sided with James II's policy of indulgence.[7] The king was trying to win over the non-conformists with a policy of toleration and a repeal of the Test acts; his move was unsuccessful since it was felt in England that the real aim was to favour Roman Catholics. In fact, Paets and Bayle were watching events in France, despairing over the persecution suffered by the Huguenots. For them the English case demonstrated that the monarch's religion need not be that of his subjects. Later still, Bayle, whose English friends were all Whigs,[8] held absolutist tenets typical of a Frenchman, and tended to treat them as of universal validity, without realising that they were inconsistent with some of the opinions of his English friends, with whom he had concurred.

It was above all on ecclesiology that the Huguenots constantly showed a complete misunderstanding of the evolution that had taken place within the Church of England. They took no account of the individuality of the Anglican *via media*, or the bitterness of the conflicts which ended in the estrangement of the Puritans. French Protestants constantly believed they had to do with the Church of England of the 1580s, and, naturally, such a misapprehension was the source of many ludicrous mistakes.

Of these I can quote an outstanding instance, which I owe to Lord Dacre who kindly put me on its track in the Public Record Office. Its hero is the French theologian, Pierre Du Moulin, senior, a man who, nevertheless, had been in England on several occasions. He had been at Cambridge University for four years (1588–92); later, he stayed twice at the Court of James I, as a privileged guest. In 1615, the King was gracious and flattering towards a man whose help he expected in his projects of reuniting the Protestant churches. Again, on the second visit, in 1624, the ailing King wanted Du Moulin to answer in his stead Cardinal Du Perron, who had criticised a royal theological work.[9] Until recently pastor of the prestigious church of Charenton — that is, of Paris — Du Moulin had become *persona non grata* in France in 1621, because the Court looked askance at his public profession of eager devotion to the King of England, so much so, that Du Moulin had been obliged to flee and take refuge in the principality of Sedan. He became Professor of Theology in the Reformed Academy there, but Du Moulin felt that so small a theatre was beneath him. He put great hopes in James I's patronage. So, on 24 October 1624, he wrote from London to Secretary of State Conway to apply for the bishopric of Gloucester, just vacant.[10]

The preposterousness of the move is all the more startling because six years earlier Du Moulin had exchanged Latin letters with the Bishop of Winchester, Lancelot Andrewes.[11] With a patronising haughtiness, the prelate condescended to accept the uneasy explanations offered by the French theologian concerning some passages of his recent book – *La vocation des pasteurs*. These had had the misfortune to displease James I and, even more, the Anglican Bishop. If we were to believe Du Moulin, it was solely the Roman episcopacy at which he had aimed his criticisms. He now desperately assured Lancelot Andrewes of his deep and respectful regard for the Anglican episcopacy, which, however, he could not consider as of Divine Right. The Bishop of Winchester closed the exchange tersely, advising Du Moulin never again to touch on episcopacy in his books. What is telling is that such a rebuke – if civil in its form – was not enough to open Du Moulin's eyes, as his request for the bishopric of Gloucester makes abundantly clear.

No doubt the Secretary of State was startled when confronted with the gaucheness of the Frenchman. However Conway answered him quite graciously on 3 November:[12] he assured Du Moulin of the steadfastness of the King's good will, that the King was sending him a present of £200 and adding a Welsh prebend *sine cura*, yielding £100 a year to the one he already possessed. However, Conway's letter did not refer at all to the pushing request made earlier by Du Moulin.[13]

The story is so much the more revealing because, contrary to what one might have some excuse for expecting, Pierre Du Moulin, senior, was anything but a fool. A learned theologian, a vigorous writer, he was also a man of the world who had assumed in a skilful way important responsibilities within the French Reformed Churches. What is telling is that such a man had not at all grasped the Anglican niceties: obviously, he considered England as a full member of this 'Calvinist International', which worked so smoothly between Leiden, Heidelberg, Geneva and France, within which pastors and professors moved easily. Obviously, if a man who had so many opportunities was still so blind to the realities across the Channel, the average Huguenot, with more excuse, could shelter strange delusions.

We must now try to describe precisely this Anglican ecclesiology, so little understood in France. Among Huguenots, the origin of this blind spot seems to be founded less on their tenet about equality among the ministers (an opinion that denied episcopacy) than in the assertion of the universal priesthood of the believers. Indeed, this last doctrine denies to the pastor the character of a *priest*, in the exact sense that sets him apart from a layman. A clergyman in the Church of England who is ordained by a bishop (and not consecrated by his peers, as in the Calvinist system) is indeed a *priest*, who takes his place in the long chain of apostolic succession. Such a distinction may appear somewhat speculative and theoretical. But let us not make a mistake, it entailed concrete and practical consequences, entirely bewildering for Huguenots. The French reformed laymen were received with open arms in Anglican parishes: nobody required from them the least disavowal of their faith. Thus, they experienced a full and easy intercommunion and were easily prone to miss the point of divergence completely. Meanwhile, things were quite different for French pastors as soon as they naïvely applied to minister to a parish in England. Indeed, when the case arose, they were asked to submit to an ordination by a bishop – a rule that in the past seems to have known exceptions, as in the case of Pierre Du Moulin – but was made absolutely binding after the Restoration.

The watchfulness of Anglican bishops on this point is easily understood if it is remembered that their basic hostility was directed against the Scottish Kirk, whose internal organisation was so close to that of the French Reformed Churches. It was this similarity between French Calvinism and Scottish Presbyterianism which made it impossible to give special favour to French pastors, even though Anglican goodwill towards Huguenots was patent. Indeed the Anglicans knew very well that historical circumstances had deprived French Protestant communities of bishops and so had reduced them to the sheer *esse* – not the *bene esse* – of Christian churches.[14] Such was the handicap characteristic of churches that were 'under the cross'. In other words, circumstances outside their power had severely maimed the Huguenots' churches: they were *non*-episcopalian, not anti-episcopalian. Meanwhile, in Scotland, the lack of episcopacy stemmed from the perverse and unforgivable obstinacy of the Presbyterians. Such an analysis, stressing the differences between France and Scotland, was well-founded since, as we have seen, Pierre Du Moulin, senior, had so few misgivings about episcopacy that he had applied for a mitre! Nevertheless, he denied that episcopacy was of divine institution, and this point is very significant. Besides, it can be assumed that his solicitation to Secretary Conway, had it been known in France, would have deeply shocked, and perhaps positively horrified, a great number of French pastors, let alone Huguenot laymen.

In the autumn of 1685, when a number of French pastors landed in England, they revealed a whole spectrum of attitudes. Already before the Revocation, more than fifty of their colleagues, some of them well-renowned, had taken Anglican orders after crossing the Channel.[15] However, 'Monsieur' Claude, morally the head of the French Protestant community, who had taken refuge in Holland, was bitterly indignant about what he considered a shameful lack of integrity.[16] In his eyes, to agree to ordination (conditional though it was) was a scandalous disparagement of the pastoral consecration previously bestowed in France. What compounded the cowardice of such treachery was that Anglicans were not requiring this of a Roman Catholic priest if he went over to the Church of England. According to Claude, to yield to the Anglican requirement was no less than a dramatic impeachment of the French Reformed Churches: these were 'unchurched' by the English demand, with which no French pastor should conceivably have been expected to comply. If we look at the matter from 'Monsieur' Claude's point of view, it is scarcely an overstatement to make some analogy between the two hindrances: from the Roman side, that presented by the dogma of transubstantiation (closely linked to the prodigious privileges claimed for a priest) and, on the Anglican side, by the doctrine of apostolic succession, which made ordination by a bishop an absolute requisite.

Naturally, Claude's position was adopted by a great number of his colleagues: by practically all those who had not taken refuge in England. However, some of the French pastors who had crossed the Channel trod in the footsteps of Allix (a colleague of Claude in Charenton) who had taken Anglican orders without misgivings once he had arrived in London. Conciliatory like Allix, they maintained that to accept Anglican orders was no more than to submit to English *civil* laws and that such an obedience was a matter of course for those taking refuge in England. Obviously, a number of French pastors who had come to England wavered, and submitted to an Anglican ordination rather reluctantly and because they had failed to find a posting in a French-speaking church which had remained non-conformist.[17] A foreign church such as the Savoy had become Anglican at the Restoration, adopting the prayer-book (translated into French) and the ritual of the Church of England, as used in the Low-Church version practised in Jersey. Discreet and gentle, but steady, pressures were applied to the communities of the refugees, to induce them to follow the example of the Savoy and to conform, even if only to a Low-Church Anglicanism. Such pressures were mostly effective with the ministers; indeed, when they went to the church 'by law established', it did not always mean an increase in their remuneration, but at least it was a guarantee that they would draw it with some regularity.

There had been Anglicans who had worried over the prospect that the flow of Huguenot refugees would strengthen dissent in England. In order to avoid this alarming eventuality, they considered diverting part of the abundant funds collected to assist Huguenots, to pay for shipping off the less compliant to the United Provinces or to Germany.[18] In fact, such fears were unfounded. Some French ministers who had arrived in England, indeed were painfully surprised and taken aback by Anglican intransigence. There is an outstanding instance of this attitude in an unpublished letter written to Pierre Bayle in October 1686. He was told the bewildering fact that when some refugee pastors were presented to Henry Compton, Bishop of London, they had to put a knee to the ground to greet him. And the same letter relates, with some mute indignation, that when two French ministers who knew Archbishop Sancroft's librarian were allowed to visit Lambeth Palace under the guidance of their friend, they were told they had to take off their hats when passing through some private rooms of the building, even in the physical absence of the prelate. The stern commentary of Bayle's anonymous correspondent was to ask rhetorically what had become of Christian humility in England![19] Pastors with this turn of mind left the country of their own accord for places more congenial for Calvinists. Meanwhile, most of the pastors who remained in English-speaking lands submitted, sooner or later, to the ordination so essential in the eyes of their hosts, and in doing so they carried along with them the greatest part, if not always the totality, of their often-reluctant congregations.[20]

It would be crude and cynical to give excessive weight to the financial considerations mentioned earlier. These seem to have played a largely unconscious part and, in any case, a secondary one, as a side-effect of conformity.

In all probability, the unquestioning reverence, the positively quasi-worship with which Frenchmen regarded their king made it easy for them to submit to Anglican requirements. Now that they had fled France, they transferred to the monarch and the authorities of their new country the devotion they had formally felt toward Louis XIV, who had forfeited it by the Revocation. Obviously, when living in France, Huguenots had suffered from the schizophrenic divisions of their loyalties between their passion for the monarch and their tenacious ties to their religious faith. It must have been a psychological strain not to belong to the king's Church. Now in England, after the Glorious Revolution, Huguenots were at last able to be Protestant *and* to profess the religion of the king! The earlier tension vanished; harmony could now reign between the two loyalties. Let us not underrate the relief it brought.

Besides, the refugees were seventeenth-century Frenchmen, brought up in a society pervaded by pomp and ceremony, both of which seemed to be sorely lacking in a Calvinist service. Perhaps, some Huguenots may have been attracted by this aspect of Anglicanism, while the anti-popish stand of the Church of England was both familiar and reassuring. Others stayed allergic to ritualism, identified for them with popery.

Moreover, at least some of the refugees who came to England had made this choice because they had met Englishmen in the past. Almost certainly, these could not have been nonconformists, the least cosmopolitan of Britons. English refugees in France during the Interregnum and, later, the great majority of travellers on the continent were upper-class Anglicans,[21] often young aristocrats escorted by their 'bear-leaders', that is, their tutors. For French people, the typical Englishman was the 'milord', obviously an Anglican.[22] So some Huguenots who chose to go to England were partially prepared to adjust to an English way of life which they had glimpsed in their dealing with English travellers in France.

The dilemma was different for pastors and for laymen. We have seen that in conforming to the Church of England, ministers found both a real difficulty – ordination – and equally real inducements. In the second generation (an observation I owe to my friend Menna Prestwich) the aspiration of well-to-do young men or pastors' sons to go to University may well have strengthened the inclination towards conformity, as Oxford and Cambridge were closed to non-Anglicans.

As for laymen, the dilemma was considerably blunted. As we have mentioned, they were unconditionally welcome in the Anglican parishes. On the one hand, many laymen were much less conciliatory than the ministers: they were often nostalgically devoted to the form of worship they had made such heavy sacrifices to preserve. The instinctive horror of change in liturgy and ritual was paramount for the majority of the expatriates, at least in the first generation. If their circumstances had changed drastically in leaving France, at least they clung to their Huguenot traditions – to the point of resisting the modernisation of the sixteenth-century wording of the Psalms, a Genevan initiative. Laymen of this type could come together in the French-speaking churches that already existed or emerged in great number, both in England and in Ireland.

Nevertheless, as the years went by, a number of refugees was inevitably driven to conformity on both sides of the Atlantic; such a change became easier and more common in the second generation, to say nothing of the third. Apparently, the doctrinal basis of this move escaped the majority of laymen. What was paramount was the need to conform, the benefices that accrued and, at the same time, the confidence in remaining true to Protestantism.

However conjectural my suggestions may be, one thing is not open to question, namely, that precisely because the integration of Huguenots into English society seemed so difficult and problematical, the greater was the effort made, so that ultimately, the success was dramatic and even premature.

In two generations, Huguenots refugees and their posterity were absorbed into English society, more rapidly, it seems, than anywhere else, with the exception of French-speaking Switzerland. The integration occurred precisely because there had been some misgivings about the possibility of it. Since it was not taken as automatic, many inducements were deployed to drive Huguenots into the Church by law established. Meanwhile, other Protestant countries did not experience the need to encourage the immigrants to mix with the local population. On the contrary, in the case of Brandenburg – where the majority of the people was Lutheran – the considerable measures of autonomy and self-government granted to the Huguenot settlements was largely inspired by the desire to prevent such mixing.[23]

The common stand of staunch Protestantism allowed the victims of the Revocation, when they came to England, finally to lose without over-painful suffering, both their nationality and their confessional particularism. For tens of thousands of people the Edict of Fontaine-bleau had frustrated their passionate yearnings – once so well expressed by Jurieu – to be simultaneously members of the Reformed Churches and Frenchmen.[24] Ironically, when they came to England, Huguenots had to abandon both these aspirations.

Notes

1. Off-the-record contacts, by means of apparently personal letters between French pastors and foreigners were a substitute, but in a civilisation so insistent upon punctilious formalism, the apparently private character of these communications necessarily weakened their authority, and in any case, was humiliating for the French Reformed Churches.

2. Translations into French of English royalist propaganda were mostly done by Huguenots: cf. Georges Ascoli, *La Grande-Bretagne devant l'opinion française au XVIIᵉ siècle* (Paris, 1930).

3. Cf. for instance, Hans Bots and Pierre Leroy (eds) *Correspondance ... d'André Rivet et de Claude Sarrau*, 3 vols. (Amsterdam, 1978–82); the French theologian in the Netherlands and his Parisian friend were both giving utmost importance to the news they could gather concerning happenings in England. Rivet had access to information reaching the Stadtholder and Sarrau had good contacts in Paris, however the scantiness of their knowledge is staggering.

4. Cf. Clarendon, *History of the Rebellion*, W. D. Lacroy (ed.) (Oxford, 1888) vol. II, p. 416, no 180.

5. Cf. *Le Pacifique royal en deuil* (Saumur, 1649) which ventured to appraise these unseasonable sermons, even if, possibly, their author made more blunt their content, when they were published, after the execution of King Charles I.

6. Hérault tried – unsuccessfully – to obtain the supervision of all foreign churches as a sort of lieutenant of the Bishop of London – a distinctly

treacherous move on his part from a Huguenot point of view. Cf. F. de Schickler, *Les Eglises du Refuge en Angleterre* (Paris, 1892) vol. II, pp. 265–9.

7. The tract – published in Latin, French and Dutch – was formally attributed to van Paets, under the title of a *Lettre de Monsieur H*[adriaan] *V*[an] *P*[aets] *à Monsieur B*[ayle] *sur les derniers troubles d'Angleterre*; it appeared in Rotterdam in September 1685, supervised by Bayle. The Dutch patrician and the French refugee were seeing eye to eye in the matter and it is quite possible that Bayle had something to do with the final version of the tract.

8. Such as the Quaker Benjamin Furly, Gilbert Burnet, John Locke and, mostly, in Bayle's last years, Anthony Ashley Cooper, third Earl of Shaftesbury.

9. Cf. Lucien Rimbault, *Pierre Du Moulin, 1568–1658, un pasteur classique à l'âge classique* (Paris, 1966) pp. 108–14. Du Perron's *Réplique au roi de la Grand' Bretagne* appeared after the death of its author: in it the cardinal was refuting – in 1120 pages folio – the *Declaration du Sérénissime roi de la Grand' Bretagne pour le droit des rois … contre la harangue de l'illustrissime cardinal Du Perron … le 15 janvier 1615 …* a quarto of 127 pages! Du Moulin answered in his *La Nouveauté du papisme …* (Sedan, 1627) a book which was only translated into English in 1664 but had had a number of editions.

10. Public Records Office, S.P. 78/73, 254 r°:

> *Monsieur les bienfaits que j'ay desja receus de vous, Et les tesmoignages de vostre affection envers moy sans l'avoir merité, me donnent la hardiesse de m'addresser à vous au besoing. Vous sçavés, Monsieur, ce que le Roy m'a promis, c'est qu'à la premiere occasion il m'accommodera et pourvoira à la necessité de ma famille. La mort de feu Monsieur l'Evesque de Gloster en presente maintenant l'occasion, laquelle je vous supplie Monsieur de ramentevoir à sa Majesté, afin que suivant son commandement Monsieur le Garde des S[c]eaux donne ordre que je sois pourveu. Vous imputerés, Monsieur, mon importunité à la necessité, Et me continuerés l'honneur de vos bonnes graces. Dieu vous veuille &c.*
>
> *Londres, ce 23 d'octobre 1624*
> *vostre tres humble et tres obeissant serviteur*
> *DU MOULIN*
> (255v°) A Monsieur
> Monsieur Edouard Conway
> Chev[ali]er Conseiller au conseil Privé, Et Principal
> Secretaire d'Estat de Sa Majesté.

The late Bishop of Gloucester, who had died on 20 October was Miles Smith, one of the translators of King James Bible. His puritan tendencies, perhaps, may explain why Du Moulin got the idea he could succeed him. To counterpoise Smith's puritan leanings, King James nominated Laud Dean of Gloucester in 1616, thus creating a bitter conflict in the cathedral. See Hugh Trevor-Roper, *Archbishop Laud*, 2nd edn (London, 1962) pp. 45–6. See also p. 64 about the pressure of

Laud's party to escape being 'swallowed up with a puritan bishopricy'. Miles Smith's successor was in fact Geoffrey Goodman, a protégé of Buckingham. 'He was perpetually at loggerheads with Laud' (Trevor-Roper, *Archbishop Laud*, p. 175) and his later career was agitated; he secretly converted to Roman Catholicism around 1636 and died in 1655 after many ups and downs.

11. In 1629, two letters from the Bishop and one from Pierre Du Moulin appeared in 'Reverendi in Christo Patris Lanceloti Episcopi Wintoniensis', Opuscula Quaedam Posthuma, pp. 161–200. These letters were translated into English in 1647: *Of Episcopacy: Three Epistles of Peter Moulin, Doctor and Professor of Divinity, Answered by the Right Reverend Father in God Lancelot Andrews [sic], Late Lord Bishop of Winchester*, translated for the benefit of the Publike. (Bodleian Library). The defence of the Calvinist doctrine by Du Moulin is so timorous that he might well have been disturbed by such a publication, had he known of it. On 5 August 1649, he wrote to the Speaker Lenthal claiming that he had never criticised the English Parliament and so would like to receive again the stipend of his Canterbury canonry (Bodleian, Tanner, LVI, 197). It is necessary to remember Du Moulin's heavy family expenses and, above all, the habits of an absolutist society, where constant begging was normal, to lessen the painful impression given by such a shabby, venal and moreover dishonest document, since there is reason to believe that Du Moulin, like his namesake and eldest son, would have wished for a royalist victory.

12. Public Records Office, SP 78/73, 277 r°:

> *Monsieur, Sa Ma[jes]té m'a commandé de vous faire sçavoir que p[ou]r l'estime qu'elle a de v[ost]re personne et des rares qualités qui reluisent en vous, elle a eu souvenance de vous en cette occurence et a disposé de toutes choses le mieux qu'elle a peu p[ou]r v[ost]re advantage, & vous a pourveu d'une donation de cent livres sterling par an de quitte, & deux cents livres en argent contant p[ou]r subvenir à vos depens. Et p[ou]r vous monstret que sa Ma[jes]té ne vous estime pas si peu qu'elle croit [sic] vous avoir pleinement satisfait en ceci, elle m'a en outre commandé de vous signifier que sa main n'est pas raccourcie ni le cours de son affection arresté, mais que sa bienvueillance et bonté soingneront tousjo[urs] apres v[ost]re bien et qu'elle se saisira de toutes les occasions ou elle v[ou]s pourra tesmoigner combien elle se plaist au ressentiment de vos vertus, et le contentement qu'elle prend en faisant bien à vous et aux vostres.*
>
> *Je suis joyeux p[ou]r le respect que je vous porte d'estre l'annonciateur des faveurs du meilleur Lieutenant de Dieu en terre a une des plus remarquables lampes en son Eglise et prie Dieu que ce soit p[ou]r sa gloire et p[ou]r v[ost]re bien, en cette esperance je demeure Monsieur ...*
>
> *A Royston ce 3e Novemb[re] 1624*

13. Pierre Du Moulin, senior, obtained the transfer of the Welsh prebend to his elder son, Pierre Du Moulin, junior, perhaps because the man who

had solicited a mitre did not want to appear content with much less. On Pierre Du Moulin, junior, a convinced Anglican and a fervent royalist, who also succeeded to his father's canonry in Canterbury at the Restoration, cf. an American dissertation (not printed) by H.G. Merrill *Milton's Secret Adversary, Du Moulin and the Politics of Protestant Humanism*, University of Tennessee, June 1959. Pierre Du Moulin senior's other son, Louis, a doctor of medicine, who settled in England, took vehemently side with Parliament and with the Cromwell regime which made him a professor in Oxford. See *Dictionary of National Biography*.

14. Cf. Norman Sykes, *Old Priest and New Presbyter, Episcopacy and Presbyterianism since the Reformation* (Cambridge, 1956, 8°).
15. Cf. F. de Schickler, *Les Eglises du Refuge en Angleterre* (Paris, 1892) vol. II, pp. 330–5.
16. Ibid, pp. 323–9.
17. After the Restoration, the young Pierre Jurieu, having just finished his theological studies in France, came to England to pay a long visit to his uncle, Pierre Du Moulin, junior. The then Canon of Canterbury urged the young man to receive Anglican orders (most probably from the hands of Thomas Barlow, Bishop of Lincoln: cf. *Revue d'histoire et de philosophie religieuses* [1978] p. 292, note 42). Back in France, Jurieu was consecrated according to the French Reformed use and became pastor and, later, professor in Sedan, before being obliged to flee to Rotterdam, in 1681. He never drew any material benefit from his Anglican ordination, which would have made his situation easy had he taken refuge in England. Devoted Anglican, Pierre Du Moulin, junior, certainly had more doctrinal motives than worldly calculations in advising his nephew, but the last were perhaps not entirely absent from his mind.
18. Cf. a letter of George Morley, Bishop of Winchester, to Henry Compton, Bishop of London, dated 14 November 1683 (Bodleian, mss Rawlinson, C 984, piece 29, 50 r°). Already Huguenot refugees were beginning to arrive in great numbers.
19. An unpublished letter (Copenhagen, Kongelike Bibliothek, Thott, 1208 b–c) addressed to Bayle in October 1686, anonymously (which Dr Knetsch suggested may have been written by Noël Aubert de Versé: cf. *Acta Historiae Neerlandica* (Leiden, 1971) vol. V, p. 233, note 1) relates:

Monsieur l'Evesque de Londres est a mon avis des plus honnestes hommes du Monde, mais j'eusse souhaité de Luy qu'il n'eust pas souffert, sans chagrin, qu'on le saluast, le genouil en terre, et que ceux qui servoient d'introducteurs aupres de Luy aux Ministres refugiés, ne leur eussent pas servi en cela de reigle et d'exemple. Je connois deux ministres françois qui dans le dessein de faire la reverence à Monsieur L'Archevesque de Cantorberi s'en allerent a sa Maison, a son hostel ou a son palais, comme il plaira à l'usage de l'appeller; ils heurterent longtemps a la porte, mais enfin quelcun de dehors les vint avertir charitablement que quand Monseigneur disnoit les portes estoient tousjours fermées, et qu'on ne les ouvroit jamais a personne.

Ils apprirent dans la suite qu'ils avoyent sujet de se consoler par l'exemple de Monsieur le Duc d'Ormont a qui la mesme chose etoit arrivée quelques années auparavant. Quand les portes furent ouvertes, les deux Ministres entrerent, ils demanderent le Bibliothe-`quaire qui estoit de leur connoissance, et qu'ils avoyent crû devoir employer, pour les présenter à l'Archevesque. L'Archevesque estoit indisposé et on ne le voyoit point ce jour la; mais encore qu'il eust esté dans une santé parfaite, le bibliothèquaire leur dit, asses franchement, qu'il n'auroit ozé les presenter à Monseigneur, que ce n'etoit pas la sa charge, et que s'ils vouloient une autrefois avoir cet honneur, ils devoient s'y faire introduire ou par Monsieur du Marais, qui vivoit encore, ou par quelque autre des ministres de l'Eglise de la Savoye. Ils virent la Bibliothèque, qui est fort belle, et comme on Leur faisoit voir aussi le reste de la Maison, si vous en exceptés la chambre ou le cabinet ou estoit Monsieur l'Archesvesque, on les avertit qu'on n'entroit point dans la Sale, et en general dans tout ce qui estoit de l'appartement de Monseigneur sans avoir la teste decouverte, encore qu'il n'y eust personne...

The 'du Marais' mentioned is Richard du Maresq, probably coming from Jersey. He was still acting as a minister in the Savoy in May 1684; the exact date of his death seems unknown. At the time the Bishop of London was Henry Compton and the Archbishop of Canterbury William Sancroft.

20. It happened also in the American colonies: cf. Jon Butler, *The Huguenots in America* (Harvard, 1983) and an earlier paper of Robert Kingdon: 'Pourquoi les Réfugiés huguenots aux colonies américaines sont-ils devenus Episcopaliens?' in *Bulletin de la Société de l'Histoire du protestantisme français*, CXV, 1969, pp. 487–509, which appeared, somewhat modified in an English version, 'Why did the Huguenot Refugees in the American colonies become Episcopalian?', in *Historical Magazine of the Protestant Episcopal Church*, 49, 1980, pp. 317–35.

21. John Cosin, future Bishop of Durham, was possibly not the only one to combine High-Church standing with warm good will towards Huguenots; some of them had helped him in many ways during his exile in France. In any case, during the Interregnum, as Huguenots were dangerously compromised by the events in England for their enemies made a simple equation between Protestantism and revolution, they strove to distance themselves from Presbyterians and Independents and to appear as close as they could to those staunch royalists, the Anglicans.

22. However, Locke's famous travels in France should not be forgotten; see John Lough (ed.) *Locke's Travels in France, 1675–1679, as related in his Journals, Correspondence and Other Papers* (Cambridge, 1953).

23. If the Great Elector offered Huguenots such exceptional conditions of settlement, it was assuredly to attract them to Berlin, but at the same time, it was to remove the fears of his Lutheran subjects – usually extremely hostile to Calvinists – and to guarantee to the pastors of the

Augsburg Confession that the newcomers would not easily 'corrupt' their congregations.
24. Cf. *Politique du clergé de France*, 1681, p. 126 (or p. 97 of the 1682 edition).

10 The Huguenots and the Edict of Nantes 1598–1629

N. M. Sutherland

My task is to provide a brief background survey of that Edict of Nantes whose ultimate revocation is the subject, or anyway the occasion, of this book. The history of the edict lies mainly between the years 1598, when it was signed, and 1629 when the Huguenots were confined to their sectarian capacity. This may sound like a well-worn subject. In fact much work remains to be done, and it is still highly controversial. I mean to pose, and to leave you with, some unanswered questions. In a wider sense, one could trace the origins of the edict from the first edict, of January 1562, which had permitted a degree of licensed coexistence. But the edict of January had failed to avert civil war and, similarly, the Edict of Nantes did not terminate the conflict. After the Peace of Alais in June 1629 there was a long coda, before the Revocation in 1685. It is perhaps partly this passage of time which explains the sense of outrage which the revocation has always aroused. Indignation is one thing, but should we really be surprised? Well before 1661 and the personal rule of Louis XIV, all the various elements of danger had drained from the issue, and it is true that the passage of time might have had a tranquillising effect. The tragedy was that those who suffered the revocation were quite unlike those who had persistently defied the king. They came to be regarded, however, as guilty by inheritance.[1] Those Catholic forces which had opposed the edict – at least as anything more than a temporary expedient – and the venomous content of the religious and ideological conflicts had survived into a larger generation. That at least is one belief and one point of view.

Whether or not the 'irrevocable' edict had ever been intended to be permanent, is not a simple question; intended by whom, and what is permanent? But, if obliged to answer simply, I would have to answer 'no'. One should, however, remember that the edict which was revoked in 1685 was no longer effectively that of 1598. The passage of time had not entailed acceptance of the Huguenots as a fact of French life, nor of the edict as a *fait accompli*. Once the Huguenot cause – which I should not care to define for the seventeenth century – had ceased to be confounded with the struggles of the nobles and gentry, the Protestants were politically null. But as a confessional minority they continued to be regarded as a reproach to the church and derogatory to royal absolutism, a foreign body lodged in the heart of the *respublica christiana*.[2] The matter is fraught with subjective and emotive elements, in particular hatred, which leave one with only inadequate explanations. There was, of course, also the Roman Catholic conviction that there could be no salvation outside the church, which must therefore keep up the pressure. The attitude of the clergy was really that of the necessary expedient. They had declared in the estates general of 1614–15 that concessions to the Huguenots should be only temporary, and other demands were inimical to the continuation of the edict. They cetainly negated the spirit of the edict and gnawed at rather more than the edges. In the reign of Louis XIV, however, it was not until 1665 that they actually proposed what amounted to its revocation: the extirpation of heresy.[3]

Reflection upon the edict has led me to feel that its ultimate destruction, when this could safely be undertaken, had always lain within the nature of things. Was it not altogether too difficult and complex an exercise to be successful, exceeding by far the administrative capacity of the crown? Its execution demanded not only constant vigilance but also positive action. Success, however, is relative, and such a proposition could doubtless be disputed. Nevertheless, the edict did pose immediate difficulties, and was easily breached and frustrated by a society which had never vouchsafed a sufficient measure of assent to any of the edicts of pacification.[4] These propositions are for your consideration, because it would appear that the régime of the Huguenots under the edicts lasted for a relatively long time – suggestive of permanence – only for circumstantial reasons. Its revocation could hardly have been possible before 1661, though to substantiate that proposition would require a separate chapter.

The Edict of Nantes has, I think, been subject to distortions and misconceptions. From necessarily simplified accounts one can easily obtain the following impressions: under Henri IV – the Huguenots' erstwhile 'Protector' – they were mainly satisfied and quiescent. After his murder in 1610 the régime collapsed under a foolish regent.[5] Finally the Huguenots were attacked by Louis XIII under ultra-Catholic influences and, in 1629, received the *coup de grâce* – in two senses[6] – from the authoritarian cardinal Richelieu, who came to power in 1624. While there are elements of truth in such statements they are, nevertheless, more misleading than accurate.

The Edict of Nantes was the last of a long series of edicts of pacification which, *ipso facto*, sprang from the civil wars of the sixteenth century.[7] Its purpose, like that of its predecessors, was to establish peace. It was *not* to sanction toleration, even though tolerance was required if that peace was to be more than an armed truce or a juridical instrument. Indeed, it was a strict legalism which undermined the Edict after 1629.

There is much to be learnt from the manner in which the edict was devised. This is too long a story to tell.[8] Nevertheless, we should be clear that while Henri had always intended to provide for the Huguenots by some such edict as already existed, Nantes, in its historic form, was not an act of grace. On the contrary, it was extorted, under duress, particularly during the siege of Amiens in 1597. The Huguenots had all but betrayed their king and country into the hands of Spain, which a less recklessly magnanimous prince than Henri IV might well have felt to be unforgivable. It follows that the Huguenots were neither loyalists, nor a defeated faction; they were still independent and still dangerous, and deeply suspicious of the king's recent generosity to the leaders and towns of the Catholic League; and the spirit of that League lived on.

If the Edict of Nantes represents the Huguenots' maximum of recognition and achievement, there was little in it that was new; it was the circumstances which had changed.[9] A full analysis would be instructive, but I must confine myself to the essentials. The king's intentions were expressed – or were they concealed – in the preamble.[10] The purpose of the edict was declared to be the provision of one general law regulating the differences between those of the two religions, for the service of God and the establishment of a durable peace. It also reaffirmed the ancient ideal of a universal church. Should this be regarded as propaganda or an ultimate objective? Perhaps it was both? Henri felt able to inform the pope that the edict was more favourable to Catholics than to Protestants; it was certainly not a Huguenot charter. Article III of the text required the restoration of mass to all places whence it had been abolished, and the restoration of church property. This resulted in a considerable liberation and resurgence of suppressed catholicism, and doubtless also in many local conflicts.[11]

The edict consisted of ninety-two general articles, plus fifty-six secret or particular articles of 13 April and 2 May respectively. The ninety-two articles consist of the religious, civil and judicial liberties, and the others cover exceptions and special cases as well as the ecclesiastical clauses. Besides complete liberty of conscience, specified places where the cult was authorised included some 3500 seigneurial *châteaux*. It was therefore weighted in favour of the dangerous nobles and gentry. While a presbyterian ecclesiastical organisation was sanctioned by Article XXXIV of the second set, the general Article LXXXII expressly forbade assemblies, and all aspects of Huguenot activity necessary for their so-called 'state within the state', and for making war. We should therefore be quite clear that the Huguenots did *not* – as has so frequently been alleged – obtain any political privileges from the edict.[12] Certainly they remained in a position to exercise political leverage; but that is quite another matter, indicative of the king's inability to impose his will.

The articles were accompanied by two royal *brevets* of 3 and 30 April, not submitted to the *parlements* for registration. The first provided for the payment of Protestant pastors. The second contained the famous guarantee clauses, limited to a period of eight years. In effect the Protestants retained about 150 towns of varying sorts, of which some sixty-four were fortified garrison towns, known as hostage towns or '*places de sûreté*'.[13] The king was obliged to agree to pay 180 000 écus per annum for their garrisons and to appoint only acceptable Protestant governors. Herein lay the power of the Huguenots and, for the king, the problem of the Huguenots.

Henri was in no position either to recover these towns or to defend the Huguenots himself. He therefore had no alternative but to permit them to keep the towns and to defend themselves. Ultimately the towns would have to be recovered but it is an ordinary technique of diplomacy to relegate insoluble problems – in this case to the following reign. The Huguenots had grave and genuine fears and their position was paradoxical. Their recognition and their edict could only come from the king and the sovereign authority of the crown. Yet their intrinsic inability to trust a Catholic king prompted indisputably insubordinate conduct between 1594 and 1629. They thereby tended to undermine precisely that authority upon which they were dependent. This was partly because they always feared that once deprived of the means of defence, they would shortly be deprived of everything else. In the event the *brevet* containing the guarantee clauses was repeatedly renewed, up to 1629, even though the crown began, with slowly increasing success, to insist upon obedience.[14] Thus, what we are primarily dealing with is a problem of authority.

It is regrettable but necessary to realise that the edict was never regarded as more than a *pis aller*, and was greeted with protests and adverse demonstrations. Nor did it effectively alter those strained relations between the crown and the Huguenots dating from the later years of the civil wars. We should therefore beware of assuming – as has so often been the case – that Henri's relations with the Huguenots were either better than, or substantially different from, those of other monarchs, except that Louis XIII did not suffer the peculiar difficulties arising from Henri's abjuration.

The edict got off to a distastrous start, and the conflict from which it had emerged continued in respect of its registration and amendment by the *parlement*, and its execution. In the second *brevet* Henri had authorised the assembly of Châtellerault, convened in June 1597 during the siege of Amiens, to establish at Saumur a committee of ten until the edict was registered.[15] Promulgation of the edict did not, however, terminate the assembly. This defiant body remained in session ostensibly to supervise the execution of an edict which prohibited all assemblies. This was a supreme paradox, and supremely inauspicious. The Huguenots feared the constraints upon the king, for which they were unwilling to make any allowances. They had no intention of submitting to his authority but, from the start, breached their edict while at the same time complaining of transgressions against themselves.

This battle of the assemblies was already virtually lost.[16] The crown never succeeded in preventing assemblies until, by about 1622, the Huguenots themselves were too weak and disrupted to mount them. Henri, who had always been exasperated by this problem,[17] concentrated on trying to control their frequency, size, composition, location, duration and competence. For their part, successive assemblies – both authorised and illegal – made a determined bid for the redress of grievances before dispersal. These innumerable grievances were most frequently not matters of dispute between the crown and the Huguenots, but simply beyond the king's power to prevent. They were usually classified under five heads: the cult; pastors; eligibility for offices; justice, and '*places de sûreté*'. I think one should add, as a sixth, burials and cemeteries.[18]

It was not until 1601, a space of some four years, that Henri finally dispatched the irregular assembly of Châtellerault, which had reconvened at Saumur in November 1599. In order to do so, he had

had to authorise the appointment of one or two deputies, known as the *députation générale*, to represent their interests at court.[19] But this constructive move afforded the Huguenots new and increased leverage. In order to elect the deputies, Henri further authorised a new assembly at Sainte-Foy in October 1601. He could not treat with a rebel assembly, and he hoped to control and constrain a new one. The proceedings at Sainte-Foy exemplified certain essential points of conflict which persisted until 1629. In the first place, it reconstituted their illegal political organisation, skilfully blending it with legal ecclesiastical bodies.[20] They also produced a *règlement* designed to make the most of the *députation générale*, using their number, selection and period of service, as well as the manner and scope of their functions, to try to extort consent for frequent, regular general assemblies backed by a legalised, nationwide organisation such as the edict expressly prohibited.[21] In certain respects the Edict of Nantes had already failed by 1601.

Here again, I cannot tell the whole story. But whatever Henri otherwise thought of assemblies, his attitude and reactions to them must be seen in a wider context. One should note the synchronicity of dangerous conspiracies,[22] the uncertainty of the succession and the frailty of Henri's own threatened life.[23] Henri commanded force, and managed to isolate the Huguenots from the nobility in arms; but only just. His court was not riven by factions or favourites, and the years 1598–1610 were free of major wars. Thus Huguenot conflicts were not exploited by others, and Henri succeeded in containing them. But he had had to temporise, and to make concessions; he was not in command. Had he lived in 1610 to wage his war in Germany, Italy and the Netherlands, the Huguenots might well have betrayed him again; they were, at least, far removed from an attitude of grateful loyalty.

If Henri IV could not control the Huguenots without jeopardising peace, it was not be expected that an unpopular regent, Marie de Medici, or a youthful king, Louis XIII, would be able to do more.[24] The principal points of conflict between the Huguenots and the crown remained the same, but in quite different circumstances in which the edict could not operate satisfactorily. In 1610 as foreign war began, the circumstances were very dangerous. Marie was known to be ultra-Catholic and to favour Spanish marriages for the king and his sister.[25] Her own marriage, hence the king's legitimacy, was questioned in some ultramontane quarters, which was purely a ploy to frighten her,[26] while the prince de Condé, a prince of the blood with claims to the throne, was in Spanish pay.

The advent of a regency inevitably entailed a struggle for power at court, and this was nefariously extended to embrace the Huguenots in factional conflicts unconnected with religion or the edict. It was doubly unfortunate that the appointment of the Huguenot deputies was held to be due, while the terminal date of their *brevet* was uncertain.[27] These divisive problems could not be turned to advantage since, as a 'party' they gradually disintegrated from lack of leadership and of any common purpose to bind their disparate elements. Only a very small number of the Huguenot provinces were to take part in the eventual hostilities of Louis's reign.[28] Furthermore, leadership gradually passed into the hands of radical, and even revolutionary elements, mainly at La Rochelle.[29] These elements could not sustain their cause elsewhere in France without the support of the nobles, who steadily defected to the crown.[30] Why the brothers Rohan and Soubise should have resisted until 1628 and 1629 respectively, is not entirely clear.[31]

The regency of Marie de Medici was neither foolish nor misguided; her priority was to avoid the awful risks of civil war. She confirmed the edict within a week,[32] authorised an assembly at Saumur in 1611 in order to elect new deputies, and renewed the two *brevets*.[33] She tried in every detail to follow the policy of Henri IV, allowing what he had allowed, and refusing what he had resisted.[34] The Huguenots' attempt to exploit her weak position provoked her to a courageous ultimatum to the assembly of Saumur, over the old issues of redress before dispersal and the nomination of deputies. Marie could not be expected to ignore the Huguenots' provocative extension of their illegal organisation.[35] If they had plenty to fear, so did she who had already witnessed their treatment of Henri IV.[36] With no bridge of confidence between them, both sides may be said to have committed errors of judgement. In 1612 Marie patched up an agreement with the duc de Rohan who had emerged at Saumur as a new leader. Their relations, however, were really governed by the impact of other events.[37]

Fears aroused by hostile demands at the estates general of 1614–15, were exploited by Huguenot activists.[38] An assembly which opened at Grenoble in 1615 began to make political demands, corresponded with foreign countries, and finally supported the second rebellion of the prince de Condé.[39] As a result the Huguenots necessarily shared some responsibility for the consequent fall of the regency government in 1616.

When Louis XIII assumed power in 1617 the Huguenots, if currently at peace, were felt to be rebels.[40] They had demonstrated how dangerous they could be, and had extracted in the Peace of Loudun 1616 a further extension of their *brevet* until 1623. Nor was it to be expected that nothing more would happen. The Edict of Nantes, if jealously defended, no longer fulfilled its essential purpose of maintaining peace. These points should be remembered in assessing Louis's attitude to the Huguenots, and the events of his reign. Louis was still too young to rule alone, and there were undoubtedly those about him who hated the Huguenots, including his own favourite, the duc de Luynes. What was Louis to do?[41]

Louis has been said to have resolved to suppress the Huguenots after they had supported the second rebellion of his mother in 1620. He then conducted three campaigns, in 1620, 1621 and 1622, emotively hailed by Catholics as crusades. This is very misleading. While Louis was probably more pious than his father, it is nevertheless doubtful whether his attitude to the Huguenots was substantially different from that of Henri IV, who did not sit idly by, charting the progress of rebellions. Louis insisted that he meant to be obeyed,[42] and it was fortunate for the Huguenots that he displayed some understanding of their fragmentation, not blaming innocent Protestants of quiet life for the faults of those who pursued their own designs and defied the king.[43] Louis was scrupulously careful to make his will and intentions clear.[44] These lay within the law, and the edict was renewed at least fifteen times between 1610 and 1629.

The civil wars of 1621 and 1622 stemmed from the issue of Béarn, a Protestant Bourbon territory. The restoration of the Catholic church in Béarn dated from the terms of the absolution of Henri IV in 1595 and was in the nature of unfinished business. A decision to proceed with this matter had been taken in council before Louis assumed the government. The Huguenots had compromised themselves by proclaiming Béarn a Huguenot province, and promising solidarity upon which, in the event, they defaulted. Louis gave Béarn ample opportunity to receive his edict of June 1617 before annexing the province in person and restoring Catholicism and church property.[45]

A section of the Huguenots reacted to this by organising rebellion from La Rochelle but supported by only a few areas of the south.[46] Again, Louis gave the illegal assembly of La Rochelle ample opportunity to conform to his will before commencing hostilities in 1621.[47] Nevertheless, the campaign had advantages, leading to the recovery of some eighty of the hostage towns, few of which offered any serious resistance.[48] The increasing probability of foreign war, since the start in Germany of what came to be the Thirty Years War, made this internal situation a more dangerous and complex matter. Parallels, real or imaginary, had been drawn between Bohemia and Béarn.[49] While Louis was halted at Montauban in 1621, the Huguenots had nevertheless collapsed as a party. The assembly of La Rochelle could not run a war, and the towns and the nobles were not behind it.

The year 1621 was a turning-point. Pockets of resistance continued, but the issues were rapidly changing. After the death of Luynes in 1621, Louis came increasingly under the influence of Richelieu, whose anxious preoccupations were the acquisition of power and the defence of France. From 1622 to 1629 the conflict primarily centred on La Rochelle.[50] It happened to be not only a Huguenot stronghold, but also a rich, independent, maritime city. La Rochelle presented an obstacle to the defence of France, and to her naval and economic progress, as well as being an impediment to the advance of royal absolutism. Furthermore, Soubise and the Rochellais rivalled the king at various times for the alliance of England and the United Provinces, and also Spain. These were issues of authority and foreign policy, not of religion or the Edict of Nantes.[51]

The Peace of Montpellier, which ended the campaign of 1622, was not a treaty but a declaration. It clinched and formalised the collapse of the illegal Huguenot 'state'. It explicitly declared the illegality of all assemblies, exhaustively listed, and required the destruction of most of their fortifications. It also proposed, at least conditionally, a recognised procedure for the election of the Protestant deputies. Louis had effectively asserted himself and in a manner which commanded respect. Were it not that the Huguenots were unlikely to restore the remaining towns upon the expiry of the *brevet* in 1625, there need not inevitably have been any further Huguenot engagements.[52] It was, at any rate, the repercussions of foreign affairs which caused the final Huguenot wars. Thus Richelieu's oft-repeated claim, made some time later, that it was he who ruined the Huguenot party is a fabrication; he was not in power until 1624 by which time the process was, at the least, very far advanced.[53]

Richelieu's real attitude to the Huguenots is still held to be controversial. It hardly seems impenetrable, although work on the subject is certainly incomplete. His priority was clearly foreign affairs, for which he needed peace in France and Protestant alliances abroad. The Huguenots had links with Germany, England and the United Provinces, as well as Spain. Thus Richelieu's Huguenot policy had to be prudent and pragmatic; in no respect was he a free agent.[54] In the event he was relieved of major decisions, since the last campaigns of 1625–6 and 1627–9 were precipitated by Huguenot rebellions, the latter involving three English expeditions to La Rochelle.[55] On the other hand, it could be claimed that the crown had been gradually closing in on La Rochelle.[56] The peace of La Rochelle, February 1626, largely destroyed the independence of the city, and it is doubtful whether the famous siege would have been necessary in order to exert the control the government desired and needed.[57] Certainly Richelieu cannot have wanted it when it occurred, clashing with the Mantuan crisis in Italy.[58]

The equally inopportune final episode in 1629 occurred in Languedoc against the duc de Rohan. Since it was unnecessary for the Huguenots to fight for what the king had so many times accorded, Rohan's objectives are not obvious. His treaty with Spain of 3 May 1629 hinted at a separate state in the Midi.[59] If this was indeed the mark he aimed at, he was not the first to do so; nevertheless, it was an undeniably far cry from the cause of religion or the Edict of Nantes.

Richelieu remained in Languedoc to make peace, and is usually credited with the wise moderation of the Grace of Alais.[60] This is rather surprising since it was obvious enough what it must contain. In once more according the religious, civil and judicial clauses of the edict, the hope was expressed for a return to Catholicism and the unity of religion. If, in 1598, that pious hope could, arguably, have been mere rhetoric, in 1629 it could not. Richelieu declared that the springs of heresy and rebellion had run dry, and it is evident that, from henceforth, he intended the Huguenots to be no more than Protestant individuals, enfeebled and vulnerable to Catholic impulsion.[61] Once the state and their own divisions had combined to destroy the Huguenots as a collectivity, it became possible for the church, and all who feared or hated them, to erode their edict and to destroy them as an heretical sect.[62]

Notes

1. E. I. Perry, *From Theology to History: French Religious Controversy and the Revocation of the Edict of Nantes* (The Hague, 1973) p. 9.
2. Perry, *From Theology to History*, p. 95.
3. P. Blet, *Le Clergé de France et la Monarchie*, 2 vols (Rome, 1959) vol. I, pp. 378–9.

4. The edicts of pacification were: the Edict of Saint-Germain, 8 August 1570; the Peace of La Rochelle [2] July 1573; the Peace of Monsieur, 6 May 1576; the Edict of Poitiers, 17 September 1577; the Treaty of Nérac, 28 February 1579 and the Treaty of Fleix, 26 November 1580.
5. Henri IV was murdered in Paris on 14 May 1610 by François Ravaillac.
6. The Grace of Alais, 27 June 1629.
7. The Edict of Nantes was indeed so described in 1610. E. Benoist, *Histoire de l'Edict de Nantes* 5 vols (Delft, 1693–5) vol. ii, recueil, pp. 3–5.
8. This process is traced in N. M. Sutherland, 'The Edit of Nantes and the Protestant State', *Annali della Fondazione italiana per la storia amministrativa*, 2 (1965) pp. 199–236.
9. It was based on the edicts of pacification which are analysed in N. M. Sutherland, *The Huguenot Struggle for Recognition* (New Haven and London, 1980) pp. 333–72. The edicts are printed, without that of Nantes, in André Stegmann, *Edits des guerres de religion* (Paris, 1979).
10. The text of the Edict of Nantes is most readily available in Roland Mousnier, *L'Assassinat de Henri IV* (Paris, 1964) pp. 294 ff.
11. M. Mullet, *The Counter Reformation*, (Lancaster pamphlets, London, 1984) p. 34, expressed the surprising opinion that the edict 'weakened the traditional role of the Catholic Church in France'.
12. See, for example, W. J. Stankiewicz, *Politics and Religion in Seventeenth Century France* (Westport, Connecticut, 1976) p. 63; A. D. Lublinskaya, *French Absolutism: the Crucial Phase, 1620–1629* (Cambridge, 1968) p. 156; M. Greengrass, *France in the Age of Henri IV* (London, 1984) p. 78 mentions the 'political status' of the Huguenots, while also indicating that political assemblies were banned; V.-L. Tapié, *France in the Age of Louis XIII and Richelieu* (Cambridge, 1984) p. 201, mentions the abolition of political privileges in 1629.
13. L. Anquez, *Histoire des assemblées politiques des réformés de France 1573–1622* (Paris, 1859) pp. 160–6, indicates four categories: *places de sûreté, places de marriages, villes libres royales* and *places particulières*.
14. It is difficult to compile an accurate list of renewals because of ambiguity about the dates from and to which the *brevet* would run. It appears to have been confirmed or extended at least seven times. Anquez, *Histoire des assemblées*, p. 430.
15. Mousnier, *L'Assassinat*, p. 334.
16. In Henri's reign there were the assemblies of Saumur 1599–1601, Sainte-Foy 1601, Châtellerault 1605 and Jargeau 1608.
17. Sutherland, 'The Edict of Nantes', p. 204.
18. Anquez, *Histoire des assemblées*, pp. 391 ff. analyses the *cahiers* under these headings.
19. Ibid, pp. 183–6. The *députation générale* lasted until the Revocation. There were usually, but not always, two deputies who served for varying terms.
20. Ibid, pp. 209–10.

21. Ibid, pp. 208–9.
22. The Biron conspiracy 1600–2, involved the Huguenot ducs de Bouillon and La Tremoille; Auvergne conspiracy 1604, Bouillon conspiracy 1605–6.
23. There are known to have been at least twenty-three attempts on the king's life before that of 1610. Greengrass, *France in the Age of Henri IV*, p. 201.
24. Marie de Medici was regent *de jure* 1610–14 and *de facto* until 1617.
25. The Spanish marriages project dated from Henri's reign, but was mooted for different reasons at different times and did not cause alarm until after Henri's death. See F.-T. Perrens, *Les Marriages espagnols* (Paris, 1869).
26. Mousnier, *L'Assassinat*, p. 152; Tapié, *France in the Age of Louis XIII*, (1984 edn) pp. 64–5.
27. L. Anquez, *Un Nouveau chapitre de l'histoire politique des réformés de France 1621–1626* (Paris, 1865) p. 25.
28. The number of Huguenot provinces represented at assemblies seems to have varied between about fifteen and twenty-five.
29. This significant and complex problem of the social composition of the Huguenots and tensions among them is discussed by Anquez, *Un Nouveau chapitre*, introduction, pp. x, ff.
30. Ibid, pp. 25–8.
31. Henri, duc de Rohan, 1597–1638; Benjamin de Rohan, seigneur de Soubise, 1583–1642. Anquez, *Un Nouveau chapitre*, pp. 28–34. Rohan is said to have been impelled by a desire to 'se faire valoir'.
32. Benoist, *Histoire de l'Edit de Nantes*, ii. Recueil, pp. 2–5, 22 May 1610, *déclaration du roi sur l'édit de pacification*.
33. The guarantee clauses were renewed for five years from January 1612.
34. For example, the assembly demanded the original edict, not that registered by the *parlements*. This demand had already been refused in 1601 and 1602. Benoist, *Histoire de l'Edit de Nantes*, ii, Recueil, pp. 9–25, 23 July 1611, *cahier de l'assemblée de Saumur*.
35. Anquez, *Histoire des assemblées*, pp. 242–3, 246 ff.; Benoist, *Histoire de l'Edit de Nantes*, ii, *Recueil*, pp. 5–9, *règlement général*, 29 August 1611.
36. The declaration on the king's majority, 10 October 1614, indicates much of what the government feared. Benoist, *Histoire de l'Edit de Nantes*, ii, Recueil, pp. 31–2.
37. J. A. Clarke, *Huguenot Warrior: The Life and Times of Henri de Rohan 1579–1638* (The Hague, 1966) pp. 38–46; Anquez, *Histoire des assemblées*, pp. 255–8.
38. On the estates general see M. J. Hayden, *France and the Estates General of 1614* (Cambridge, 1974).
39. Anquez, *Histoire des assemblées*, pp. 263–7; Benoist, *Histoire de l'Edit de Nantes*, vol. ii, recueil, pp. 35–8, 10 November 1615, *déclaration sur la prise des armes*.
40. Peace was made by the Treaty of Loudun, 3 May 1616, Anquez, *Histoire des assembliés*, pp. 287–9.
41. The counter-reformation atmosphere in which Louis XIII grew up is

discussed by Tapié who poses the question: 'would the young king try to obstruct the movement in favour of Catholics and Catholicism, or would he, on the contrary, enlarge its field of action'? *France in the Age of Louis XIII* (1984 edn) p. 88 and chap. 3; J. Viénot, a Protestant historian, emphasised the influence of Père Joseph and other Catholics at court, making all the Protestant churches feel directly menaced. It was believed by some that there was a court intention to destroy them by war. *Histoire de la Réforme française de l'édit de Nantes à sa Revocation*, 2 vols (Paris, 1934) vol. i, chap. 8.

42. Obedience, not persecution was implicit in the whole question of Béarn. Similarly the *déclaration sur la paix*, 19 October 1622 stressed that Louis had been forced to take up arms to defend his authority. Benoist, *Histoire de l'Edit de Nantes*, ii, Recueil, pp. 60–3.

43. See, for example, 10 November 1615, *déclaration sur la prise des armes*. Louis distinguished between those of Protestant conscience and those of faction; the faults of the few were not to be imputed to the many. The *déclaration* of 24 April 1621 in favour of obedient Protestants made a similar distinction. Benoist, *Histoire de l'Edit de Nantes*, ii, Recueil, pp. 35, 53–5.

44. There are numerous examples of this: a declaration of 30 April 1615 reassured the Huguenots on matters arising from the estates general; the Edict of Blois, May 1616, confirmed the liberty of the Gallican church and assured the Huguenots that the king had not approved the clergy's acceptance of the decrees of Trent; the Edict of Paris, 20 July 1616 reassured the Huguenots on the matter of the coronation oath. Benoist, *Histoire de l'Edit de Nantes*, ii, Recueil, pp. 33–5, 39 ff.; Anquez, *Histoire des assemblées*, pp. 290, 403.

45. Anquez, *Histoire des assemblées*, pp. 299 ff.; Viénot indicates that the Catholics saw this campaign and the subsequent wars as a Catholic crusade. *Histoire de la Réforme*, i, pp. 173–9; Tapié, *France in the Age of Louis XIII* (1984 edn) pp. 117–19.

46. Anquez, *Histoire des assemblées*, pp. 330 ff. Resistance centred in Saintonge, Guyenne, Quercy and Languedoc. Clarke, *Huguenot Warrior*, 80.

47. Declarations of 24 April and 7 June 1621. On 27 May 1621 Louis appealed to loyal Huguenots to disavow the assembly of La Rochelle. Benoist, *Histoire de l'Edit de Nantes*, ii, *Recueil*, pp. 53–5, 56–8; Anquez, *Historie des assemblées*, p. 353.

48. Clarke, *Huguenot Warrior*, pp. 81–93.

49. Tapié, *France in the Age of Louis XIII* (1984 edn) part I, chap. 3 shows how the issues raised by the Bohemian revolt in 1618 became linked with those of the Protestants in Béarn. They excused themselves in the same terms as those in Bohemia and 'quoted recent events in Prague as evidence that the Jesuits were plotting against the reformed religion in every country in Europe'. In December 1619 the emperor sought to bring France into the struggle both at home and in Europe and in 1622 Louis was congratulated by the Pope. Viénot, *Histoire de la Réforme*, vol. I, pp. 238 ff.

50. On the whole question of La Rochelle, see D. Parker, *La Rochelle and the French Monarchy* (London, 1980).
51. On 28 July 1622 Rohan appealed to James I of England. Clarke, *Huguenot Warrior*, p. 102.
52. *Déclaration sur la paix*, 19 October 1622. The Peace of Montpellier was supplemented by *brevets* of 24 and 25 October 1622 on the demolition of fortifications. Anquez, *Histoire des assemblées*, pp. 385–9; Anquez, *Un Nouveau chapitre*, pp. 19–27.
53. This is based on a well-known passage in Richelieu's *Political Testament*. H. B. Hill (ed.) *The Political Testament of Cardinal Richelieu* (Madison, 1961) p. 11. Tapié, *France in the Age of Louis XIII*, (edn 1984) pp. 140–1, points out that the celebrated passage has been the starting-point for a disastrous scholastic tradition.
54. Tapié, *France in the Age of Louis XIII* (1984 edn) pp. 143 ff.
55. War with England rendered inevitable war with the Huguenots at La Rochelle and at sea.
56. Much conflict centred on Fort Louis, a royal fortification begun in 1622 which threatened La Rochelle. Anquez, *Un Nouveau chapitre*, pp. 94 ff; Clarke, *Huguenot Warrior*, chap. 6.
57. The peace of La Rochelle concerned only La Rochelle for which it was very harsh. This shows the government to have been in a strong position. By the Peace of Paris Rohan received confirmation of certain stale articles and no formal treaty at all. Clarke, *Huguenot Warrior*, p. 134; P. Grillon, *Les Papiers de Richelieu*, vol. I, 1624–6 (Paris, 1975) pp. 287–8.
58. The assumption that the siege of La Rochelle was always intended – a controversial matter – appears to be deduced from preparations in the area. Parker, *La Rochelle*, pp. 14–15; Clarke, *Huguenot Warrior*, pp. 136–7, 140–1. These preparations could well have been made because Soubise was in England obtaining English help. Richelieu obviously did not intend to weaken the government's position but he had tried in 1625 to win over Rohan and Soubise as other nobles had been seduced. Had he succeeded, the siege might not have been necessary. Furthermore, the declaration of 5 August 1627 against Soubise was evidently an effort to detach him from La Rochelle. Benoist, *Histoire de l'Edit de Nantes*, ii, Recueil, pp. 87–90.
59. Clarke, *Huguenot Warrior*, p. 175.
60. Benoist, *Histoire de l'Edit de Nantes*, ii, Recueil, pp. 92 ff, Grace of Alais, 27 June 1629 issued as an edict in July. One opinion is that the alleged moderation of Alais rested on a belief in the existence of a strong Huguenot party. Stankiewicz, *Politics and Religion*, pp. 112–14. The point was not their strength, which was shattered, if left with a cause, they could be exploited either by noblemen or by foreign enemies, endangering Richelieu and embarrassing the government. 1629 was the year in which the emperor attained the height of his power in Europe and Richelieu's position at court was insecure.
61. Tapié, *France in the Age of Louis XIII*, (1984 edn) p. 202; Benoist, *Histoire de l'Edit de Nantes*, ii, Recueil, p. 502.

62.   Richelieu's concern was to restore peace and not to offend allies not, at that moment, whether the Huguenots and their edict would survive. Benoist, *Histoire de l'Edit de Nantes*, p. 499.

Map 11.1 **Geographical distribution of Calvinists in France c. 1630–70**

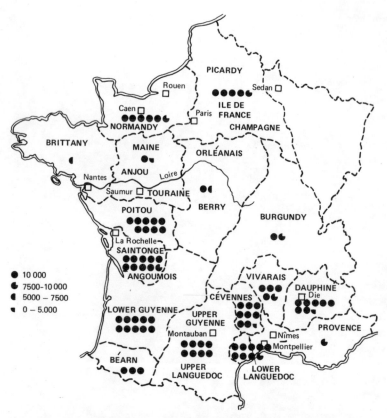

PICARDY

Rouen □

Sedan □

Caen □

Paris ●●●●●

ILE DE FRANCE

NORMANDY ●●●●●●

CHAMPAGNE

BRITTANY

MAINE ●●

ORLÉANAIS

ANJOU

Nantes

Loire

Saumur □ TOURAINE ●●

BERRY

POITOU ●●●●● ●●●●

BURGUNDY ●●

La Rochelle

SAINTONGE ●●●●● ●●●●

● 10 000
● 7500–10 000
● 5000 – 7500
● 0 – 5.000

ANGOUMOIS

VIVARAIS ●●●

DAUPHINÉ ●●●●

Die □

CÉVENNES ●●●● ●●

LOWER GUYENNE ●●●●● ●●●●

UPPER GUYENNE

PROVENCE ●

Montauban □

□ Nîmes

Montpellier □ ●

BÉARN ●●●

UPPER LANGUEDOC ●●●● ●●●●

LOWER LANGUEDOC ●●●● ●●●●

Source: after H. Bots, G. H. M. Posthumus Meyjes, F. Wieringa, *Vlucht naar de vrijheid de Hugenoten en de Nederlanden* (Amsterdam, 1985) p. 15, based on S. Mours, *Le Protestantisme en France au XVIIe siècle* (Paris, 1967) and drawn by T. Brouwer. The numbers are approximate and do not include those for Alsace, Metz and Sedan. The dotted lines show the synodal provinces.

11 The Huguenots under Richelieu and Mazarin, 1629–61: A Golden Age?

Menna Prestwich

In 1629 the Peace of Alès marked the final military defeat of the Huguenots and ended the Wars of Religion. This last war had seen the siege of La Rochelle and the campaigns of the duc de Rohan, as destructive as any operations in the wars of the sixteenth century. In the course of these Huguenot strength had come to be concentrated in the south-west and south, behind a crescent whose tips touched La Rochelle on the western seaboard and the small towns of mountainous Dauphiné in the east. The 'United Provinces of the Midi',[1] as they have been termed, gave the Huguenots the military and political leverage to extract from Henri IV, once their leader, the Edict of Nantes in 1598 and to defend that edict in the revolt of Rohan.

The Edict of Nantes should have ended the Wars of Religion. In the preamble the edict was stated to be irrevocable and perpetual, and the liberty of conscience it accorded to Calvinists made France a pioneer in granting toleration. But in reality the Edict of Nantes was an armistice; it was pragmatic and its many clauses – especially the appendix of secret clauses – reflected particular claims and circumstances. Although liberty of conscience was accorded, liberty of worship was restricted to places where temples existed in 1597, to fiefs where the seigneur was a Calvinist, and to a limited number of towns. But the edict legalised consistories and synods and granted Calvinists full rights of citizenship, with access to all offices and to membership of gilds and corporations. Besides, Calvinists enjoyed legal privileges through the new *chambres mi-parties*, courts with Huguenot representation which dealt with litigation arising from the application of the edict. Further, royal warrants, separate from the main body of the edict, gave the Huguenots the right to hold over a hundred fortresses, fortified towns and manors, thus legalising the strategic defences of the West and South.

Sir George Carew, the English ambassador at the court of Henri IV, commented that 'the body of those of the Reformed Religion is a great thorn in his foot', and he saw a danger of the Huguenots trying to 'cantonise themselves in Guienne'.[2] Professor E. G. Léonard, the leading authority of the last generation on French Protestantism, considered that the Edict of Nantes produced 'a disadvantaged religious confession and a privileged social and political body'.[3] Neither Catholics, fired by Counter-Reformation piety which had fuelled the violence of the Paris *Ligue*, nor Huguenots, who still looked forward to the triumph of their religion, were prepared to accept the edict as final. The resulting tensions account for the last war of religion, a decisive one, since, as Professor Chaunu has observed, 'until the fall of La Rochelle in 1628 the Catholic future of France was neither solidly nor irreversibly assured', while for his part Léonard saw Rohan fighting the last battle of a lost cause.[4] Infractions of the edict could be countered only by litigation in the *chambres mi-parties*, by representations to the king from the General Synods which from 1629 met only infrequently, and by the influence that the *Députés-Généraux*, appointed under the terms of the edict as a quasi-ambassador for the Huguenots at the court, could or cared to exercise. The thorn remained in the king's foot, but it no longer festered and could be extracted if or when he chose.

Léonard held that the Edict of Nantes closed like a tomb upon the Calvinists and that the Peace of Alès, which affixed the final seal, ushered in a period which saw *'le Protestantisme en léthargie'*.[5] Calvinist sermons, which harped on the plight of the Huguenots as a punishment meted out by God for their failure to meet the standards expected of the Elect and which preached passive obedience and the divine calling of kings in terms which could compete with Catholic apologists, did not raise morale. Yet recent historians, such as Elisabeth Labrousse, have been more sympathetic towards seventeenth-century French Calvinism, and Janine Garrisson has written that although the Protestant community between 1630 and 1656 is difficult to describe and to understand, it was not the sick man of France and showed signs of health and vitality. Yet again, in contrast, the view has been taken by Solange Deyon that in the twenty years between 1629 and 1649 French Protestantism was at its least dynamic.[6]

The claim has also been advanced that this was a triumphant age for Calvinist businessmen, merchants and bankers, described as 'the most dynamic sector of Calvinism'.[7] In towns such as Nîmes, La Rochelle, Caen, and Rouen, Calvinist notables and businessmen dominated urban life, just as they dominated the consistories. They conformed to the same social patterns as their Catholic counterparts, building up fortunes, acquiring offices and landed estates, though financial offices were easier for them to acquire than the more prestigious legal ones. Under Henri IV Sully had staffed the Treasury with his Calvinist co-religionists. Under Mazarin, Barthélemy Hervart, whose father had come from Augsburg, was the financial colossus whose loans had made possible the French acquisition of Alsace and who became *contrôleur-général*. He too had his Protestant clientele in the Treasury. Indeed, under his patronage the Protestant moneyed interest in these years anticipated the legendary *haute société protestante* of the Third Republic.[8]

Such varying opinions make it desirable to reconsider the state of Protestantism between the Peace of Alès and the beginning of Louis XIV's personal rule, and to ask how far these decades were a golden age for Calvinism. In this period Calvinism should be assessed not in the perspective of the Revocation but in terms of its own achievements and role in French society. How far the coexistence envisaged by the edict could prove viable after 1629 is an open question. Michelet, a passionate advocate of the Huguenot cause and values, sombrely considered that from the start the seventeenth century gravitated inexorably towards the Revocation. Elisabeth Labrousse has seen the Revocation as more or less probable from the Peace of Alès.[9] Coexistence depended pre-eminently upon the policies of the Crown and the attitude of the Catholic Church. Calvinism drew its political strength from its links with provincial particularism, but after the conquest of Languedoc Richelieu no longer had any reason to fear Calvinism offering a challenge to his centralising policies, particularly in view of the abjurations of Calvinist nobles. He could afford to wait and to hope for peaceful conversion, a policy in any case made necessary by his Habsburg war and consequent Protestant alliances. But if Richelieu's approach was empirical and dilatory, these were also the years which saw an invigorated Catholic church with a reformed clergy, a cluster of saints and cohorts of Capuchins and Jesuits pursuing missionary campaigns. The respite for the Huguenots would end when the interests of the state and the fervour of the Church coincided.

One of the greatest changes affecting French Calvinism after the accession of Henri IV was the return of the Huguenots to Paris from which they had fled after the Massacre of St Bartholomew. The new Parisian Calvinism had a more fashionable and sophisticated tone than that of the provinces, and the divide between north and south was clear when the Huguenot church at Charenton refused to back the revolts of La Rochelle and Rohan. Léonard deprecated the view that this new Parisian Calvinism was a source of strength,[10] but nevertheless much depended upon the nature and strength of Calvinism in Paris. Colbert was later to write to his son, Seignelay, that *'Paris, étant la capitale du royaume et le séjour des rois, il est certain qu'elle donne le mouvement à tout le reste du royaume, que toutes les affaires du dedans commencent par elle'.*[11]

The church at Charenton, built a few miles outside Paris in conformity with the edict, drew on a community of some 20–30 000 Calvinists. The high social status of its members gave it prestige, and although Calvin had laid down that no one church should take precedence over another, the four or five pastors of Charenton had something of the standing of bishops. Paris was the stage-setting for the Bourbon monarchy and the court was the political and administrative centre from which patronage radiated. When Henri IV ruled, Charenton was almost an annexe of the court, and under Richelieu and Mazarin its congregation continued to include nobles, office-holders, financiers and tax-farmers, goldsmiths, artists and architects.[12]

In 1652 Jean Daillé, one of the the Charenton ministers, preached that there were two Jerusalems. One was the Church of Christ, but the other to be loved as tenderly was France and Paris itself, larger and much better situated, frequented by all nations as the mother of arts and letters and the glory of the West. When Daillé's son wrote the biography of his father, he spoke with nostalgia of the golden age of Richelieu and Mazarin when the church at Charenton had enjoyed *'la belle saison, les années de bénédiction et de prosperité'*, and had shone with so lustrous a splendour that it had been a beacon for the provincial temples.[13] Madame des Loges, who reigned over a Paris salon in the late 1620s and who was a firm Calvinist, wittily commented on the changed tone when she wrote that 'We have now reached the point that even amongst our greatest adversaries, we no longer pass for monsters and savages. We are regarded not only as reasonable persons, but also as Christians. If our enemies make the same efforts against us as in the past, it is now possible to believe that they will not be able to obtain the same success'.[14]

Madame des Loges may have been over-optimistic, and a tour of provincial Calvinism needs to be made to see whether it showed decline or dynamic and how far after 1629 tension was giving way to coexistence. In the year of the Edict of Nantes the number of Calvinists was put at 1·2 million, roughly 6 per cent of the population of France. At a provincial synod in Poitou in 1663 it was said that the number of Calvinists had increased by a third up to the time of Richelieu, but since then momentum had flagged. The number of Calvinists around 1670 has been estimated as 856 000, that is 4·3 per cent of the French population.[15] Whether the figures represent a slow decline from the Peace of Alès or a rapid fall after the beginning of Louis XIV's personal rule is uncertain. The regional variations give a clearer picture and allow a qualitative as well as a quantitative assessment.

Of the provinces north of the Loire Normandy stood out in the early seventeenth century as having a large Calvinist population, with seigneurial Protestantism in the countryside and big agglomerations in towns and ports such as Rouen, Caen, Le Havre, and Dieppe, dominated by a wealthy Calvinist bourgeoisie. But Normandy saw a decline in Protestant numbers. Calvinist seigneurs, according to the intendant of the generality of Caen in 1666, numbered only 74 out of a total of 877, while in Caen itself Calvinists fell from 7000 in 1608 to 4000 in 1664.[16] The leading minister of the church in Caen, Pierre de Bosc, admonished his congregation in 1658 against worldly ambition, thundering against the lure of office which made men not only abandon their sovereign, the King of Kings, but prefer thirty pieces of silver to all the treasures of God's grace, and put the possession of a landed estate before all the delights of His heaven.[17] Another reason for the decline in Calvinist numbers lay in the success of the Catholic missions. In 1643 St Jean Eudes, Norman by birth, founded in Caen a new society of priests, the *Congrégation de Jésus et de Marie*, and his rules laid down that his priests should occupy themselves with the poor rather than with the rich. He himself had interceded with Chancellor Séguier in 1640 on behalf of the prisoners taken in the revolt of the *Nu-Pieds* of the previous year, and he instructed his priests that when they heard the confessions of tax-collectors they should ask them whether they had been too harsh in securing their returns. In the mission field emotional chords were plucked; there was insistence on confession, followed by community celebrations with fêtes and pilgrimages. Success was the greater because of the concern shown for the poor in contrast to the élitism of Calvinist employers, town notables and skilled artisans.[18]

Yet although overall numbers declined in Normandy, many Calvinists remained faithful, emigrating in 1685 or privately preserving their beliefs when, under the pressure of the *dragonnades*, they conformed outwardly as *nouveaux convertis*. Pierre Bayle was later to speak of Caen as *'la ville de France qui a produit le plus de beaux esprits'*. Pierre du Bosc has been described as the best Calvinist preacher in France, while the pastorate at Caen possessed also the great Hebrew scholar and orientalist, Samuel Bochart, whom Queen Christina invited to her court in Sweden in 1652. It was in that year that Jacques Moisant de Brieux, the brother-in-law of Pierre du Bosc, founded an academy or club to discuss current affairs and literature on the lines of the Paris Academy, inaugurated in 1634. These gatherings show coexistence among the cultivated circles in Caen, since they were not confined to Protestants, and de Brieux informed the intendant that religion would not be discussed unless in terms of the general principles of Christianity to which everyone subscribed. In this discretion of the Calvinists combined with their lack of proselytising zeal Léonard detected weakness, and Normandy illustrates his point in the contrast between the cultured circle of de Brieux and the worker-priests and missions of St Jean Eudes.[19]

In western France Calvinism had struck strong roots in Lower Poitou, a textile area, where three-quarters of the rural nobility was Calvinist, according to a report to the government in 1664. Although subjected to Capuchin missions from 1617 the region showed such obstinacy that it was to have the distinction in 1681 of being the first to experience the brutality of the *dragonnades*. The social pattern along the western seaboard was similar to that in Normandy, Calvinist merchants and craftsmen exercising in the towns a dominance disproportionate to their numbers. In the 1650s Catholics were loudly complaining that Protestants were in the ascendant everywhere and flaunting their wealth. Indeed in the Ile de Ré 79 per cent of the salt-pans belonged to Protestants, while the work-force was overwhelmingly Catholic. In La Rochelle Calvinism showed great tenacity, even though it was particularly disadvantaged, since no Protestants were allowed to become citizens or to carry on business unless they had been domiciled in the town before 1625. There were very few conversions on either side after the siege, and it was immigration which led to the number of Catholics rising from 4000 in 1600 to 10 500 – that is 55 per cent of the population – in 1648. Catholic immigrants held about 90 per cent of the judicial and municipal offices, though

Protestants dominated the commercial life of the town. The big confessional change did not come until 1661, when 2200 Protestants who had entered illegally since 1628 were ordered to leave, followed by massive Catholic immigration.[20]

Protestant energy and initiative had done much to build up the wealth of La Rochelle. The Tallemants, refugees from Flanders, had settled there in 1561 and branched out from trade into maritime insurance. In 1615 Pierre Tallemant was mayor and lived in style in a mansion a few doors from the temple. His brother, Gédéon, had left for Paris in 1612, buying the office of *secrétaire du roi*, which carried minimal duties but brought ennoblement, and entered the world of tax-farming. The Tallemant brothers sealed their business interests by a double marriage with the Rambouillets, a prominent merchant and banking family of Rouen, and this consortium became the most spectacularly successful of all Protestant firms in the age of Richelieu. In 1623, when La Rochelle was being swept into the politics of rebellion, Pierre Tallemant prudently moved his main business to Bordeaux, leaving a subsidiary branch behind. He put business before religious fervour, acting as intermediary for the Crown during the siege, while Nicolas Rambouillet in Paris handled part of Richelieu's fortune. In 1632 the firm reached the pinnacle of success when the lease of the *Cinq Grosses Fermes* was secured for 2 640 000 livres. Two years later Pierre Tallemant left Bordeaux for Paris, and his son, Gédéon, faithful to the family tradition, married a Rambouillet, and, taking his name from the estate settled upon him, became known as Tallemant des Réaux. He, however, refused to go into the counting-house, but drew an income which enabled him to cut a figure on the Parisian social scene and to have the leisure to describe it with elegance, wit and malice in his *Historiettes*.[21]

The firm emerges as a forerunner of the *haute société protestante* of the Third Republic, but there were other families in Rouen and the west which also achieved great wealth by the mixture of trade and state finance. Olivier Bidé of Nantes had shares in twenty-five tax-farming syndicates between 1639 and 1658 a halcyon decade for financiers and was ennobled in 1658 when he bought the office of *secrétaire du roi*. Georges Pellissari from Lyon was a financial giant, who married into a notable Rochelle family, the Bibauds, connected with the Tallemants. He controlled the highly lucrative administration of the navy, including contracts for purveyance, from 1648 until his death in 1676. He was a dominant figure in Colbert's administration through his investment in and direction of various commercial and industrial enterprises. Twenty-one of the twenty-five leading shipowners of La Rochelle were Calvinist. Louis Pagès was the most prominent and the leading merchant in the trades to northern Europe and the Baltic in association with the Formont brothers from Rouen. This group which enjoyed the patronage of Barthélemy Hervart, the brother-in-law of Nicolas Formont, moved smoothly into the orbit of Colbert from 1661 and supplied the funds and directors for the *Compagnie du Nord*, established in 1669 with headquarters at La Rochelle. Colbert's dramatic take-over of power in 1661 gave Hervart a golden retirement, but destroyed Fouquet and his clients, including his secretary and business agent, the Protestant Jacques Amproux de Lorme from Nantes, who had been at the centre of the web of tax-farming, contracts and Treasury borrowing.[22]

Calvinism had been at its strongest in the Midi and it now remains to test its resilience there. Montauban, like La Rochelle had been a Calvinist bastion, and the siege of 1621 had been resisted with the same rich mixture of religious fervour and civic pride. The Bishop of Montauban in a letter to Richelieu after the Peace of Alès said that since his return to the town he had often been in danger of his life, but he now felt happier because the demolition of the fortifications had begun, while Jesuits and Capuchins were hard at work on conversion. Furthermore, he himself was busily engaged with attracting '*colonies catholiques*' into the town.[23] The tactics were the same as for La Rochelle, a resort to immigration in face of Protestant obduracy. But immigration was slow in Montauban, a textile town where Calvinists controlled entry into the gilds. When the Landgrave of Hesse visited Montauban at Easter 1647 he reported that with Calvinist congregations of some 6000 it had been necessary to celebrate the Lord's Supper in two temples and that even then two days had been required.[24] Feelings against conversion ran high and exploded in 1657 when the body of Jeanne Moisset, a Catholic convert on marriage who recanted on her death-bed, was snatched for burial in a Protestant cemetery in a riot which saw a mob taking to the streets and demanding that the clergy should be expelled, the Jesuits thrown into the river and Catholics exterminated.

Such outbreaks showed that the Protestant majority felt threatened and indeed Richelieu pursued a policy of undermining Protestant control of municipalities by ordering that the senior magistrate should be a Catholic. But the fiscal administration was in Protestant hands. Pierre Dalibert, originally from Languedoc, held the lucrative office of *trésorier de France*. He invested in tax-farms and in 1660 became farmer-general of the *gabelles* in the Lyonnais, Provence and Dauphiné. Dalibert was a client of Colbert and a friend of Descartes, and in 1648 was seeking support for a technical institute to which artisans could go for instruction outside their working hours, an example of Calvinist interest in self-help. Samuel Daliès de la Tour came from a Montauban family. His grandfather had been a receiver of the *tailles* there and his father became a *trésorier de France*, engaging in some thirty tax-farms. Samuel received his apprenticeship in the family *tailles* office and then went to Paris, where as a result of Colbert's patronage he became a receiver of the revenues of Dauphiné. He became a key-figure in Colbert's commercial and industrial enterprises, having interests which ranged from the Levant company to Languedoc textiles and armaments factories in Dauphiné. Daliès, a business tycoon and industrialist, has been described as *'l'archetype le plus achevé du grand financier'*.[25]

If Calvinism showed obdurate resistance in the generality of Montauban, in Lower Languedoc it was characterised by thrusting energy. The recent study of the diocese of Nîmes refutes for this area Léonard's view of an enfeebled Calvinism and demonstrates that here after 1629 *'la Réforme resta conquérante'*. By 1663 the Catholics were in as much of a minority as they had been at the end of Henri IV's reign, while the geographical pattern of the two religions remained identical. Calvinism had struck deep roots in the Cévennes and in the little towns of the plain between Montpellier and Nîmes, but in Nîmes itself there was a big change. There Protestant numbers remained steady at around 12 000, but the number of Catholics rose from around 3000 to 8000, as a result of the immigration of Catholic workers, resulting in strain and tension. The Calvinists fought strenuously against any weakening in their hold over the town, and the consistory kept a record of conversions from Catholicism, obtaining 300 between 1632 and 1652, and 509 between 1652 and 1672. Nîmes was dominated by an aristocracy of Protestant merchants, who controlled the textile and silk industries and whose business tentacles stretched to the Cévennes. They favoured the employment of their co-religionists, as indeed they were exhorted to do by the consistory, leading to loud Catholic complaints against closed-shop practices.[26]

The destruction of churches and images during the wars of Rohan faced the bishops of Nîmes with formidable tasks, and the work of conversion was especially difficult in the Cévennes where intrusive Catholic missionaries were attacked. In 1646 when the intendant Baltazar installed a Jesuit mission in Anduze, a Calvinist bastion closely linked by trade to Nîmes, he hoped for quick results, but within a month the disconsolate Fathers were beating a retreat and their few converts soon relapsed. In 1659 the priest at St Hippolyte ostentatiously abjured in the Protestant temple and soon afterwards married a Protestant. The conversion by Jesuit teachers of a Calvinist schoolboy who took refuge in the bishop's palace in Nîmes sparked off an ugly riot in 1650. More riots seven years later led a notary to write in his diary that 'poor Catholics can hardly go out in the streets for fear of being killed', and he foresaw a new war of religion. In 1658 the Bishop left Nîmes, lamenting that God had not permitted him to see the end of the Huguenots, and informed the king that sixty new temples had been built in the years of the royal minority.[27]

Léonard was right to say that the dynamic of conversion was missing, for in general this was so, apart from Lower Languedoc and some areas in Dauphiné. He also contended that there was a decline in the quality of French Calvinism. He deplored the strict discipline of the consistories, which by enforcing a code of manners tended to make Calvinism a religion of works rather than of faith. Although he conceded that there were pastors eminent for their piety, learning and oratory, such as Charles Drelincourt of Charenton, Pierre du Moulin of Charenton and Sedan, Daniel Chamier in Dauphiné and Montauban, and Paul Ferry in Metz, he held that in general there was *'une crise pastorale et spirituelle du Protestantisme'*. He considered that Calvinism had become an arid religion when sermons were intellectual dissertations, dwelling on the faults of the children of Israel and weakening moral fibre by preaching the divine calling of kings, and passive obedience.[28]

But were Léonard's strictures justified? He criticised the pastors for their lack of vocation and for entering the ministry merely as a profession, but since he also stressed how ill-paid they were, his argument becomes paradoxical. It was conventional for sermons to revolve round a text and the absence of emotive hot-gospelling can be regarded as a point in favour of Calvinist pastors who preached instructive sermons, which stimulated not only 'mocking incredulity towards Popish miracles' and witchcraft, but also raised the educational level of congregations by including information on subjects ranging from cosmology to medicine.[29] It is true that there was heavy emphasis on chastisement from Heaven, but this was a sign of God's care for his Elect, who were to be strengthened by these ordeals. Certainly Du Bosc and others preached the divine calling of kings, and passive obedience, but since the maintenance of the Edict of Nantes was dependent on the royal word it was vital to expunge the taint of republicanism which still clung to Calvinism. Lastly, Calvinists did not lack pride in the achievements of the Bourbon monarchy, especially since Huguenot nobles, following the traditional careers of their social order, served in the royal armies. Indeed one of their number, Jean de Gassion, rose to be a marshal of France, taking a prominent part in the battle of Rocroi in 1643.

Recent work on consistory records suggests that the enforcement of morals was less strict than in the sixteenth century. There was still the denunciation of loose living and dancing, but consistories could impose moral sanctions, only and undue rigour might result in delinquents seceding entirely. In the sixteenth century the strict Calvinist discipline had been disruptive of local communities, for Huguenots opted out when they shunned carnivals and fêtes, dancing and taverns. However, Huguenot domestic scenes in the Paris of Louis XIII as portrayed by Abraham Bosse do not suggest great austerity, though there is a touch of this in the will of Moisant de Brieux, the founder of the Caen Academy, who gave instructions that his daughter should be brought up simply and modestly, and should not go to comedies and balls, nor read novels, nor wear low-necked dresses. Private dances in the homes of nobles and notables were permitted by the consistory of Die in Dauphiné, but the comte d'Harcourt in Normandy was furious when, planning to give a ball to celebrate the end of the Fronde, he found the Huguenots, loyal as they had been, refusing to attend this frivolous occasion.[30]

In the seventeenth century the Counter-Reformation caught up with Calvinism. The 1630s saw the foundation of the *Compagnie du Saint-Sacrament*, a secret society of Catholic laymen who scented out moral lapses, while reforming bishops campaigned against drinking and taverns, carnivals and fêtes. With social controls employed by both religions, the Huguenots should have been the less marginal, except for their steadfast refusal to recognise the feasts of the Church. As a result, Huguenots put up their shutters and refused to decorate the exterior of their houses in honour of the processions which passed, a highly sensitive point of friction between the two religions.

Léonard also considered that Calvinism deteriorated because of the inadequate teaching in the Protestant academies, and his strictures, although severe, are not unjustified. Theology was taught very narrowly and with so much emphasis on exegetical controversy that the Academy of Geneva protested in 1637 to the Synod of Alençon that students were engaging in vain disputes when their time should have been spent on pastoral training. There were eight academies in France, an ambitious number since there were only fifteen universities, but four academies alone became important: Saumur, Montauban, Sedan, and Die in Dauphiné. The academies played their role in educating the sons of local nobles and notables. In Die only 20 per cent of the students became pastors, while Saumur attracted an international clientele, particularly young Englishmen on the Grand Tour. The main problem for the academies lay in their lack of endowment, especially when the royal grants promised under the Edict of Nantes ceased after 1632. The academy of Die was poor but showed great vitality, and its struggles illustrate the importance of regional support. The academy was placed by its charter under the control of the town *consuls*, who fought tenaciously in the 1630s against attempts to suppress it, raising funds for deputations to Paris by house-to-house collections.[31] The college at Nîmes was less successful, for in 1634 it failed to withstand an assault by the Jesuits, who took over half the appointments and moreover were subsidised by donations from the cathedral and funds siphoned off from the *gabelles* of Languedoc. There was inevitably friction, for consistories and synods exhorted the faithful to withdraw their children from Jesuit courses.[32]

In general, there were problems of under-staffing in the academies where stipends were low, so that the teaching of Greek was much weakened after 1626 and the knowledge of Hebrew declined. Further, allegations of idleness and dissolute conduct in the academies were made in the synods, but these are perennial charges levelled against students and are to be found in the model letters of thirteenth-century France, in one of which a father told his son 'you live dissolutely and slothfully, preferring license to restraint and play to work'.[33]

Saumur was the leading academy, but it had the good fortune to have been endowed by Duplessis-Mornay and could afford to pay full-time professors. Saumur was especially famous for the liberal views of its school of theology, directed first by the Scot, John Cameron, and then by Moïse Amyraut. The Saumur school was attacked at the time by Pierre du Moulin, a strictly orthodox Calvinist, and later criticised by Léonard for weakening the moral fibre of Calvinism and making conversions to Rome easier. Yet Richard Stauffer has recently argued that the Saumur professors were 'the representatives of a Calvinism which, faced by the frozen orthodoxies of Sedan and Geneva, was sensitive to the questions being asked in the seventeenth century'.[34] The synod of Dort, the equivalent of the Council of Trent for the Calvinist churches, had in 1618 condemned the latitudinarian views of Arminius and upheld as orthodox the strict double-predestination tenets of Beza. The French Reformed churches, although forbidden to send representatives to Dort, subscribed unequivocally to the canons of the synod. Amyraut did not adopt the full Arminian position, but produced his variation on the theme of predestination: hypothetical universalism. By this he maintained that faith was basic for salvation and that although Christ's death was sufficient to redeem all men, in effect he had died only for the Elect. Although Amyraut argued that his theology was that of Calvin, Pierre du Moulin condemned his views as deviationist. The controversy, which generated more heat than light, was smoothed over in the 1640s, since the French Reformed churches could not afford to indulge in theological quarrelling.[35]

Apart from these technical theological questions, the importance of the Saumur school lay in its humanism, which linked it on the one hand to the Erasmian tradition and on the other to the Enlightenment. In accordance with Calvinist orthodoxy Amyraut insisted that a single page of the Bible carried more weight than any Church council, but he also stressed the overriding necessity for a scholarly scrutiny of the texts and for placing these in their historical context. He thus gave precedence to the New over the Old Testament and rejected the latter as the norm of Christian existence, a revolution for Calvinist fundamentalists who saw the Elect as the Children of Israel, and employed the language of Canaan. Amyraut was influenced by the teaching of Grotius on Natural Law and believed in the sociability of man. He gave preference to the New Testament on a second count – that it separated politics from religion, in contrast to the Old Testament which confounded the two. Amyraut was, in effect, seeking to find a formula for tolerance.[36]

Amyraut raised questions which Pierre du Moulin found disturbing and dangerous, and indeed the most modern verdict on Amyraut from a sympathetic pen is that by raising problems he weakened Calvinism. This was the view of the consistory of Nîmes which was quick to silence supporters of Amyraut. But both Amyraut and du Moulin found common ground in denouncing rebellion and advocating passive obedience. In his *Apologie pour ceux de La Religion*, published in 1647, Amyraut sought to set right the political record of the Huguenots who, he contended, had never attacked royal authority nor sought to set up a state within a state, and his *Discours sur la*

Souveraineté des Rois of 1650 condemned the execution of Charles I. Amyraut was apparently a better writer than a preacher, for his erudite and sophisticated sermons were said to lull his audiences to sleep. He was however at his best in society and moved in the highest circles, being on visiting terms with Mazarin and staying in Turenne's hôtel when he came to Paris. Guez de Balzac, the fashionable man of letters and exponent of absolute monarchy, wrote approvingly of the *Apologie*, which he considered '*très bon et très raisonable*', and, mixing his metaphors, said that Amyraut knew how to dance on a tightrope but never dashed himself on the rocks. Indeed Balzac paid his highest tribute to Amyraut when he said that he showed the qualities of the court rather than of the consistory.[37]

Amyraut was an important link between Saumur and Paris, and it is to Paris that we must now turn, for if ever there was a golden age for French Calvinism it is to be found in the Paris of Richelieu and Mazarin. The temple at Charenton was built in 1623 by Salomon de Brosse, a Protestant and the greatest architect of the age of Henri IV and of the Regent, Marie de Médicis, and who played a key role in the development of French classicism. He was commissioned to build for Marie de Médicis the palace of the Luxembourg, and the gardens there were designed by Jacques Boyceau, the son of a minor Calvinist noble from Saintonge. Boyceau, *intendant des jardins du roi*, was also the landscape gardener for the Tuileries and for St Germain-en-Laye, and in 1636 published his *Traité du jardinage selon les raisons de la nature et de l'art*. He never married, but his family remained Calvinist, three great-nephews emigrating at the Revocation.

Commissions crowded in on de Brosse, who established a firm of architects consisting of his highly-talented relatives who came, as he had done, from the little Calvinist town of Verneuil-sur-Oise. His first cousin, Jean Androuet du Cerceau, became in 1617 *architecte des bâtiments du roi* and built hôtels of great splendour in Paris for wealthy clients, who included the Protestant duc de Sully and the Catholic Chancellor Séguier, appointed to the office in 1633. Charles du Ry, de Brosse's brother-in-law, headed another branch of the firm, and his son was employed on urban projects in Paris by Richelieu. The du Rys were still practising in Paris until 1685, but they then emigrated to Cassel, where they flourished as court architects.[38]

Protestant artists also formed a highly talented group in Paris at this time and received patronage irrespective of their religion. The whitewashed walls of Calvinist churches were denied to artists, but Calvin's views of art were not such as to stunt their talents nor to inhibit their activities. Calvinist artists responded to the dictates of Geneva, but they also bowed to the canons of taste imported into Paris from a Rome denounced from Calvinist pulpits as Babylon. Calvinism was a minority movement with a separate ethos but not a separate culture. Protestant artists tended to live in the Faubourg St Germain and were closely linked by their ties with Charenton and by intermarriage. Many had been trained in the studio of Simon Vouet, who returned from Rome in 1627, and were drawn closer together with the founding in 1648 of the *Académie Royale de Peinture*. It is worth noting that at this date when the *dévot* movement was in full ascendancy, seven of the twenty-three members of the *Académie* (nearly a third) were Protestants. This was a golden age for painters whose talents were in demand for huge canvasses, ceiling decoration, murals and paintings for a court ambitious to make Paris a new Rome, for a proselytising Church which lavishly commissioned visual aids to piety and for a wealthy clientele of courtiers, members of the *robe*, financiers and administrators, enriched by the swollen profits of office and tax-farming.[39]

The first secretary of the *Académie* was Louis Testelin, whose father had been a Catholic but his mother a Protestant, and the children were christened at Charenton. Louis Testelin specialised in decorative painting and was commissioned by Philippe de Champaigne, a devout Catholic and the official portraitist of Richelieu, to paint murals for the Palais Cardinal, while it was Philippe de Champaigne who was commissioned to paint a portrait of Amyraut. Testelin's brother, Henri, was secretary of the *Académie* from 1650, and he painted not only the Chancellor Séguier but also, in 1648 a charming portrait of Louis XIV, then aged ten. He was a close friend of Le Brun and a director of the Gobelins tapestry factory run under the auspices of Colbert. But Testelin, who had painted the boy-king, was excluded with other Protestants from the *Académie* in 1684 and took the road to exile in Holland. Protestant artists in the *Académie* included the two Elles, father and son, fashionable portrait-painters, and two miniaturists, Samuel Bernard, whose six children were christened in the Dutch embassy in Paris, and Louis de Guernier, who painted for the court. Jean Michelin painted attractive street scenes, some of which have been attributed to Louis Le Nain. Abraham Bosse was the accomplished engraver of Paris scenes, notable both for their realism and for the moral message they often carried. His membership of the *Académie* was short, not for reasons of religion, but because of his rigid stand over the rules of perspective.

The most distinguished and prolific Protestant member of the *Académie* was Sébastien Bourdon, who was immensely talented, but who has never achieved an unquestioned place in the first rank. He came from Montpellier, was taken as a child to Paris by his father, and contrived to get to Rome – the Mecca of French artists – when Poussin and Claude were painting there. Rome was potentially dangerous for a Calvinist and Bourdon left after a brawl, but in the company of Louis Hesselin, a wealthy courtier and patron of the arts, under whose protection he visited Venice and returned to Paris in 1637. There Bourdon enjoyed rapid success and in 1641 married Suzanne Guernier, the sister of the miniaturist, at Charenton. In the marriage contract he was described as resident in the *galeries u Louvre*, and the witnesses included goldsmiths and jewellers, characteristic of Huguenot Parisian society. Bourdon painted religious subjects for churches, murals for the hôtels of the wealthy, portraits, landscapes, and also small *genre* pictures which sold cheaply and well. He had exceptional talent as a copyist, painting in different styles, but having his closest affiliation with Poussin. Indeed it has been said of Bourdon that in his versatility and ability to capture a whole spectrum of styles and moods that he epitomises the art-culture of Paris in these brilliant decades.[40] Bourdon was fortunate in his generation, since in these years there was coexistence in the worlds of art and architecture. Bourdon was given the commission to paint St Vincent de Paul, as remarkable a choice of artist as was that of Philippe de Champaigne for Amyraut. Catholic patrons of taste, such as Hesselin, employed the Calvinist Bourdon, while the Protestant bankers, Gédéon Talle-mant and Barthélemy Hervart, commissioned the Catholic artists La Hyre and Mignard. Bourdon had an international reputation, for in 1652 he was invited to Sweden by Queen Christina. He died in 1671 while painting a ceiling in the Tuileries. He never wavered in his Calvinism, and his daughter was faithful to her father's religion, escaping to England at the second attempt in 1687.

Coexistence was made easier in Paris when St François de Sales was advocating urbanity and good manners in controversy and in social life, while Moïse Amyraut was encouraging the Elect not to set themselves apart but to practise '*une affabilité qui nous rend facilement accessible les uns aux autres*'.[41] In the literary world of the 1630s which saw great emphasis on purity of language and the foundation of the *Académie Française* under the stimulus of Richelieu, Valentin Conrart played a role like that of Henri Testelin, secretary to the *Académie de Peinture*. Conrart was a wealthy young

Calvinist who bought the office of *secrétaire du roi* in 1627, and who had the leisure and the income to cut a literary figure. In 1629 a literary circle began to meet and dine regularly in his house, and the evenings were later looked back upon as a golden age by those who had enjoyed his hospitality. Richelieu saw how this circle could be pressed into the service of the monarchy, and in 1634 the *Académie Française* was founded with Conrart as secretary, a post which he occupied for the next forty years. Conrart's literary interests had an Italian stamp, just as Bourdon's art derived from Rome, but he was also an elder of Charenton and translated Marot's psalms into modern classical French. Conrart was both tolerant and discreet. He objected to the term 'Huguenot' as derogatory, and subscribed to the cult of monarchy and passive obedience, as extolled by Charenton and by his fashionable friend, the writer, Guez de Balzac. As the friend of Daillé and of Amyraut, he provided another link between Paris and Saumur, while his friendship with Moisant de Brieux stimulated the latter to start his academy in Caen. Through Conrart, Perrot D'Ablancourt, a translator of classical texts and a very discreet Calvinist, was admitted to the *Académie*, as was Paul Pellisson, a clever young man from the Huguenot town of Castres, who in 1652 wrote an elegant account of the *Académie*, but who later abjured to earn notoriety as a convert and converter.[42]

Madame des Loges, as we have seen, thought that Calvinism had become an alternative religion, and among those who frequented her salon had been Guez de Balzac, who called her *'cette céleste, divine, dixième Muse'* and paid homage to the elegant prose of her letters. Cultivated circles in Saumur, Caen and even Nîmes responded to this climate of détente, but in general south of the Loire tension prevailed. In the final resort coexistence depended upon the attitude of the Crown to the Edict of Nantes which came under ceaseless attack from the Assemblies of the Clergy and the *dévots*. A royal decree in 1634 which excluded from the Edict the subsidiary churches or *annexes*, vital for rural Protestantism, caused maximum irritation and inconvenience. But the war against the Habsburgs dominated Richelieu's policies, and involved not only Protestant alliances but also the recruitment of Protestant nobles and soldiers. Thus the conversion campaign of the Bishop of Nîmes was necessarily checked when he had to recruit from the Cévennes, a reservoir of manpower, soldiers 'with the courage of lions', led by 'incomparable commanders and officers, fed on the milk of Monsieur de Rohan'.[43] Richelieu came to toy with the idea of giving the Calvinists minor consessions, for instance, by condemning indulgences and 'indecorous images' in churches, and luring them into a Gallican church of which he would be Patriarch. At this time Grotius, whose Arminian views had caused him to be an exile in Paris, was also pressing an oecumenical programme. Papal nuncios and Calvinist ministers showed keen apprehension, but irenical schemes died with Richelieu in 1642.[44]

His successor, Cardinal Mazarin, had more urgent preoccupations during the minority of Louis XIV and could not afford to offend the Huguenots, however strong the pressure from the Assemblies of the Clergy. He chose to continue the war against the Habsburgs and between 1648 and 1653 was faced by the crisis years of the Fronde. Calvinists appeared to many Catholics an aggressive minority, whereas they saw themselves on the defensive, fighting to preserve their status under the Edict of Nantes. Immediately upon the establishment of the Regency in 1643, the Calvinist sense of insecurity surfaced and the temple at Charenton glittered with drawn swords and resounded with hysterical lamentations provoked by a rumour that a mob was on its way from Paris with the intent of burning down the temple as in 1621. In the event the Porte St Antoine was closed and the congregation returned to Paris, protected by Swiss guards sent by the government, which provided a military escort again in 1648. Indeed in July 1643 the Regent reaffirmed the edicts of pacification, while in 1645 the *Chambres de l'Edit* were instructed to send information of any infractions of the edict.

The anger of the clergy rose in a crescendo and in 1650 the Assembly claimed that Protestants were gaining ground, that they were building new temples and schools, besides flooding into offices, and asked that the civil power should come to the aid of the Church and repress heresy. But it was in these years that Protestant loyalty rallied to a government faced by near-civil war. Montauban and La Rochelle took energetic measures of defence against the Prince de Condé mobilising troops in the south-west, and, following the lead of Amyraut, the Huguenots distanced themselves from their co-religionists in England, engaged on the trial of their king. Moreover, Mazarin was dependent for his survival both on the loyalty of the Protestant general, Turenne, and on the loans of the Protestant financier, Barthélemy Hervart, who was praised in a government declaration of 1649 for 'saving France and preserving the crown for the king, services which should never be forgotten'.[45] Lastly, Mazarin needed the alliance of the English Commonwealth to bring the war against Spain to an end. In 1652 Mazarin's 'little flock', as he called the Huguenots, gained their reward when a declaration specifically praising their loyalty, reaffirmed the Edict of Nantes, and annulled all judgements made by the *parlements* against the letter and spirit of the Edict. This was the greatest gain of the century for the Huguenots and a triumph for coexistence.

The triumph was momentary and had been achieved only because of the weakness of the Crown. In 1656, with the Fronde over and the English alliance secured, Mazarin issued a declaration full of menace for the Huguenots by which two commissioners, one a Catholic and one a Protestant, were at some future date to be appointed for each province to enquire into infractions of the edict. In 1659 at the persuasion of Turenne, Mazarin allowed a National Synod to assemble at Loudun, but this was declared to be the last, a lethal blow to the functioning of the Calvinist churches. In the same year Huguenots were forbidden to sing psalms in public places, on main roads and rivers, aiming in this last case at the boatloads going to Charenton.

It is true that Mazarin was in a stronger position, but the change of policy can also be explained by subversive activities of Huguenots in the South. Persistent reports had come in from the intendants that Lower Languedoc was a powder-keg about to explode. A year after the 1652 Declaration, and probably encouraged by it, a conflict over the rebuilding of a temple at Vals in the hills above the Rhône valley led to the setting-up of an armed camp of some 6000 men, including some infantry and cavalry sent by Nîmes, which resounded to militant psalms.[46] The Charenton pastors had deplored the support given by the Midi to Rohan, and the difference between quiescent and minority Calvinism in the north and turbulent, often majority Calvinism in the south still remained. In 1660 Turenne, who eight years later was to become a convert, was outraged on a visit to the Midi to find pastors talking enthusiastically of 'the wars of M. de Rohan', and he told his wife that he considered this attitude 'incompatible with the tranquility of a state such as this'.[47] Turenne was expressing the view that Louis XIV came to adopt, and could afford to adopt, because the Peace of the Pyrenees at last ended the war with Spain. In 1661 he put into effect the Declaration of 1656 and the destruction of the temples began.

It is tempting to hold that from the promulgation of the Edict of Nantes its revocation was probable, even inevitable, that there could be no accommodation between an intolerant Catholicism and an equally intolerant Calvinism. But under Richelieu and Mazarin the state's need for Protestant allies abroad and Protestant troops and financiers at home was too great for it to capitulate to the clamour of intransigent Catholics. French Calvinism was an indigenous growth, lacking the harsh austerity of the Genevan and Scottish variety; and during the years 1629–61 it seemed to many in the cultivated élites of Paris, Saumur, Caen, and Nîmes that a common French culture could accommodate, perhaps even reconcile, confessional differences. Moreover in communities not exposed to the missionary activities of Capuchins and Jesuits, nor to large-scale Catholic immigration, sentiments of local solidarity could be stronger than those of religious bigotry.

Evidence from two widely-seaprated regions may be cited, not as typical, but as illustrations of the benefits and pleasures enjoyed by fortunate individuals in these years when illusory hopes could still be entertained. Peiresc in Provence was one of the leading spirits in the European Republic of Letters. He included in his vast circle of friends and correspondents the Calvinist Samuel Petit, a theologian and Hebrew scholar of the College of Nîmes, and introduced him to intellectuals in Paris, among them being the friar and scientist Mersenne. Another of Peiresc's friends in Nîmes was the Protestant architect, Isaac Péladan, the author of a work on the antiquities of Nîmes which he proposed to dedicate to Cardinal Barberini. The cardinal's ungracious refusal of this offering by a Huguenot evidently surprised Péladan, unused to this churlishness. Péladan's comment to the Bishop of Vaison was that 'for men of learning religion ought not to be an obstacle'.[48] It was no obstacle for the canons of Montpellier when in 1654 they invited Sébastien Bourdon to return to his birthplace and paint a picture for the high altar in the cathedral which was being reconstructed after the destruction of the wars of Rohan.

The memoirs of a Norman squire, Isaac Dumont de Bostaquet, introduce us to the very different pleasures of rural life. Born in 1632, he was educated at Saumur, returning to his estates near Dieppe to indulge in his passion for hunting and to relax in musical evenings which he particularly enjoyed. At the age of 20, he followed the traditional career of a noble, enlisting under the duc de Longueville and serving on the north-eastern front. In 1657 he yielded to his mother's wishes that he should marry since, as he tells us, 'I was the only son and fond of the opposite sex, which made her fear that I might commit some youthful folly'. A Calvinist bride with a suitable dowry was chosen, and there followed a halcyon summer filled with *'parties de plaisir, de chasse, de repas'*, and dancing. This independent country gentleman, born and bred as a Calvinist but showing no particular interest in theology and averse to austerity, went into exile in 1685,

succeeding in reaching Holland at the second attempt. There he
enlisted in the army of William of Orange. He died in Ireland in
1709.[49] For him at least his youth in the time of Mazarin had seemed a
golden age indeed.

Notes

1. J. Delumeau, *Naissance et affirmation de la Réforme* (Paris, 1965)
   p. 181.
2. *A Relation of the State of France under Henri IV in 1609*, T. Birch (ed.)
   (London, 1749) pp. 441, 445.
3. E. G. Léonard, *Le Protestant français* (Paris, 1955) p. 32.
4. P. Chaunu, 'Le XVIIᵉ siècle religieux. Réflexions préalables',
   Annales ESC (1967) 291; E. G. Léonard, 'Le Protestantisme français
   au XVIIᵉ siècle', *Revue Historique* (1948) p. 166.
5. E. G. Léonard, *Histoire générale du protestantisme* (Paris, 1961), vol.
   II, p. 331.
6. Elisabeth Labrousse, *Une foi, une loi, un roi?* (Geneva, Paris, 1985); E.
   Labrousse, 'Calvinism in France, 1598–1685' in Menna Prestwich (ed.)
   International Calvinism 1541–1715 (Oxford, 1985); Janine Garrisson,
   L'Edit de Nantes et sa Révocation: Histoire d'une intolérance (Paris,
   1985) pp. 108, 114–15; Solange Deyon, *Du Loyalisme au Refus: les
   protestants français et leur député-général entre la Fronde et la
   Révocation* (Lille, 1976) p. 27.
7. B. Dompnier, *Le venin de l'hérésie: Image du protestantisme et combat
   catholique an XVIIᵉ siècle* (Paris, 1985) p. 17; D. Ligou, *Le
   Protestantisme en France de 1598 à 1715* (Paris, 1968) p. 197.
8. G. B. Depping, 'Un banquier protestant en France au xviiᵉ siècle,
   Barthélemy Herwarth', *Revue Historique* (1879) vol. X pp. 285–338
   (1879) vol. XI pp. 63–80.
9. Prestwich, *International Calvinism*, p. 301.
10. Léonard, 'Le Protestantisme français, p. 165.
11. Quoted by Inès Murat, *Colbert* (Paris, 1980) p. 166.
12. J. Pannier, *L'Eglise Réformée de Paris sous Louis XIII* (Paris, 1932)
    pp. 324–436.
13. J. Pannier, *L'Eglise Réformée de Paris sous Henri IV* (Paris, 1911) pp.
    5–6; O. Douen, *La Révocation de l'Edit de Nantes à Paris*, vol. I
    (Paris, 1894) p. 195.
14. Léonard, *Histoire générale*, vol. II, p. 333.
15. Labrousse, *Révocation*, p. 28; S. Mours, *Le Protestantisme en France
    an XVIIᵉ Siècle* (Paris, 1967) p. 86. In both cases the total French
    population is taken at 20 million, while Mours does not include Alsace,
    Metz and Sedan in his Calvinist count.
16. M. de Bouard (ed.) *Histoire de la Normandie* (Toulouse, 1970) p. 367; A.

Galland, *Essai sur l'Histoire du Protestantisme à Caen et en Basse-Normandie, 1598–1791* (Paris, 1898) p. 156.

17. Galland, *Normandie* p. 157.
18. P. Milcent, 'Spiritualité de la Charité envers les pauvres selon Saint Jean Eudes', *XVIIe Siècle*, (1971) 48–50, 53–4; Galland, *Normandie*, p. 370.
19. Léonard, vol. II, pp. 341, 335; Galland, *Normandie*, p. 119.
20. L. Pérouas, *Le Diocèse de la Rochelle de 1648 à 1724: Sociologie et Pastorale* (Paris, 1964) pp. 136–9, 142, 206, 302, 304.
21. E. Magne, *La Joyeuse Jeunesse de Tallemant des Réaux* (Paris, 1921) chaps 1–2; J. Meyer, *Colbert* (Paris, 1981) pp. 65–6; Tallemant des Réaux, *Historiettes* A. Adam, ed, 2 vols. (Paris, 1960).
22. D. Dessert, *Argent, pouvoir et société au Grand Siècle* (Paris, 1984) pp. 539, 667–8, 521, 605; P. Boissonnade, *Histoire des premiers essais de relations économiques directes entre la France et l'Etat prussien pendant le règne de Louis XIV, 1643–1715* (Paris, 1912) chap. 5.
23. P. Grillon (ed.) *Les Papiers de Richelieu* (Paris, 1980) vol. IV, p. 598.
24. C. Schmidt, 'Le voyage d'un prince allemand en France, 1646–1648', *Bulletin de la Société de l'Histoire du Protestantisme français*, 48 (1899).
25. Dessert, *Argent*, pp. 566–9.
26. Léonard, 'Le Protestantisme français', pp. 153–79; R. Sauzet, *Contre-Reforme et Réforme Catholique en Bas–Languedoc: Le diocèse de Nîmes au XVIIe siècle* (Paris, 1979) pp. 255, 359–61, 256–61.
27. Ligou, *Le Protestantisme en France*, p. 118; Sauzet, *Nîmes*, pp. 257, 305–7, 315, 318, 303.
28. Léonard, 'Le Protestantisme français', pp. 161–2.
29. Labrousse in *International Calvinism*, p. 292.
30. Galland, *Normandie*, p. 79.
31. Béatrice Causse, *Die en Dauphiné* (thesis, 1979) pp. 47, 70–7, copy in Paris, Bibliothèque de la Sociéte de l'Histoire du Protestantisme français.
32. Sauzet, *Nîmes*, pp. 276–8, 291.
33. C. H. Haskins, *Mediaeval Culture* (Oxford, 1929) pp. 15–16.
34. Léonard, 'Le Protestantisme français', pp. 169–170; R. Stauffer, 'Le Calvinisme et les universités', *Bulletin de la Société de l'Histoire du Protestantisme français*. (1980) 44.
35. F. Laplanche, *Orthodoxie et Predication* (Paris, 1965) pp. 60–71; B. Armstrong, *Calvinism and the Amyraut heresy* (Wisconsin, 1969).
36. F. Laplanche, 'Tradition et modernité au XVIIe siècle: L'exégèse biblique des protestants français', *Annales ESC* (1985).
37. Laplanche, *Orthodoxie*, pp. 334, 371.
38. R. Coupe, *Salomon de Brosse and the Development of the Classical Style in French Architecture from 1565 to 1630* (London, 1972).
39. For Protestant artists see Menna Prestwich, 'Patronage and the Protestants in France, 1598–1661: Architects and Painters', in J. Mesnard and R. Mousnier (eds) *L'Age d'Or du Mécénat, 1598–1661* (Paris, 1985).

40. P. Rosenberg *et al.*, *La Peinture française du XVIIe siècle dans les collections americaines* (Paris, 1982) introduction by M. Fumaroli, p. 28.
41. Léonard, *Histoire générale*, vol. II, pp. 336–7.
42. R. Kerviller, *Valentin Conrart: sa vie et sa correspondence* (Paris, 1881).
43. Sauzet, *Nîmes*, pp. 295–6.
44. J. Orcibal, *Louis XIV et les Protestants* (Paris, 1951) p. 31; P. Blet, 'Le plan de Richelieu pour la réunion des protestants', *Gregorianum* (1967).
45. Depping, 'Un banquier protestant', p. 303.
46. Garrisson, *L'Edit de Nantes*, p. 114.
47. E. Labrousse, 'Passé et conjoncture politique: Les raisons d'une discretion' in P. Joutard (ed.) *La Saint-Barthélemy ou les Resonances d'un Massacre* (Neuchâtel, 1976) p. 84.
48. Sauzet, *Nîmes*, pp. 270–1.
49. Isaac Dumont de Bostaquet, *Mémoires sur les temps qui ont procédé et suivi la Revocation de l'Edit de Nantes* (M. Richard, ed.) (Paris, 1968), pp. 28, 42, 45.

12 Louis XIV and the Persecution of Huguenots: The Role of the Ministers and Royal Officials

Roger Mettam

So much has been written on the Revocation of the Edict of Nantes that it has seemed wise, in this short paper, to concentrate on one aspect where it is still possible to produce new evidence and to offer a reinterpretation of earlier historical judgements. Accordingly the argument will centre on the role of the secular officials, both the ministers at the court and the various levels of royal agents and bureaucrats in the provinces, in order to discover their views on the problem of Protestantism in the years before and after 1685. The picture which emerges, as so often in recent studies of *ancien régime* France, is one of confusion, contradiction and inconsistency, varying from province to province, from town to town and even from family to family. In a single community or household, the presence of two religions might cause little or no difficulty, but sometimes it gave rise to extreme bitterness between citizens and between close relatives.

During the personal rule of Louis XIV – the period beginning with the death of Mazarin in 1661 when the king announced that he would appoint no successor to the cardinal as *premier ministre* and would henceforth take personal responsibility for all the decisions of his ministers – royal policy towards the Huguenots underwent a number of changes. There was a brief flurry of repressive pronouncements against them in the early 1660s, followed by a spell of indifference on the part of the crown towards these heretical subjects in the middle years of that decade. A further period of activity in 1669–71 was again followed by apparent governmental inertia, and it was only after 1678 that many Frenchmen became aware of a seemingly new royal determination to eradicate heresy from the realm. On closer examination, it can be clearly seen that the ministers, and even the King himself, were far from uninterested in the Calvinist minority during the calmer days of the mid 1660s and 1670s. Indeed they were positively encouraging many aspects of Huguenot and foreign Protestant enterprise within France, greatly valuing the services of these most hard-working and inventive subjects and visitors. Royal acknowledgement of their vital contribution to industry and commerce makes the subsequent persecution even more difficult to explain.

Fortunately for the historian, Louis XIV has bequeathed a convenient starting-point for an investigation of this topic, in the form of his *mémoires* for the year 1661. These reflections on his reign were designed, not as propaganda for public consumption, but as a private instruction manual for his heir. They were not entirely the unprompted thoughts of the monarch himself, because some points were suggested to him by his advisers, especially by Colbert, and much of the drafting was done by his secretaries. Nevertheless they were approved by Louis as an account of his rule which accorded with his own views. After some preliminary observations on kingship, he describes the first year of his personal rule by isolating the serious problems facing the crown and then reviewing the other internal and external aspects where there was no cause for concern. Beginning his catalogue of troubles with the now celebrated phrase, *'le désordre règne partout'*, he identifies the disorderly state of both the court and the patronage system as the first evil, although the depletion of the royal finances was scarcely less alarming. A third source of grave disquiet was the condition of the church. The clergy, as he remarked, were embroiled as usual in theological disputes, but a new and very real danger was the threat of open schism because of the rising tide of Jansenism. This sect had recently become more subversive through the support it was receiving from the seditious cardinal de Retz and his followers. In fact Louis was applying the term Jansenist rather loosely, including some groups who were undoubtedly calling for ecclesiastical reform but were not of this brotherhood. Terminology apart, the king was genuinely worried that the church, whose hierarchical structure was often helpful to him in ruling the country, was afflicted by internal tensions, and that seditious priests, interfering popes and the treacherous Retz were eagerly fomenting them. Neither here nor at any other point on the list of the disorders of 1661 is there any mention of the Huguenots or of Protestants in general.

It is only when the king passes on to consider all those matters which were not problematic in the opening months of his personal rule that they make some fleeting appearances. After a brief survey of other European states, Louis describes in detail the new administrative structure which he has created at the centre, and the ministers and secretaries who were to staff it. The machinery and the personnel of government are portrayed at some length until he comes to the secretaries of state for the navy and for the Protestants. He refers to them within a single sentence, mentioning their names but not their responsibilities, saying merely that they held portfolios in which nothing was happening of any importance. Further on still, having listed the many decisions he took in this first year, he does remark that in the past Spain has aided rebellious Huguenots, but this aside is in the context of a general attack on Spanish untrustworthiness. After many more pages he at last describes the Huguenots as they were in 1661. Noting that they are no longer in any way to be feared, he is saddened that they continue to be present in a Catholic kingdom. Accordingly he has decided to set in motion a plan for bringing them into the true church, although he totally rejects those counsels which have advocated some violent means of persuading them to convert. Indeed he acknowledges that Luther and the early reformers spoke many wise words, against a church that was in a scandalously corrupt and worldly state, and he further accepts that the reformed religions gained much status and success simply because they were a useful weapon for more politically orientated rulers and ministers to exploit in the turbulent circumstances of the sixteenth century. He also knew, although he did not say so overtly in his *mémoires*, that the Huguenots had been supportive of the crown in the recent civil wars of the Frondes, especially in providing vital financial assistance, and he was aware that many of them held offices in the bureaucracy where they acquitted themselves honourably, while others were essential to a variety of industrial and commercial enterprises. Louis therefore felt that gentle proselytising was the only means of persuading these useful and loyal, but regretfully heretical, subjects into orthodoxy.

The *mémoires* for the year 1661 were not compiled until around 1666, when the initial flurry of royal declarations against the Huguenots, mostly issued in 1662 and 1663, had passed and no more pronouncements seemed to be forthcoming. Those early reactions to the problem of Protestantism had been largely designed to prevent any extension of the powers and privileges already granted to the *religion prétendue réformée* (RPR) by Henri IV or Louis XIII, both by proscribing those which had crept in during the recent past and by emphasising that no such innovations would be permitted in the years ahead. At the same time Louis XIV committed himself to upholding those rights which had been legitimately established by his two predecessors. Yet he was simultaneously beginning to use one of his gently persuasive methods, the granting of substantial sums to men who were prepared to convert. This was not done in the general terms which would be employed some twenty years later, when offers of fiscal concessions would be made to any Huguenot who would sincerely abjure. In these earlier days the bribes were held out to worthy individuals, whose names had been notified to the court by local officials. Thus, in 1663, the king was prepared to give 3000 livres to a talented young *avocat* if he would embrace the true faith.

As well as these requests for royal largesse, there were many other petitions asking for favour to be shown to, or action taken against, Huguenots in the early 1660s. Once again the initiative seldom came from the court but was a response to pressure from bureaucrats in the localities or from citizens, often those who held office in one of the municipal hierarchies or corporations. If the proposal asked for a restriction on Protestant activity, the ministers immediately responded with the caution that no action could be taken unless it were strictly legal, and the government was not always immediately certain of all the detailed regulations which had been agreed in preceding years. In 1664 a suggestion that there were too many Protestant temples in the pays de Gex prompted the swift royal reply that nothing must be done until all the treaties relating to that province had been scrutinised thoroughly, lest the demolition of some reformed churches be a violation of their provisions. One further example of the royal attitude to the Huguenots in the early personal rule introduces a new dimension to the problem, sufficiently important for the king to mention it in his *mémoires* for the year 1666. At that time, he was trying to set up the *grands jours*, a grand assize, in the province of Languedoc, and had entrusted its conduct to the fiercely anti-Protestant *parlement* of Toulouse. Within the jurisdiction of that court was the town of Castres, where the citizenry included adherents of both religions and had long felt deep mistrust for the arrogant Toulousains. The Castrais therefore demanded that their *chambre de l'édit* – the chamber, staffed by men of both faiths, which monitored the observance of the Edict of Nantes within the municipality – should be represented on the *grands jours*, fearing that Huguenot interests would be sacrificed by the *parlement* of Toulouse. Normally, argued the king in his *mémoires*, I would have taken such a difficulty in my stride, because local bodies were always at odds over their respective powers and jurisdictions. Yet I was currently at war with the English, and I thought it most unwise to give the Huguenots any cause to believe that their privileges were being attenuated at such a sensitive international moment. The *grands jours* of Toulouse therefore never became a reality.

Two conclusions can be drawn from an examination of the brief period in the early 1660s when Louis XIV took an interest in the question of the Huguenots. The first is that many French towns did not feel that they had a religious problem. In some of them there were no members of the reformed faith, in others a small minority of Protestant citizens or even a larger one, and in a few a Huguenot majority. In certain urban centres the RPR was dominant chiefly among the merchants, who coexisted with, but did not directly challenge, the Catholic magisterial and municipal administrative élites. Elsewhere there were Protestant officials and town councillors, occasionally even outnumbering the Catholics. Yet whatever the widely differing ratios between the two confessional groups, there was not necessarily any religious or civil tension. Indeed there were still mixed marriages, and many men of both faiths shared a common dislike of the militant Catholicism and zealous rigorism of the *dévots*. Only in a few towns did special circumstances lead to religious friction, sometimes causing one or both sides to demand government intervention. The second conclusion to be drawn is that, after the king had stated his intention that the Huguenots should not be permitted to extend the privileges which his father and grandfather had granted to them, the intendants and other royal officials did not exert themselves unduly in implementing the wishes of the sovereign – unless they were serving in a town where there was religious turmoil. Twenty years later many bureaucrats would take strong measures against Protestant communities because they knew that this would be pleasing to the king, but in the early 1660s it is evident that such tactics were not generally considered to be a sure way of obtaining royal approval. Indeed it was possible to maintain the opposite point of view because Colbert, the minister in whom Louis had openly declared that he had every confidence, was keenly granting privileges to Huguenots who were willing to establish new industries and to increase trade. Similarly Protestant foreigners were being offered lavish incentives to settle in France, bringing their wealth and their skills, and were accorded favours and monopolies which made them élite members of society.

If Louis XIV had expressed his general desire that Huguenots be persuaded to convert, this wish was not included on the long list of exhortations to the intendants in which their principal responsibilities were spelled out. Their fiscal, commercial, industrial, judicial and jurisdictional tasks were clearly more urgent and important. The bishops, in contrast, were not only aware of the royal attitude to the RPR, but needed no reminding of the desirability of obtaining conversions to their own true faith – so much so that Louis had to warn them on more than one occasion that forceful methods must not be used. It was largely pressure from over-zealous clerics which prompted the second flurry of governmental interest in the Protestant problem in the years 1669–71. Until the Peace of Clement IX in 1668, when a compromise was reached on the thorny question of Jansenism, the disputes about that sect had dominated the minds of the clergy. Very soon after, it became evident that Protestantism had replaced it as the principal concern of many prelates. The king was soon drawn into this matter, but much of his contribution to it was as a moderator of excessive zeal. There are a number of letters like that of 1671 to the Bishop of Amiens, in which Colbert expressed the annoyance of his master that a militant Capuchin was harassing Huguenots in an attempt to convert them. Such behaviour was to cease at once because these were economically useful citizens, and they were to be protected rather than alienated. At the same time Louis did make some more general offers of help to those who would voluntarily renounce their faith. For example he announced that, where he had the right to nominate oblates in convents, he would give preference to girls who had converted from the RPR. Colbert, on the other hand, continued to restrain or encourage Protestants on an individual basis, making no general statements. In 1670 he replied to an enquiry from an intendant that the exemptions from certain taxes which were to be granted to fathers of large families, in the belief that a growing population meant a healthier economy, should not apply to non-Catholic households. Yet he did not suggest to other intendants that they should make the same distinction, and he included no reference to it in the declarations which created this right of fiscal relief. Again writing to individuals and not to the whole corps of intendants, he told one of them in 1672 that public Protestant preaching should not be allowed in places where it had not hitherto been authorised, and in the same year instructed another to do everything in his power to protect the Protestant Netherlander Van Robais, whose industrial contribution had already been so valuable and who was being harassed by hostile Catholics in his place of residence. Nevertheless these, and other similarly varied letters, formed a minimal part of ministerial correspondence at the beginning of the 1670s. Louis XIV could still have honestly said, as he had in the *mémoires* for 1661, that nothing of much importance was happening in the portfolio of the secretary of state for the reformed religion.

It has been suggested that the outbreak of war against the Calvinist Dutch Republic in 1672 changed the mood of both king and country towards the Huguenots, as they were now co-religionaries of the enemy, but there is little evidence that this was so. One correspondent, writing to Colbert in 1672, did say that the Protestants of Montauban were talking insolently about the king and were behaving like Dutchmen, but the Montabanais had always been fiercely Huguenot, and had frequently voiced grievances against the authority of the crown, the governor and the provincial Estates. The comparison with Dutchmen was the invention of the writer, and there is no evidence that the citizens of Montauban were planning to conspire with the enemies of the king, however hostile they were being towards the royal and provincial administrations.

The Dutch had been the allies of France for much of the century, and it was only after the French invasion of Flanders in the 1667–8 War of Devolution that the Republic, despite reassurances from Paris, began to seek a network of European allies in order to contain what it now regarded as an expansionist France. When the war came in 1672, it was the only international conflict welcomed by Colbert, because he hoped it would emasculate or destroy the most serious threat to his plans for French economic growth. Yet the minister was quick to reassure both Huguenots and resident foreign Protestants that they were still in high favour with the king, who valued their contribution to the economy and especially to the armaments industry. Louis XIV himself – in his new set of military *mémoires*, which were revised many times as the war dragged on unexpectedly and as policies yielded unforeseen results – did not dwell at all on the Protestantism of the enemy. The Dutch and their allies were considered solely in terms of the strategic, military and diplomatic danger they presented to his consolidation of his eastern and north-eastern frontiers. His irritation with the Dutch was centred on the fact that, at the peace conferences of 1668 and 1678–9, the French monarch and his aristocratic envoys had been compelled to make concessions to their bourgeois negotiators and to address these social inferiors as political equals. Moreover he and his ambassadors, who put forward an agreed French position, found it difficult to fathom the behaviour of the self-styled 'hogen-mogen' men, Their High Mightinesses the Staten-generaal, let alone the States of Holland and the princes of Orange, all of whom seemed to speak with many voices, with none able to negotiate on behalf of the whole Republic.

In the middle years of the war, in 1675–6, there was therefore still no sign of a militant royal initiative against the Huguenots, and yet from 1678 it began to be one of the dominant topics in ministerial correspondence with the provinces. Some historians have provided a ready, and unfortunately too glib, explanation for this growing hostility – namely the rise of the new minister of war, the marquis de Louvois. They have portrayed the years 1672–83 as a battle in the royal council between Colbert on the one hand, and Louvois and his father Le Tellier on the other, the latter faction ultimately gaining the upper hand. The Le Telliers were in favour of war and glory, Colbert preferring peace and economic expansion. This interpretation is simplistic for a number of reasons. Colbert, himself originally a client of the Le Telliers, had undoubtedly established his family as a force in politics, at a time when power at all levels was organised in the form of rival dynasties with their associated clientage and patronage networks. Louis XIV had determined that during personal rule no single group should dominate the government, as had happened with disastrous consequences in the past.

By 1679, when many Frenchmen felt that the persecution of Huguenots had begun in earnest, the Le Telliers had not in any sense defeated the Colberts. Louvois had not wholeheartedly pleased the king during the conflict with the Dutch. The minister had caused much friction between the royal council and the army commanders by his high-handed behaviour, the war had lasted much longer than had been anticipated, and France had obtained a negotiated peace only by conceding points which had been fundamental aims at the outset of the hostilities. Thus, when a new foreign minister was needed in 1679, Louis appointed one of the Colberts, to balance the Le Tellier faction which now had Louvois as secretary of state for war and his father as Chancellor. There were also genuine disagreements between the groups, many determined by the different portfolios they held. Colbert had wanted a short war against the Dutch, but now saw France involved in a lengthy European conflict, and he was alarmed that many of his plans for fiscal reform and economic expansion were now in ruins because of these costly international campaigns. Louvois therefore felt that he had to fight an obstructive Colbert for every penny he needed, at a time when it was vital to maintain the momentum of the war. Yet the argument about the role of Louvois as a leading persecutor of Huguenots must turn on his own attitude to the reformed religion, and here historians like Orcibal and Scoville seems plainly to have been mistaken.

Louvois and his father were primarily concerned to reform the French army, and, although neither achieved as much as he had hoped, they were able to begin the implementation of many ambitious plans. Throughout this process Louvois was eager to ensure that religion did not become a divisive issue. Many of the best soldiers were Huguenots, and foreign Protestants formed the larger part of some crack regiments, the celebrated Swiss above all. His only worry, and it was a serious one, was that members of the reformed faith might be a danger in frontier provinces where they might make common cause with their co-religionaries in enemy countries at times of war. Elsewhere in the kingdom, he judged a man by his military skills, not by his beliefs, and it was only when it became clear that the king had hardened his attitude to the Huguenots that the minister had to espouse this policy. Yet he continued to advocate moderation, caution and persuasion, and had some success in tempering the ardour of Louis XIV.

The first sign of the religious priorities of Louvois can be seen in the compilation and enforcement of the rules for life in the new hospital of the Invalides, a spectacular Parisian building which was meant both to demonstrate royal care for the aged and wounded military and to inspire other towns to make similar provisions. These regulations, drawn up in 1674, prescribed a régime for the inmates which, as in all charitable institutions at this time, was to be highly moral and was to be organised around profit-making crafts for those who had the strength to work. Louvois ordered that Protestant invalided soldiers should be admitted on the promise that they would be prepared to convert. Yet this minister, who kept a close watch on the Invalides and was renowned for his meticulous attention to detail, never enquired about these conversions. As a result, many wounded or aged Protestants lived out their remaining years within its walls and were not questioned further about their beliefs. In the early 1680s, when persecution increased, Louvois will be seen more clearly as a minister who was out of sympathy with a forcefully imposed orthodoxy. If that is accepted, then the historian must look elsewhere for an explanation of increasing governmental concern over the problem of religious dissent in the last years of the Dutch War. From 1678 the RPR became the dominant preoccupation in royal and ministerial correspondence.

During the 1660s and early 1670s resentment against Protestants had been growing slowly in some French towns, but many more remained free of such discord. Although a minority of bishops concentrated on raising the standards of the Catholic clergy, a significant number of them had been offering financial incentives to converts and had often introduced such token tests of orthodoxy that the process of embracing the true faith did not require too much soul-searching. Royal officials continued to proffer bribes to individuals, and increasingly showed a willingness to grant fiscal incentives, with exemption from some of the many different taxes which were levied on the French people. The Dutch War was therefore of crucial significance. As the wartime tax burden rose sharply, the prospect of exemptions appeared to be more attractive, and increasing numbers of Huguenots succumbed to these temptations. Unfortunately for the Catholic population, the whole community was responsible for honouring the fiscal assessment placed upon it. The larger the number who converted and gained exemption, the greater was the amount which the remaining Protestant and Catholic taxpayers had to find, and they were already affected by the general rise in taxes occasioned by the war. Some Huguenots, who could not bring themselves to abjure, were disgusted by these new converts who had betrayed their faith. Nor did many Catholics approve of them, because the true follower of Catholicism was being offered no fiscal relief while the former heretic was now benefiting financially from his renunciation of a long and blasphemous life. Even more offensive was the knowledge that many converts had not really abandoned their faith, although they were now receiving the financial rewards because they had gone through the motions of conversion. Equally objectionable were certain Catholics who swore that they had always been secret Huguenots but were now ready to embrace the Roman creed, thereby qualifying for the fiscal reliefs. It was often difficult for ecclesiastical and royal agents to unmask these pretenders because they did not know them as individuals and had only their sworn affirmations as a guide. The neighbours of the abjuring Huguenots and of the doubly-converting Catholics had a much clearer idea about their sincerity, and it was therefore here, in the streets of the towns, that tension began to mount. Hostility was also increasing against one group of Huguenots and foreign Protestants who refused to convert the successful merchants and craftsmen. These entrepreneurs, who enjoyed a privileged position, accorded to them by the crown for their contribution to the French economy, were in some instances offensively prosperous. They were also able, through the monopolies they had been granted, to exclude others who wished to start similar enterprises. To be fair to them, many of the foreigners had come to France when Colbert could not find eager indigenous craftsmen in certain important industries, and he had chosen to shower them with privileges in order to entice them to stay. Nevertheless these visitors had sometimes become so successful that they had awakened Frenchmen to the possibility of making similar profits but had at the same time used their monopolies to exclude native newcomers from participating in their trade or craft.

Thus, around the year 1676, the government began to receive reports of tensions and even overt confrontations, involving Catholics, Protestants and converts, in a number of French towns. As there had been, in the preceding year, two major revolts in Brittany and in the Bordelais, at the very moment when the crown wanted the country to be united against the Dutch and their European allies, the prospect of further disorder alarmed the ministers. Louvois in particular had a loathing for internal insurrection, especially when it threatened international military campaigns. So he and Colbert began to pay increasing attention to religious matters, although it is not until early 1679 that it can be said to be their dominant concern. Their letters of the preceding two years conform to no obvious pattern where the Huguenots are concerned, because the ministers were responding to a wide range of detailed issues which were being raised by royal and municipal officials in the provinces. For example one report told of a Huguenot who had turned Catholic but had subsequently lapsed, and Colbert wrote to insist that he be pursued by the relevant authorities because such behaviour was already forbidden by earlier regulations. Another man, a Catholic man who had joined the RPR, was to be persuaded by every possible means to rejoin the true church. Only a few of these letters resulted from a royal, rather than a provincial, initiative, as in 1678 when Colbert wrote to say that the king was unhappy that a Protestant concierge was employed in the gardens of his palace at Blois. As the man had purchased this office, the king had no intention of dismissing him *tout court*, but the officials of the town were exhorted to find a suitable person who would purchase it from him.

It is in 1679 that, quite suddenly, the Huguenots seem to have become the principal topic in governmental correspondence, even before the signing in that year of the Nijmegen peace which ended the international preoccupations of the crown. It is not the intention here to explain why Louis XIV drastically changed his perception of the Huguenot problem, for that would require a lengthy exposition and would remain highly speculative. Historians have not been able to prove that specific events caused the king to adopt a more militant attitude towards his heretical subjects, although courtiers noted that he was exhibiting a new piety and seemed repentant for his promiscuous life-style and for the distress it had inflicted upon the queen. Although the Nijmegen settlement was officially proclaimed as a great victory for French arms, close confidants knew that Louis was not so euphoric in private, feeling that God had not favoured his purposes and was indeed punishing him for his past misdeeds. Whatever the causal factors, there is no doubt that Colbert and Louvois were soon aware that the restoration of religious uniformity throughout the realm had become a royal obsession, and they were alarmed that valuable members of the reformed faith were being harassed excessively. In their letters the ministers began to make frequent use of phrases like 'on this matter His Majesty is totally inflexible', as they suggested subtle ways of circumventing the rigour of some new royal prescription or proscription about Protestants.

The king himself did not always use heavy-handed methods, especially when the jealously-guarded rights of local institutions might be affected. However strong his desire to convert the heretics, he did not want to provoke more of those tiresome jurisdictional clashes which distracted officials from their duties. Thus in 1679 he instructed an intendant to thwart the admission of a Huguenot craftsman to a gild. The best method was to persuade the mayor to use his influence with the gildsmen and convince them that they should reject the applicant, because the king deemed it imprudent that he or his agent should intervene directly in a decision which was rightfully the prerogative of the gild.

One striking difference can be seen in the attitude of the crown to the Huguenots after the year 1679. Before then, most correspondence on that subject had referred to specific individuals or events. Now there began to be a host of more general pronouncements, some asking for information, others commanding royal officials to take action throughout the kingdom. New Protestant institutions were to be closed, and those which were well established were to be scrutinised with extreme care in order to ensure that they were not adding to their legitimate functions. There was always the danger that secret preaching might be taking place in Huguenot libraries, hospitals and poor-houses. It was decreed that members of the RPR should not be appointed to certain judicial offices, and this prohibition was soon extended to include many other posts. Colbert himself remarked that he would appoint fewer Huguenots to offices which lay in his gift.

It should immediately be observed that these royal bans on entry into office for Protestants were far from effective. Frequently the proscription was simply disobeyed, and many local officials seemed disinclined to enforce it. When one of the forbidden posts was already in Huguenot hands, it was now required that the holder should convert or sell his position to a Catholic. Often it proved impossible to find such a purchaser, in which case the crown had two alternative courses of action, neither of which was practicable. The government could buy the office itself or could arbitrarily suppress it without compensation. The former course would be costly, and Colbert was unwilling to permit it. Much revenue was being lost from the policy of granting fiscal exemptions to converts, because the local communities were not making good the lost taxes. The treasury simply could not have borne this additional burden. As for dismissing a venal officer without reimbursing him, that was the kind of high-handed action which had provoked the first Fronde of 1648–9 and might again prompt bureaucrats, of both faiths, to unite against such a threat to their security of tenure. Privately Colbert was pleased that it was therefore difficult to remove some of these officials, because many of them were able and skilled bureaucrats.

While these general proscriptions continued to be widely ignored, others were promulgated. In 1680 it was forbidden for midwives to be of the reformed faith, lest they prevent the Catholic baptism of children who were likely to die soon after birth. Later that year mixed marriages were banned, as was conversion from Catholicism to Protestantism. Nor were Huguenots permitted to send their children abroad to be educated, and it was decreed that 7 years old was a sufficiently mature age for a child to be sincerely converted to the Church of Rome. These new regulations were flouted in many parts of the kingdom, and many royal officials deemed it unwise to demand their implementation lest it provoke dissent or, even worse, emphasise the point that royal orders were hollow because they could be openly ignored.

Other bureaucrats took a very different line, hoping to gain favour with the king by carrying out his wishes. This was an easier task in strongly Catholic areas, where intendants and other officials could play the part of crusaders against heresy. In less amenable territories, they pretended to be taking a militant stance when they dared not do so in reality. As a result the ministers received much misinformation about the religious climate and the rate of conversion. Yet the zealous intendants soon discovered that their proud claims, whether factual or imaginary, received a cool welcome from Colbert and Louvois. The ministers frequently counselled greater caution, and sometimes sent stinging rebukes. One luckless recipient of Colbertian wrath was the intendant of the navy at Rochefort, who was told in 1680 that he was too militant in his methods for converting Protestant sailors. The minister reminded him that he had been severely warned about this on previous occasions, with the clear implication that this was his last chance to mend his ways. The intendant was therefore being more aggressive than his king, who that same year had expressed his own wish that there be no Protestant officers on his ships, but had prescribed gentle persuasion as the only permissible method, ruling out the use of force or outright dismissal. The expanded French fleet was very dear to Colbert, and he confided to friends that this declaration, although still worrying, was less strident than the personal inclinations of the king would have dictated.

Louvois was experiencing similar problems with the army, where he had to support the çause of religious uniformity but managed to exert a moderating influence on the formulation and implementation of the new royal regulations. In 1680, approximately one-tenth of the soldiery was Huguenot, and there were also the Swiss and other foreign Protestant regiments to consider. The reformed faith provided many distinguished members of the officer corps, and some vital manufacturers of sophisticated weaponry. Louvois therefore pursued a dual policy – seeking to eradicate potentially treacherous Protestants in the frontier provinces, and calming the fears of those in other parts of the realm. As a minister in a very expensive department of government, he shared the concern of Colbert at the amount of money being spent on bribes and fiscal incentives, and now both men received even worse news. Numerous reports came in that French and foreign Protestants were selling their property and leaving the kingdom, taking with them their valuable skills as manufacturers and successful traders. Such an exodus had never been envisaged as part of the conversion policy, and new regulations were drafted to forbid such emigration. Protestant ministers were encouraged to leave, French laymen ordered to remain and foreigners reassured that they were welcome. These announcements soon rebounded on the king and his ministers, because the promises were not believed and the regulations could not be enforced.

The exact scale of this emigration is difficult to calculate, because many men had different reasons for distorting the true figures, often raising or diminishing them in order to make the most desirable impact on the readers of their reports. In 1679 it was stated that, during the last three years in the province of Languedoc, the sum of 20 000–25 000 écus had been spent on favours, bribes and other financial incentives, and that since 1678 3000 converts had come forward. This process, it should be noted, had been largely organised by the Languedocien clergy, not by the secular officials. Yet despite this and other similar claims, there were still many Protestants within the kingdom in 1681 and, notwithstanding the series of royal prohibitions, there were numerous Huguenot officials in the financial and judicial administrations. Moreover, although the number of families fleeing the country was, and remains, difficult to calculate, the government certainly thought that it was dangerously high. Therefore two new elements entered into royal policy in 1681. If it was difficult to exclude Protestants from office, regulations were now issued which would make their lives more unpleasant. For example it was decreed in April 1682 that Huguenot lawyers should lose their rights of precedence over Catholic colleagues, which had hitherto rested solely on the criterion of seniority. As the most lucrative business in the courts was assigned to the senior judges and advocates, this was a serious financial blow. The crown hoped that this change would be welcomed by Catholics, who would gain status through the demotion of their Protestant fellows, rather than provoking a united reaction of all lawyers against arbitrary royal interference in the rules of office-holding. To discourage further emigration, it was announced that Huguenots should not be allowed to sell their furniture, nor to take out of the country any child over the age of seven, nor to leave with any of their French domestic servants. All these rules were widely ignored and were hard to enforce. In commerce and industry no new Huguenot enterprises were to be permitted, although those which were already established should be subjected to pressure and persuasion rather than legislation. The crown did not want this valuable section of the economy to be crushed. The continuing attempts to prevent the admission of Huguenots to gilds were still fiercely resisted in some areas, so that in Tours thirteen out of the fifteen goldsmiths were Protestant in 1681 and the corporation was steadfastly refusing to admit any more Catholics.

The most celebrated development of 1681 was the invention by Marillac, the intendant in Poitou, of the *dragonnades* – the savage billeting of disorderly troops on Huguenots in the hope of persuading them to convert. This initiative, the best-known and most-widely condemned aspect of the persecution, was not well received at the time by the ministers in Paris. Colbert was already irritated with Marillac, and had earlier warned him that a policy of remitting half the *taille*, the principal direct tax, for three years to those who converted would inflame the Catholic population, which would have to shoulder this additional burden. Accordingly Marillac tried another stratagem, that of taxing recalcitrant Protestants more heavily than other citizens. This plan produced different but equally undesirable consequences. The aggrieved Huguenots appealed against the assessment to the *cour des aides*, whose judges shared the general dislike of the sovereign courts for the intendants. The court promptly annulled the extra levy, alarming Colbert who did not want a local jurisdictional battle to complicate an already thorny problem. Marillac therefore embarked upon his third and most brutal remedy for persistent heresy, the *dragonnades*, and immediately brought down on his own head the wrath of Colbert and some stinging observations from Louvois. The intendant had boasted that, under the pressure of resident dragoons, many Protestants had converted, while others had sold their goods and departed. The religious problem was solved. He was no doubt exaggerating this success, and he abruptly changed his tone when he received a fierce letter from Colbert, informing him that an exodus of Huguenots was emphatically not the purpose of royal policy. Marillac hastily replied that he had made further investigations and had initially made a mista e. Some of those families which seemed to have left the area had merely gone into the countryside around the town, and had either returned or were still residing there. Also many of those who had sold furniture had done so merely because they were planning to buy newer designs, which they had now purchased.

Louvois, as his private letters reveal, was in a real dilemma. As questionable statistics about increasing conversions came in from many parts of the kingdom, many courtiers – especially the court clergy – were in a state of euphoria which the king found infectious. To Louis XIV, Marillac seemed to have many merits. Nevertheless Louvois persuaded his royal master to denounce the brutality of the *dragonnades*, and as war minister he rapidly withdrew the troops which had been used for this tyranny. Soon Marillac himself was recalled and sent to another posting. Yet the king was now convinced that a strong military presence was the most effective of the methods which had been used in converting the heretics, and Louvois had no alternative but to acquiesce. All he could do was to inform the civil and military authorities that they must supervise these troops very carefully, ensuring that the strict rules for their conduct were scrupulously observed. As on many occasions, these ministerial directives were not fully obeyed, and much brutality continued.

The minister was equally exercised, during this period of growing royal, clerical and courtly hostility to the Huguenots, with two other problems. He was determined not to lose the excellent Protestant soldiers, native and foreign, from the army, and reminded the bishops that their clergy should be instructed to make the tests of conversion as nominal as possible. Also, on the death of Colbert in 1683, he succeeded him as secretary of state for arts and manufactures, and was therefore now fully briefed on the Protestant contribution to every aspect of commerce and industry. He had long been aware of his debt to the reformed religion in the field of weaponry, but he had not fully realised the threat to the economy as a whole if a massive exodus were not prevented.

Louvois became really alarmed during the summer of 1685. The king did not consult his advisers on war, economics and foreign affairs about a purely religious matter, and it was soon evident that the clerical counsellors had given Louis the resolve to revoke the Edict of Nantes. Once the decision was taken, the legal details were entrusted to the Chancellor, Le Tellier, the father of Louvois himself. On 3 September the war minister left the court for Chambord, where he drew up his plans for mitigating the worst consequences of the Revocation. For the forty-seven days preceding the signing of the Edict of Fontainebleau, which reversed the Nantes agreement, he was away from Versailles, and it was a further ten days before he returned to sit by the deathbed of his father. Then he took swift, and obviously well-prepared, action.

The Edict of Fontainebleau had not denied the right of Huguenots to remain in France, although it had forbidden all their religious practices. So Louvois was not technically breaching the edict, as he now wrote numerous letters of reassurance to members of the RPR. He had been doing so for many years, but now he greatly increased his efforts. Intendants and other officials were to reassure native and foreign Protestants that, as they were economically useful to the crown, no harm would come to them. He also wrote to ambassadors abroad, urging them to persuade those who had emigrated to return home, where they would be treated kindly. More instructions went to governors, intendants, military officials and bishops, exhorting them all to convert the soldiery by the most gentle and ambiguous means, because he was not sure at this moment that Louis would tolerate any Protestants in his army. On conversion, every soldier would receive

24 livres, and a sergeant twice that amount. Officers were offered an annual pension of 200 livres for a lieutenant and 300–600 livres for a captain, depending on seniority.

Louvois was disappointed with the results of these efforts. Huguenot soldiers and officers left the royal service in considerable numbers, many enlisting in foreign armies which, in 1688, would take the field against France. Ambassadors had little success in persuading émigrés to return, and even more families departed. By skilful counselling, the minister prompted Louis to exempt German and Swiss Protestant soldiers from the religious restrictions, and they continued to serve in their crack regiments, but a further concession in 1686, which permitted foreign Protestant merchants to trade freely within France, was not well received and the effect on international commerce remained crippling. In one crucial way, Louvois himself was thought to have failed in his duty. He had devoted his early ministry to reinforcing the frontiers of France, and yet, if they now seemed effective for excluding enemy armies, they had proved inadequate for keeping Huguenots within the realm. It had never been the intention of Louis XIV that there should be a mass exodus of Protestants, and yet it had happened.

Before and after the Revocation, Louvois had continually urged the king to be critical of the new wave of conversions, warning him that many were converts only in name and many more were the invention of officials who wished to curry favour with their sovereign. If few had chosen, or dared, to voice similar reservations before 1685, in 1686 such feelings were widely held and openly stated. The courtly and clerical euphoria quickly gave way to doubt and alarm. It was not just the flight of soldiers, weapon-makers, craftsmen and traders into other countries. Nor that the Revocation further soured relations with Rome, where Innocent XI saw it not as a desirable crusade against heresy but as one more example of arrogant gallicanism on the part of Louis XIV. The real fear was that within France there were still many overt Huguenots, and many more who had converted insincerely and were awaiting their opportunity to resume their old faith, and even to take revenge on their persecutor. As war drew near in 1688, and as England acquired a Protestant king, there were many French officials who feared that these religious dissidents might become a fifth column within the kingdom.

The Revocation only increased the despair already felt by many French bureaucrats that the crown was issuing numerous regulations which simply could not be enforced and were therefore bringing discredit on the royal administration as a whole. After 1685, there were more and more examples of disobedience by provincial officials, who preferred to calm their areas rather than inflame them further. Many bishops openly admitted that forced conversions had been a major mistake, and renewed their call for a reform of the Catholic church as a prelude to a new campaign of persuading Protestants to abjure. One close confidant of the king, the duc de Noailles, has left considerable evidence about the policy of religious repression in Languedoc, the province where he was the governor. He pressed his clerical friends to reform the church with all speed, and to use only the mildest tests as proof of conversion from Protestantism. He made a spectacular gesture of obedience to the king by destroying the temple at Montpellier, but was much less ardent in pursuing the Huguenot faithful. Although claiming that he was using every possible means at his disposal, he had to explain to Versailles that the difficult terrain of the Cévennes into which they had retreated had defeated him, because they commanded the vantage points over narrow defiles and made troop movements impossible. To his friends he confided that he had been quite successful in establishing some respect for royal authority in the Cévenol villages, and had no intention of throwing away this advantage through the implementation of a religious policy of which he disapproved. This did not mean, of course, that there was no further persecution in Languedoc, because the *parlement* of Toulouse and many members of the provincial Estates remained implacable opponents of heterodoxy.

All that this chapter seeks to argue, therefore, is that many ministers and senior royal officials during the personal rule of Louis XIV were either unconcerned about the Huguenots until the mid-1670s, or positively valued them as citizens. When tensions began to be reported in the provinces, and when the king and the clergy became fervent advocates of forced conversion after the year 1679, these civil administrators tried to mitigate the worst effects of a policy which they could not change. The results of the Revocation of the Edict of Nantes were not only as bad, but even worse, than they had feared.

13 Patterns in the Study of Huguenot Refugees in Britain: Past, Present and Future

Robin D. Gwynn

Now glory to the Lord of Hosts, from whom all glories are!
And glory to our Sovereign Liege, King Henry of Navarre!
Now let there be the merry sound of music and of dance,
Through thy corn-fields green and sunny vines, oh pleasant land of
France!
And thou, Rochelle, our own Rochelle, proud city of the waters,
Again let rapture light the eyes of all thy mourning daughters.
As thou wert constant in our ills, be joyous in our joy,
For cold and stiff, and still are they who wrought thy walls annoy.
Hurrah! Hurrah! a single field hath turned the chance of war,
Hurrah! Hurrah! for Ivry, and Henry of Navarre.

There are not many modern historians of England who are also poets, but amongst the select few who share the skills of both it is difficult to believe that any would feel inclined to write a narrative poem about the battle of Ivry in 1590, a battle some 35 miles from Paris in which Henry of Navarre defeated the forces of the Catholic League. Yet that is what no less an historian than Lord Macaulay did in the nineteenth century. His awareness of the history of the Huguenots was much greater than that of most of his modern British professional successors, and when he came to write his *History of England from the Accession of James the Second* he thought it worthwhile to include a good deal about the impact of refugees from Louis XIV's France.[1]

It might seem curious, then, that Macaulay's great French contemporary Jules Michelet chose to reproach him precisely on the score of *neglecting* the Huguenots. In 1860, he expressed amazement that Macaulay should have seen fit to leave unremarked the role of the Huguenots in the army with which William III invaded England:

Surely great England, with all her glories, her lineage of ancient liberties, will acknowledge handsomely the part played by us French in her deliverance. In his homeric account of William's companions, the historian includes everyone: English, Germans, Dutch, Swedes, Swiss, with picturesque details about weapons and uniforms, down to 300 negroes in turbans with white plumes in the trains of rich Englishmen and Dutchmen. He doesn't see our men. Evidently our expatriates paid little honour to William by their costume. A number, no doubt, wore the clothing in which they had taken refuge, dusty, shabby, tattered.[2]

As a result of the writings of people of the calibre of Macaulay and Michelet, still more as a result of the enormous popularity of those of Samuel Smiles, no Victorian historian of the later Stuart and early Georgian period could have ignored the contribution made by the Huguenot refugees. That does not seem unreasonable, for amongst the remarkable mixture of different inheritances that go to make up an 'Englishman', the Huguenots have a special place. There were many of them; some 40–50 000 from Louis XIV's France alone,[3] with others who had come over the previous century, and more dribbling across the Channel for much of the eighteenth century – a far larger number than any other group of peaceful immigrants before the reign of Queen Victoria. Their impact on silk-weaving, furniture, silversmithing and the economy has been discussed in previous chapters. But there has not been space to look at their influence in many other spheres: in the arts (Gosset, Le Marchand, Mercier, Roubiliac); in skilled crafts like watch-making and gun-making (Amyot, de Bauffre, Gorgo, Monlong); in banking and insurance (Houblon, Janssen, Bosanquet, Minet); in the theatre (Garrick); in the Anglican, Methodist and Unitarian churches (Allix, Dubourdieu, Perronet, Martineau); in law (Romilly, Maseres, Sylvestre); in paper-making (Fourdrinier, Portal); in medicine and science (Chamberlen; Dollond; Six); in the army (Schomberg, Galway, Ligonier), and so on. Nor have we heard about their effect on the development in England of Friendly Societies, poor relief, cooking, freemasonry or flower shows. To have attempted to cover all these fields in a single book would manifestly have been impossible. But clearly the refugees in Britain are worth study, and not merely because they are the outstanding example in this country's history of the successful integration of a large immigrant minority.

The encouragement of such study is one major reason why the Huguenot Society of London was founded, in 1885. Curiously, however, its foundation marked a peak of awareness of the Huguenots' contribution, rather than the discovery of new horizons anticipated by the Society's founding fathers. For people in Britain today are less aware (perhaps one should say, *were* less aware before the comme- morations that marked 1985, the tercentenary year) of who the Huguenots were, than at any time since the reign of the first Queen Elizabeth. Experience gained from addressing over forty groups around the country[4] during 1985 suggests that this is especially true of the young. People educated before the Second World War normally do know what is meant by 'Huguenot', and at least something about why some Huguenots came to England as refugees and what they did here. By and large this is not true of those educated since 1945; indeed, people in the younger age groups to whom the word means anything normally think solely of the French context, and tend to be unaware that there was ever any Huguenot presence in the British Isles. This prompts questions about the way changing perceptions develop. The purpose of this chapter is to investigate how the Huguenots in Britain have been viewed since the time of the later Stuarts, to account for the widespread ignorance about them that has existed of late, and to explore prospects for Huguenot studies in the future.

*   *   *

The arrival of so many refugees in the sixteenth and seventeenth centuries could hardly escape the notice of Englishmen. They were the subject of sympathy, sometimes of opposition, but in any case of frequent and often heated discussion. Especially in the 1680s – a crucial decade, because it saw the removal of the Roman Catholic James II and the 'Glorious Revolution' – their sufferings and plight were considered in a stream of pamphlets and recounted in innumer- able newsletters.[5] Their presence was a significant aspect of ordinary British life, especially in the south and east of England where most of them settled, and contemporary historians like Gilbert Burnet or White Kennett treated them accordingly. Nor could they be forgotten in the eighteenth century, when (in reference particularly to the success of many London merchants of Huguenot extraction) it became a popular saying that a drop of Huguenot blood in the veins was worth £1000 a year. The most obvious tendency that can be detected in eighteenth-century writings about the Huguenots is the exaggeration of their numbers, partly perhaps in reaction to their prominence in national commercial life, partly the inevitable result of intermarriage which increased the number of those who claimed Huguenot descent through either the male or the female line. The highest estimate was proffered in a letter written by Jacob Bourdillon in 1785, asserting that some 150 000 refugees came to Britain after the Revocation.[6]

By the time of the Napoleonic wars, the Huguenots had been virtually completely integrated into British society, and government expenditure on their relief was drawing to a close. That is, they were becoming an historical rather than a present consideration. Accordingly, in the nineteenth century attention was paid to their history, the ground being prepared by John Southerden Burn, who rescued many of the registers of the French churches. His work was developed subsequently by Samuel Smiles of *Self-Help* fame, whose book, *The Huguenots: Their Settlements, Churches, and Industries in England and Ireland* went through repeated editions after its initial publication in London in 1867; by D. C. A. Agnew with his more antiquarian *Protestant Exiles from France*, first published in 1866; and by Reginald Lane Poole with his *History of the Huguenots of the Dispersion at the Recall of the Edict of Nantes* (London, 1880). These authors prepared the way for the foundation of the Huguenot Society of London in 1885. Interest in the Huguenots was capped, in scholarly terms, by the appearance in Paris in the last decade of the century of a magisterial three-volume history of the French churches in England before the Revocation, by Baron de Schickler. At the same time there was published a remarkable collection of primary source material, the archives of the Dutch Church of London, edited by J. H. Hessels, of value for the history of the French as well as Dutch Protestant communities.[7]

So, it might be thought, the stage had been set for an expansion of historical scholarship in the twentieth century. After all, with the growth of university postgraduate studies there have been far more professional historians at work than in the Victorian era. And after a hundred years of its existence the Huguenot Society is into its twenty-fourth volume of *Proceedings* which include many useful articles, and has produced no fewer than fifty-seven Quarto Series publications, so that printed editions of all known French church registers (and much else besides) have been available for the past thirty years.

Yet in fact, outside the pages of the *Proceedings* there has been almost a void in historical writing on the Huguenots in Britain since the days of Schickler, even though his terminal date of 1685 was an open invitation for the period after the Revocation to be reviewed in similar depth. If one excludes a first-class study of the Huguenots in Canterbury, produced in the Huguenot Society Quarto Series in 1898, my *Huguenot Heritage* published in 1985 is the first book-length engagement with the history of the Huguenots in Britain to have appeared in English for a century. How is such a void to be explained? The answer has to be sought on several different levels: in the problems inherent in pursuing the subject; in the very existence of the Society itself; and in the changing interests and values of the modern world.

There is indeed a number of problems confronting those wanting to work on the Huguenots. One of the most obvious is the requirement for a working knowledge of French, and – while it says little for the British educational system – some would-be researchers have undoubtedly been deterred because they have felt their French to be inadequate. Another is getting access to relevant records, especially those concerning what was by far the largest foreign community, in the capital. The French Church of London now in Soho Square possesses a remarkable set of archives going back to the 1560s, but it remains a working church and the archives are in its Consistory room, and so not readily available. The Library of the Huguenot Society and French Protestant Hospital is lodged in University College, London, but the Society lacks full-time staff, and the library is intended solely for the use of Fellows of the Society – though in practice serious academics will not normally encounter difficulty in obtaining access. Such problems are real, but they scarcely account for the neglect that has been the Huguenots' lot for so many years. As far as I am aware, no one who has attempted to use these archives has finally failed to do so; and, in Mr Charles Marmoy and Miss Irene Scouloudi, the Society has for the last quarter century been served by an Honorary Librarian and an Honorary Secretary devotedly willing to assist, as many researchers (like myself) have cause to remember with gratitude.

Until recently, there were substantial problems in finding out what was available. When I worked through the records of the French Church of London in the late 1960s, there was no adequate catalogue. Consequently it was necessary to start with the first manuscript on the upper shelf in the cupboard in one corner of the room, and work round until the last bottom shelf in the far corner had been reached. The process was exceedingly time-consuming, although it had the advantage of teaching a great deal about the church, how it operated, and what mattered to its officers. The manuscript records of the Huguenot

Library were likewise then not adequately listed. But over the past sixteen years, three substantial printed handlists have appeared in the Society's Quarto Series, one covering the records of the French Church of London (vol. L), the other two those of the Huguenot Library (vol. LI, LVI). So this problem no longer exists; and, again, it cannot really be held responsible for the lack of interest shown in the Huguenot refugees. Material in most of the other important collections – in the British Museum, for instance, or the Bodleian Library, the Canterbury Cathedral archives or the Public Record Office – has long been readily accessible in the ordinary way.

Inevitably, specific problems exist that have to do with the loss of records over time. Huguenot settlements in Devon were substantial – some 3000 refugees may have gone there – but little is known about them;[8] here the loss of Bishop Lamplugh's papers and many church registers is particularly serious. One wishes there were more original memoirs to set alongside those by Jacques Fontaine, Dumont de Bostaquet and others that have survived. Some have disappeared from view even over the past century; where are all the sources known and used by Smiles? How much more would we know about the small but old-established community at Southampton if we had the original minute book of the church there covering the period of the sixteenth and seventeenth centuries! And the historian and genealogist can only join in bemoaning the fact that the Huguenots did not keep burial registers with the same care with which they maintained baptismal and marriage records, which would have allowed the profitable technique of family reconstitution to be used with illuminating effect.

Next, there is the usual historians' problem that it is times of conflict that generate most records, but the resulting picture may be far from typical. If one looks at the French Church of Southampton in the eighteenth century, for instance, the remarkably long pastorate of Isaac Jean Barnouin (1736–97) with its decades of peaceful, caring ministry, is overwhelmed in terms of records by the debates caused by the difficult personality of St Denis (1719–23).[9] However, like the existence of gaps in the records ideally required for a study, this problem is not peculiar to the sources available for the Huguenots; to counter such difficulties is an inescapable part of the historian's craft.

The same observation can be made with reference to the more subtle problem of finding the right balance between the priorities of the Huguenots themselves and the interests of modern historians, but this is worth a little reflection. It was religion which motivated most Huguenots who settled outside France to leave their home country.

Most, but not all; amongst them were some whose commercial needs called them from France or whose special skills meant that they were in international demand. It was, unquestionably, easier for Huguenots who already had overseas links to make the decision to move than for those who did not. Isaac Minet, for example, who left Calais in 1686 and settled in Dover, had previously been sent to Dover as a young teenager for some twenty-one months, to learn the English language and something of English commercial practice.[10] The sculptor Roubiliac may have been a Huguenot, but it would be stretching a point to call him a refugee. It is still more true of those reaching Elizabethan England that their motivation was mixed. The returns of aliens for London for 1573, the year after the Massacre of St Bartholomew, suggest that many members of the foreign Protestant churches of London had come 'not for religion, as by their owne confession dothe appeare' but 'to seeke lyvinge'.[11] Even with these reservations in mind, though, it is safe to say that most Huguenots reaching England between the sixteenth and eighteenth centuries were religious refugees. This is particularly true of those leaving Louis XIV's France. Isaac Minet may have had the advantage of knowing English when the Revocation and the *dragonnades* turned his world upside down, but without his religious belief he would have lived and died at Calais, not in Dover.

The point is obvious, but it has to be made. It tends to be obscured by the fact that the more prominent Huguenots are precisely those whose religious motivation is least apparent; attention is naturally concentrated on the wealth of a Janssen or a Seignoret or the skills of a Harache or an Oliver, rather than on their beliefs. More importantly, the secular interests of many modern historians lead them to ignore or distrust religious motivation. Writing in the *Guardian* earlier this year and remarking that the past does not have to be boring unless we want it to be, Christopher Driver continued 'This now applies with especial force to the history of religion. We have a deep need to find it boring, because most of us are no longer interested in making it.'[12] There is a truth here to which we shall return. For the moment we need only note that the balance between the priorities of modern historians and of their Huguenot subjects is not easy to strike.

After reciting these obstacles to research, it seems strange to turn to the existence of the Huguenot Society of London, a Society which has devoted itself with great effect to publishing information on the Huguenots in Britain. Nevertheless, it has to be said that in some ways the very existence of the Society has restricted the scholarship it has tried to encourage. It is not that the Society failed to live up to its intentions; on the contrary, as its numerous volumes of *Proceedings* and Quarto Series publication bear witness, it has been consistently active. Rather it is as though the existence of the Society has allowed professional historians to divorce themselves from the subject, to assume that it can be left to a special interest group. It will be seen from Figure 13.1 that published works on the Huguenots in England, other than those in the Huguenot Society Quarto Series, ceased rather than blossomed after the Society's foundation. That would not have mattered had all county or university libraries subscribed to the Society's publications, nor if historians had joined the Society in large numbers. But neither of these things happened. Even today, there are astonishing gaps in the Society's list of subscribing libraries, and – just to draw examples from areas of dense Huguenot settlement – the list shows no Devon library subscribing before 1952, no Kent library before 1978, no Norfolk or Suffolk library subscribing at all. Perhaps the misleading suggestion implicit in the Society's name, that its interests are primarily to do with London, has been partly responsible. As for individual historians, they have tended – wrongly – to believe that the Society exists exclusively for descendants of the Huguenots. It does not; there is no need to be of Huguenot descent to join or hold office in the Society, or neither Miss Scouloudi nor I would be here today. But a widespread belief that it *is* necessary has increased the isolation of the Society (and its publications) from the attention of historians who have not been members.

The paradox then, is, that in 1884 the Huguenot Society of London did not exist, yet awareness of the Huguenots was high. A century later, despite all the Society's endeavours, awareness was lower than it had ever been. The results are plain to see in the general historical writing of the twentieth century. The contribution and assimilation of England's first 'refugiés', indeed their very existence, has ceased to interest historians concerned with the mainstream of English history. Over the past fifty years, neglect has reached the point of distortion. It is astonishing that scholars of the calibre of Professors J. P. Kenyon or J. R. Jones can refer to the arrival of the Huguenots in the later Stuart period, if at all, virtually solely in terms of growing English hatred of foreigners.[13] Only when refugee influence has been inescapable within a confined subject area like the 'financial revolution' have historians seriously confronted the subject.[14] Consequently a survey like the recent Oxford Children's History (1983) can find no place even to mention the Huguenot refugees in its two volumes and 700 pages.

Figure 13.1 British interest in the Huguenots: a visual impression

~ ~	(Premier of Meyerbeer's *Les Huguenots* in Paris 1836.)	1836-40
~ □		1841-5
		1846-50
~ BURN □ □ □	Millais's *The Huguenot*	
~ ~ ~ ~ □ □ □ □ □	exhibited at the Royal Academy 1852.	1851-5
~ □ □ □	Millais's *The Huguenot* engraved 1856.	1856-60
~ ~ ~ □ □ □ □ □		1861-5
~ ~ ~ AGNEW (1st edn): SMILES (1st, 2nd, 3rd and 4th edns) □ □ □ □		1866-70
~ ~ ~ AGNEW (2nd edn) □ □ □ □ □		1871-5
~ ~ ~ SMILES (Two 'new' edns): POOLE □ □ □ □ □		1876-80
~ ~ KERSHAW □ □ □ □	Foundation of Huguenot Society of London 1885.	1881-5
~ ~ AGNEW (3rd edn): SMILES ('6th' edn) □ □ □ □ □		1886-90
~ ~ ~ ~ ~ ~ ~ (SCHICKLER) □ □ □ □ □		1891-5
~ ~ ~ ~ ~ ~ ~ ~ ~ ~ ~ □ □ □ □		1896-1900
~ ~ ~ ~ ~ ~ □ □		1901-5
~ ~ ~ ~ ~ □ □ □		1906-10
~ □ □		1911-15
		1916-20
~ ~		1921-5
□		1926-30
		1931-5
		1936-40
		1941-5
		1946-50
~ ~ ~ ~		1951-5
		1956-60
~		1961-5
~		1966-70
		1971-5
		1976-80
GWYNN: (COTTRET) HUGUENOT HERITAGE: *The Quiet Conquest* and over 20 other displays and exhibitions related to the Huguenots 1985.		1981-5

Key: ~ Each symbol represents the first edition in English of a work of historical fiction based on Huguenot themes
□ Each symbol represents a year in which Meyerbeer's opera *Les Huguenots* was performed at Covent Garden

If the Huguenots have largely disappeared from general assess-
ments of English history, it is more astonishing that they have been
neglected in many works with a regional basis. Consider three good
books by thoroughly competent historians. Perhaps W. G.
Hoskins, writing a study of *Industry, Trade and People in Exeter in 1688–1800*
published in Manchester in 1935, had the reasonable excuse that the
sources available on the several hundred refugees who went there
were poor. But what does one say when confronted by John T. Evans's
otherwise enlightening *Seventeenth-Century Norwich: Politics, Religion, and Government, 1620–1690* (Oxford, 1979)? How can it be
proper for him to ignore the aliens and their descendants in Norwich, a
city where there were both Dutch and French/Walloon communities
and where in the 1570s and 1580s the strangers had comprised about a
third of the city's population?[16] Or look at the influential work by
Peter Clark in Clark and Slack, *Crisis and Order in English Towns
1500–1700* (London, 1972). He took as models for a study of internal
migration in early modern England the Kent towns of Canterbury,
Faversham and Maidstone. The first and last of these were notable for
substantial foreign populations; but there is no discussion of the effects
this might have on English migrants' choices and movements.

An interesting feature of the chart is that it shows academic and
popular interest riding in tandem. It must be emphasised that Figure
13.1 is exactly what it is headed, a 'visual impression', and has no
claims to statistical purity. Some historical novels have almost
certainly been overlooked. But impressionistic or not, it is indicative.
The majority of teachers expect to pass on to their pupils what they
read and discussed as live issues in their youth, and this will explain
why knowledge of the Huguenots in England remains strong in those
educated in the 1920s and 1930s. Otherwise, the chart suggests, real
interest declined at around the time of the First World War. If
academic and popular awareness of the Huguenots declined simultaneously, then other reasons besides the lack of interest shown by
professional historians must have had a bearing. One, no doubt, is that
so many immigrants have reached Britain's shores during the last
century that the Huguenots have in a sense lost their distinctiveness –
although it might have been expected that this would have created
greater interest in how they came to be assimilated so successfully.
Even joining the European Economic Community had not (before
1985) promoted interest in a diaspora from France which profoundly
affected not only England but other European countries including
Ireland, the Netherlands, Switzerland and West Germany.

However, more important than either large-scale recent immigration or insularity in accounting for changing perceptions are the new attitudes, interests and values of the modern world. We have to return especially to the wave of religious disinterest that has swept the West. Of course it has not affected England alone; and interestingly, of the countries just mentioned, only for Ireland have reasonable general histories of the Huguenot refugees been produced this century before the 1980s.[17] It is very difficult to focus clearly on the Huguenots through the secular telescopes of the twentieth century. Modern western writers on Aztec civilisation, we are told, are likely to seek to penetrate 'beneath the religious cloak to the underlying material causes and issues'.[18] This is no less true for historians of seventeenth-century England. Huguenot willingness to flee rather than accept Catholicism suggests, though, that the approach is flawed: twentieth-century vision has to be partially abandoned if the actions of the refugees are to be understood. Indeed, since particular attention has been paid to the atypical minority who had extensive resources or outstanding skills, the need today may be to penetrate beneath the *secular* cloak to the underlying *religious* causes and issues. If historians took this line, they might also come to understand better the apparent foolishness of both James II, whose policies so antagonised the English nation, and William of Orange, prepared to trust the tarnished word of seven English leaders and to lead an inferior force in an invasion of England which, by strictly rational criteria, was at best a gamble of outrageous proportions and at worst, sheer folly. The fact is that both James and William believed that their paths were prepared by God himself, and acted accordingly. In other words, religious motivation mattered deeply in the 1680s.

It is a truth that we in our age recognise (if at all) with our minds rather than in our hearts. That, perhaps more than anything else, explains why the spotlight of history has avoided the Huguenots for so long. The Victorians warmed readily to the remarkable stories of escape so effectively retold by Samuel Smiles; but in our age most people simply feel bewildered by the phenomenon of so much hardship endured when it could so easily have been avoided. The essential difference lies in changing attitudes to religious commitment.

The opera *Les Huguenots* was last performed at Covent Garden in 1927. Its rendering left much to be desired. 'One badly sung aria succeeded another', a critic observed. 'Some of the soloists improved as the evening went on, though after all that is not to be wondered at, for they could hardly have been worse than they were in the first two acts'.[19] Sad, indeed, but a reason to employ better performers rather than to abandon the opera. Granted it is too long and in need of abbreviation, is Meyerbeer's work so much worse than others performed today? The true reason for its neglect seems to lie in modern attitudes to the subject-matter as much as in any inherent weaknesses in composition. Or consider a twentieth-century historical novelist tackling a refugee subject. It is much easier for him to evoke the pull of a close personal liaison or the ferocity of political persuasion than to convey why the Huguenots acted as they did. How are the novelist's readers, mostly unread in the New Testament let alone in the Psalms, to sympathise with a Huguenot subject motivated largely by the Scriptures? Michelet had the necessary insight when he contrasted the Huguenot refugees of the 1680s with those fleeing in the aftermath of the French Revolution:

> Let the Protestant but say one word, and he would keep his belongings and his homeland, would be spared terrible dangers. The émigré of 1793 sought to save his life; that of 1685, to safeguard his conscience.[20]

It is an insight all too often missing from modern English writings.

Of course, the study of ecclesiastical history has not disappeared this century. Roman Catholics, Presbyterians, Quakers and other dissenters in later Stuart England have been the subject of detailed studies, even if the Huguenot refugees have not. In consequence, they appear in the textbooks, and sixth-formers and undergraduates are likely to learn something about them. Such studies are encouraged by the fact that modern Christians of those denominations want to know something of the history of their predecessors, whereas the Huguenots created no new separate faith to endure the process of assimilation. From the point of view of historical perspective, the problem here is that the refugees were probably more numerous than the Quakers, perhaps not very much less numerous than the Catholics,[21] and considerably more important than either for England's survival in the difficult years around 1700.

The number of people attending this Huguenot Society's Conference and those in France, Germany, Ireland, the Netherlands and North America in 1985 suggests that scholarly interest in the Huguenots is at last reviving, just as the numbers attending lectures and exhibitions would indicate that popular interest has been somnolent rather than dead. There are many avenues for research which could profitably be explored if indeed the will and manpower are available. What is important is that any effort be well-directed. In the past some university students interested in writing M.A. theses have been offered subjects impossibly broad in such a complex field, subjects like 'The Huguenots in Britain 1560–1760'. Not surprisingly, such unreasonable projects do not get completed. It is to be hoped that the numerous works and articles which appeared in 1985 will ensure that there will be no repetition of such folly.

There are plenty of interesting subjects awaiting investigation. There has, for instance, been no detailed historical and sociological study of the assimilation of the refugees and their descendants into English society during the eighteenth century, other than one by Dr Ronald Mayo of the Huguenots in Bristol;[22] but sufficient material for such studies must exist in other areas, such as the east or west London suburbs. Refugee poor relief could profitably be contrasted with its English counterpart in Elizabethan and Stuart Canterbury, London and Norwich.[23] The Huguenots of the 1680s have been strangely neglected in relation to the growth of Friendly Societies in England; in terms of the development of organised state charity on a national level; and in their contribution to the armed forces of William and Anne fighting against Louis XIV. Their relationship with the descendants of earlier, mostly Walloon, refugees would make a most interesting study in relation to a number of ventures which in the war years at the close of the seventeenth century required both skills and capital: papermaking in Hampshire, silk-weaving in Canterbury and Spitalfields, and funds and stocks in the City. The impact of the refugees in England could add a new strand to the debate on religion and the rise of capitalism – especially in the light of H. R. Trevor-Roper's contribution to that debate in *Religion, the Reformation and Social Change* in 1967. Finally, hardly any work has been done on the changing religious inclinations of the refugees and their descendants in the eighteenth century. How much did they contribute to early Methodism or to the Presbyterian church in England? Was there any tendency for the children or grandchildren of refugees to move away from the non-conformity which the majority of their ancestors preferred, and to become Anglicans?

These suggestions are far from exhausting the fields that deserve exploration. No mention has been made of comparative studies involving other immigrant groups, for instance, or of examination of the connections maintained by refugees with their families in France or dispersed elsewhere in Europe. Yet there clearly exists scope for work on the relations and links between the French communities in England

and their hosts. It will be noticed that most of the suggestions apply to the second main wave of Huguenot immigration rather than the first, to the refugees from Louis XIV's France rather than those arriving in later Tudor England. This is because it is the more numerous (and more strictly Huguenot) refugees of the late seventeenth century who have suffered far greater neglect. For the sixteenth-century period, the heavyweight Victorian scholarship of Baron de Schickler and J. H. Hessels provides a firm and certain base. There is no equivalent for the later period; nor is there any equivalent to the Returns of Aliens so insistently demanded by the late Tudor and early Stuart authorities. In the last few years attention to the earlier refugees has been renewed from a variety of perspectives, in Patrick Collinson, *Archbishop Grindal, 1519–1583* (London, 1979); Bernard Cottret, *Terre d'Exil* (Paris, 1985); Philippe Denis's Liège University thesis (1973–4) '*Les Eglises d'étrangers à Londres jusqu'à la mort de Calvin*'; Beate Magen, *Die Wallonengemeinde in Canterbury von ihrer Gründung bis zum Jahre 1635* (Berne and Frankfurt/Mainz, 1973); Andrew Pettegree's Oxford D.Phil. thesis (1983) '*The Strangers and their Churches in London, 1550–1580*'; and Joan Thirsk, *Economic Policy and Projects* (Oxford, 1978). As far as knowledge in France about the situation of refugees in England is concerned, the situation is now most curious. While two books in French – by Schickler and Cottret – have examined the situation in the sixteenth and seventeenth centuries, they both stop short precisely at the point when most refugees went to England. Consequently the impression from this side of the Channel is that many French scholars appear unaware that, after the Netherlands, Britain was the most important centre of refuge around the time of the Revocation;[24] and they are more likely to talk of Germany or Switzerland than of England as a home for the Huguenots. This underlines the need for England to be actively involved in the European-wide project recently mounted to computerise information about the refugees.

In the search for answers to some of the interesting questions about the Huguenots in England, it would be helpful to have certain information and records more readily available. The regional records of quarter sessions for 1709–11 need to be thoroughly searched, to supplement the records of denization and naturalisation already published.[25] An analysis of the leadership of the French Protestant community in England, taking as its core all known church officers, lay elders and deacons as well as ministers, would be valuable.[26] A focus on lay church officers would cover a high percentage of families important in society or the economy; of merchants mentioned in Dr Roseveare's paper, for instance, members of the families of Coulon, David, Lethieullier, Marescoe, Reneu and Trinquand were officers of the French Church of Threadneedle Street in the late seventeenth century. Above all, two important sources remain hard of access: the minutes of the French church consistories, and the 'Royal Bounty' papers.

The Bounty records offer information about assistance to the refugees, the Consistory minutes about matters of church organisation and discipline. Both give further information about individuals not available in published church registers: for example, the fact that Abel Boyer was assisted from Bounty funds as a *proposant* or trainee minister in 1690,[27] or the long service given as an elder by the watchmaker David Bouquet to the French Church of London.[28] If Consistory minutes and associated records are investigated, we can say of him that he served once as deacon and at least three times as elder, that he was often employed on deputations to public figures, that he held doctrinal views, and that he was considered to have particularly strong links with powerful Englishmen – he was consulted at a moment of crisis in 1702 because he had 'a very great acquaintance with many Lords and Commons and ... was capable and no doubt willing to do his best to preserve the liberties and priviledges [*sic*] of the Dutch and French Churches'.[29] Such information can help to fill out the picture of his economic activities.

Information about individuals of lesser significance is helpful in a context wider than family history alone because it enables the process of assimilation to be plotted more accurately. Attention to the Bounty papers would emphasise the poverty of so many refugees, setting straight the record distorted by inevitable attention to the wealthy and successful minority. As for the consistory minutes, the information within them could be used in a number of unexpected directions. The changing geographical limits of the administrative divisions or *quartiers* of the French Church of London in the seventeenth century, for example, offer a new means of charting the growth of the metropolis. At present only the minutes of the London church in the 1560s and 1570s and those for Southampton 1702–1939 are available in print. The great bulk of what remains untouched concerns the French Church of London at Threadneedle Street. By far the largest foreign congregation in England from the mid-seventeenth century onwards, it was the single most important magnet in England for refugees, setting the tone for all the French non-conformist churches in the country and keeping a watching brief on their interests. Its records are massive, a fitting target for the second century of the Huguenot Society's endeavours as the various French church registers were for the first. The entries in the minutes for the years immediately after the Revocation are of especial interest, for they include hundreds of *reconnaissances* or professions of faith made by new arrivals. These fell into the category of consistory business as a matter of church discipline because the refugees in question had been unable to bring the usual *témoignages* from their old churches in France, which had, of course, been demolished. For researchers, the result is that here is an untouched source which would provide the date of arrival of many refugees, waiting to be set alongside the valuable *témoignages* recorded by the church which have already been published.

Perhaps I may be allowed to end on a personal note. For over a year now, I have been freed from my usual duties in my New Zealand university to act as Director of *Huguenot Heritage* in Britain – the activities arranged to commemorate the tercentenary of the Revocation of the Edict of Nantes. This chapter arose from the number of times I have had to explain what someone from New Zealand should be doing in this capacity, especially someone with a Welsh name and of 'Anglo'-Irish, not Huguenot descent. The short answer is that there has long been a sad lack of academics in this country working on the Huguenots in Britain. There was a phrase used at the Dublin Colloquium earlier in 1985, not once but several times: 'Huguenot History'. I am not particularly interested in 'Huguenot History' *per se*, but I am very interested indeed in the history of the Huguenots as part of English history, or Irish history, or European history. It is significant, and it has been overlooked. The scope of the many exhibitions and displays that were held in 1985, the Museum of London catalogue for *The Quiet Conquest* and the papers delivered to this conference show that this is no mere 'fringe' interest but a subject of unusual challenge and breadth. The process of reappraising and reintegrating the Huguenot refugees into the mainstream of British history may already have begun with Barry Coward's textbook *The Stuart Age* (London, 1980). It is very much to be hoped that it will gather momentum, now that the tercentenary has been passed.

Notes

1. Illustrated edition; (ed.) C. H. Firth 6 vols. (London, 1913–15) vol. II, pp. 675–81, 732–4, 868; vol. III, pp. 1074–7, 1084; vol. IV, pp. 1678–80, 1690, 1875, 1880–1.
2. J. Michelet, *Louis XIV et la Révocation de l'Edit de Nantes* (Paris, 1860) pp. 418–19. Translation by the present writer.
3. R. Gwynn, 'The Number of Huguenot Immigrants in England in the Late Seventeenth Century', *Journal of Historical Geography*, vol. 9 no. 4 (1983) pp. 384–95.
4. Widely spread geographically, from Jersey to Sunderland and from Exeter and Swansea to Chelmsford and Sandwich.
5. R. D. Gwynn, *Huguenot Heritage*, (London, 1985) pp. 126–7.
6. Lambeth Palace Library, Fulham Palace mss, Box 'French Protestants', papers regarding the French chapel at Hoxton.
7. Baron F. de Schickler, *Les Eglises du Refuge en Angleterre*, 3 vols, (Paris, 1892); J. H. Hessels (ed.) *Ecclesiae Londino-Batavae Archivum*, 3 vols, (vol. III in two parts), (Cambridge, 1887–97).
8. For the present state of knowledge, see an article by A. Grant and R. Gwynn, 'The Huguenots of Devon', *Transactions of the Devonshire Association for the Advancement of Science*, 117 (1985) pp. 161–94.
9. See E. Welch (ed.) *The Minute Book of the French Church at Southampton 1702–1939*, Southampton Records Series, vol. 23, (Southampton, 1979).
10. W. Minet, *Some Account of the Huguenot Family of Minet*, (London, 1892) p. 24.
11. Huguenot Society of London Quarto Series, vol. X (1902) pt 2, p. 156. It should be noted that we are not told what questions the aliens were asked, nor how their answers were evaluated. It is not easy to reconcile all the figures given; and some aliens may have chosen to emphasise their economic contribution in the belief that the government would value it more than their religious motivation.
12. C. Driver, *The Guardian*, 20 May 1985.
13. J. P. Kenyon, *The Stuarts* (London, 1958; and 1966) and *Stuart England* (London, 1978) does not think them worth mentioning at all. The most recent university textbook devoted to the period when the Huguenots came over in their greatest numbers finds no place for 'Huguenot' or 'refugee' in the index; and though they are in fact mentioned in the book, it is normally in the context of xenophobia (J. R. Jones, *Country and Court: England 1658–1714*, (London, 1978) for instance pp. 93, 306–7).
14. P. G. M. Dickson, *The Financial Revolution in England* (London, 1967); A. C. Carter, *Getting, Spending, and Investing in Early Modern Times* (Assen, 1975).
15. Each 'historical novel' symbol represents the first edition in English or English translation of a work of historical fiction based on Huguenot themes, as recorded by C. F. A. Marmoy, 'The Historical Novel and the Huguenots', *Proceedings of the Huguenot Society of London* (1978) vol. XXIII, pp. 69–78, or in notes kindly loaned by Mr Marmoy. The lack of

entries for the 1930s may reflect only the lack of any suitable available guide (p. 76). Each 'opera' symbol represents a year in which Meyerbeer's *Les Huguenots* was performed at Covent Garden, as recorded in H. Rosenthal, *Two Centuries of Opera at Covent Garden* (London, 1958) appendix II. As far as books are concerned, the Huguenot Society of London Quarto Series publications have not been included: those by Moens (1885–6), Cross (1898) and Gwynn (1979) have significant historical commentaries as well as documents. Also omitted are three works not directly on the Huguenot refugees in England, but which might have been expected to encourage interest in them: W. Cunningham, *Alien Immigrants to England* (London, 1897); G. L. Lee, *The Huguenot Settlements in Ireland* (London, 1936); and W. C. Scoville, *The Persecution of Huguenots and French Economic Development 1680–1720* (Berkeley and Los Angeles, 1960). Books not previously mentioned in this paper which are shown on the chart are J. S. Burn, *The History of the French, Walloon, Dutch and other Foreign Protestant Refugees settled in England* (London, 1846); S. W. Kershaw, *Protestants from France, in their English Home* (London, 1885); B. Cottret, *Terre d'Exil: l'Angleterre et ses réfugiés ... 1550–1700* (Paris, 1985).

16. Gwynn, *Huguenot Heritage*, p. 30; W. J. C. Moens, *The Walloons and their Church at Norwich*, Huguenot Society of London Quarto Series (1887–8) vol. I, pp. 34, 36, 44–5; *Proceedings of the Huguenot Society of London*, (1984) vol. XXIV, p. 132.

17. Lee, *Huguenot Settlements in Ireland*; Albert Carré, *L'Influence des Huguenots Français en Irlande aux XVIIe et XVIIIe Siècles* (Paris, 1937). However, even for Ireland modern general histories pay little attention to the Huguenots other than in connection with the battle of the Boyne. Across the Atlantic, there is a similar void between C. W. Baird, *History of the Huguenot Emigration to America* (New York, 1885) and J. Butler, *The Huguenots in America* (Harvard, 1984).

18. *Past and Present* (1985) no. 107 p. 61.

19. Rosenthal, *Two Centuries of Opera*, p. 450.

20. Michelet, *Louis XIV et la Révocation*, p. 351.

21. It has been authoritatively suggested that there were about 60000 Roman Catholics, although older estimates are much higher; J. Miller, *Popery and Politics in England 1660–1688*, (Cambridge, 1973) pp. 11–12.

22. R. Mayo, 'Les Huguenots à Bristol 1681–1791', unpublished Lille University doctoral thesis, 1966. See also R. Mayo, *The Huguenots in Bristol*, pamphlet 61, published 1985 by the Bristol Branch of the Historical Association.

23. J. Campbell made a start with Caroline Canterbury in his unpublished Wisconsin University Ph.D. thesis (1970), *The Walloon Community in Canterbury, 1625–1649*.

24. For example, P. Joutard, 'The Revocation of the Edict of Nantes: End or Renewal of French Protestantism', in Menna Prestwich (ed.) *International Calvinism 1541–1715* (Oxford, 1985) p. 354, claims that twenty-six new churches were founded in England as a result of Louis

XIV's persecution. Where was this figure obtained? In 1680 there were two French churches in the area of modern Greater London; by 1700 there were at least twenty-eight. That makes twenty-six new churches in London alone, and there were another fourteen in the country, so the total should be not less than forty. The difference is the more significant in that Joutard goes on to argue that the figure of twenty-six new churches, while not negligible, 'is ten less than that of churches founded in Holland, which logically presupposes a markedly smaller number of refugees'.

25. In the Huguenot Society of London Quarto Series volumes VIII, XVIII, XXVII and XXXV. Between the passing of the General Naturalisation Act of 1709 (7 Anne, cap. 5) and its repeal by 10 Anne, cap. 9 in 1711, any Protestant alien could obtain naturalisation simply by taking the sacrament, subscribing the oaths of allegiance and supremacy and making a declaration. For the extent and limitations of the lists currently in print, see Huguenot Society of London Quarto Series, vol. XVIII p. xi; vol. XXVII pp. 72–3; and vol. XXXV p. 11.

26. A beginning has been made in appendix 1B of R. D. Gwynn, *The Ecclesiastical Organization of French Protestants in England in the Later Seventeenth Century, with Special Reference to London*, unpublished London University Ph.D. thesis (1976).

27. Huguenot Library, University College, London, Bounty ms.6, 8 October 1690.

28. Ms.5 of the library of the French Church of London, now in Soho Square, shows that Bouquet served as an elder 1637–40, 1644–7, 1653–6 and 1659–62, and died in 1665.

29. R. D. Gwynn, *Ecclesiastical Organization*, p. 444.

Index

Page references in *italics* indicate Figures; those in **bold** type Tables.

Académie Française 190–1
Académie Royale de Peinture 189–90
Addison, Joseph 27
adultery 84
Agace, Obadiah 138n.–17
Agace, Zachariah 128, 135
agate 95
aggravation of strangers 67
Agnew, Rev.D.C.A. xvi, 220
Alais, Grace of (Peace of Alès) 167, 175–6
Alençon, Synod of 185
Alès, Peace of (Grace of Alais) 167, 175–6
Allard 116, 121
Allix, Pastor 149
altar-plate 97
Althorp 100
Amiens 203
Amsterdam 84, 127
Amyraut, Moïse 186–9, 190–2
Ancaster, Earl of 100
Andrewes, Bishop Lancelot 146
Androuet de Cerceau, Jean 188
Anduze 183
anglicisation of names 58, 67–8, 74
Anglo-Dutch Wars 74, 75
Anne, Queen 11–12, 100
anti-alien feelings 91, 136
Antwerp 75, 90, 93, 94
Antwerp, John of 90–1
apostolic succession 149
apothecaries 26–7, 47
apprenticeships 49–51, 54n.38, 90, 103
Archambo, Peter 108
architects 116, 188
Arighi, Domenico 99
armchair 118
Arminius 187
Arnaud, Peter 128
artists 189
Aspremont-Lynden Ewer 94
assaying 92
Athlone 6
Atholl, 1st Duke of 116

Austin Friars Church 75
Austrians 8

Bache, John 102
Baker, Captain John 137n.5, 140n.34
Baltazar, intendant 183
Baltic trade 74, 77, 80, 82
Balzac, Guez de 188, 191
Bancroft, Anthony 52
banking and insurance 218
Banning, Paul 44
Barberini, Cardinal 194
Barber-Surgeons' Company 100
Barbeyrac, Jean 32
Barbut, Stephen 139n.20
Barillon, Paul 6
Barker, Cresfer 49–50
Barker, Isabell 52
Barnouin, Isaac Jean 222
baroque furniture 115, 121
Basnage, Jacques 9
Basnage de Beauval, Henri 4–5, 9, 21–2, 23
Bas Poitou 129, 135, 180
Batchelor, Ham and Perigal 134
Baudrine *alias* Poitevin, Jean 115
Baudouin, Christopher 133–4
Bayle, Pierre 3–5, 21, 25, 31–3, 145, 149, 180
Beckwith, General xvi
Beharel, Simon 61
Belchier, Jean 121
Belgium 89, 93
Beningborough Hall 116
Bentinck, Hans Willem, Earl of Portland 7, 9
Béarn 165–6; and revolt in Bohemia 170n.49
bequests 67, 77; subterfuges on 47
Berlin Academy of Sciences 28
Bernard, Jacques 21
Bernard, Samuel 189
Beuzelin, Benjamin 83
Buezelin, François 83
Beza *see* De Bèze
Bibaud family 181

Bibliothèque Anglaise 5
Bibliothèque Germanique 5
Bidé, Olivier 181
Bissell, James 68
Blair Castle 115
Blathwayt, William 116
Blenheim 113
Blois 107
Bochart, Samuel 180
Bodendick, Jacob 97
Boeve *alias* Bovey, Jaques 74
Bolbec 136
Bolingbroke, Lord 12, 14
Bolle, Francis 56
bookkeeping 76
Booth, George, Earl of Warrington 106
Booth Cup 95
Bordeaux 144
Bordelaise 208
Bosse, Abraham 185, 189
Bossuet, Bishop 3, 9
Bougeac, Jean Jaques 13n.8
Boughton 115, 119, 120–1
Boujet, Mr 118–19
boulle furniture 119–20
Bouquet, David 231
Bourdillon, Jacob 220
Bourdon, Nicholas 136
Bourdon, Sébastien 19, 194
Bowes, Sir Martin 94
Bowes Cup 93–4
Boyceau, Jacques 188
Boyer, Abel 32–5, 231
Boyne, battle of 6
Boys, John 57
Brandenburg 152
Bristol 229
British interest in Huguenots xvii, *225*, 226
British knowledge of Huguenots 219, 222, 226, 230
British Museum xvii, 222
Brittany 208
Browning, Arthur Giraud xvi
Brussels 105
Bucerus, Jacob 57
Buck, John 74
Buissière, Paul 28
Bunce, C.R. 59–60
Burlemachi, Philip 47
Burn, John Southerden 220
Burnet, Gilbert 6, 14, 28, 219

cabinet-makers 119–21
Cadiz 72

Caen 128, 177, 179–80, 191, 194
calico, campaign against 127
Calloway, John 139n.20
Calvinist International 143, 147
Calvinists 150; in France 174 (map), 175–80, 182–91, 193–4
Cameron, John 186
Campart, Peter 127, 140n.34
Canterbury 57–9, 127, 133, 136; aliens and natives in **64**; baptisms of foreign children **63**; benefits from strangers 70; Cathedral 59–60; cloth industry 69–70; French Churches 61–2, **63**, 64; Huguenot families in **131**; numbers of Walloons 62–3; *passants* 64, **65**; Politic Men 60–1, 66; poor relief 63, **64**, 66, 68; rents 67; weavers in 128–9, 130, 132; wills proved 66–7
Capuchins 180, 182, 194, 203
Carew, Sir George 176
Carlton, Charles 87n.28
Caron, Israel 67
Carte, Thomas 16
caryatid candlestands 120–1
Casbert, Jean 114
Cassel 188
Castel, Jean 89
Castres 32, 191
Catholics 3; refugees 83, 234n.21; *see also* France
Cecil, Sir Robert 47
Cévennes 183, 191, 216
Cervantes, Miguel de 26
Chambres de l'Edit 6, 192, 201
chambres mi-parties 175–6
Chamier, Daniel 184
Champaigne, Philippe de 190
Châtellerault assembly 162
Charenton 178, 184, 188–9, 191–3
charities 135
Charles I, King 96, 144–5
Charles II, King 96–8
Charles II bounty 46–7, 231
Chartier, Jean 107, 108
Chatsworth 100, 116, 119
Chaunu, P. 176
Cheveney, Peter 134, 137n.8
Christ Church 135
Christina, Queen 180, 190
Christ's Hospital 78
Church of England; attitude to Huguenots 144, 148–9; Huguenot attitude to 144–7, 150

churches, membership of foreign 45, 94
City of London 47, 48–9, 50–1, 72;
    freemen of 49, 59, 74, 98–9, 102,
    104, 106, 107, 136n.2; Orphans
    Court 81; Restrictions on
    strangers 50
civilisation, England's lack of 8
Clagny 119
Clandon Park 118
Clarendon, First Earl of 13
Claude, Monsieur 148–9
Clausen, Nicholas 105
Clement IX, Peace of 203
Cleves 10
clothes making 48–9
cloth-making 48–9, 56, 59, 68–9
Clothworkers' Company 74
Cockus, Jean-Gérard 96–7
Cocqueau, David 75
Colbert, Jean-Baptiste 178, 181–3, 189,
    199, 203–5, 208, 210–11, 213–14
Collinson, Patrick 230
commentators 22
Compagnie du Nord 182
Compagnie du Saint-Sacrement 185
Compton, Bishop Henry 149
Condé, Prince de 163–4, 192
Congrégation de Jésus et de Marie 179
Conrart, Valentin 190–1
convertisseurs 6
Conway, Secretary of State 146–8
cooking 218
Cosimo III of Tuscany 114
cottons 73
Cottret, Bernard 230
Coulon, Moses 76, 78, 83
Coulon family 231
Counter-Reformation 185
Courtauld, Augustine 108
Coventry 128
Coward, Barry 232
craftsmen 218, 223; alien, attitude
    to 96–7, 99
Crespin, Paul 108
Croft cups 105
Crommelin, Catherine 75
Cromwell, Sir Oliver 47
Cromwell, Thomas 91
culture: English 20; Huguenot
    intermediaries 21–3
Cumberland plate 101
Cuny, Louis 107

D'Ablancourt, Perrot 191
Dacre, Lord 146

Daillé, Jean 178
Dalbiac, Charles 139n.20
Dalibert, Pierre 182–3
Daliès de la Tour, Samuel 183
Dalkeith Palace 119
damask 133, 135
Dandridge, Joseph 133, 140n.32
Dangre, Christian 129
Dauphiné 184, 185
David, Isabella 84
David, Jacob 76, 78–80, 81–3, 84, 85
David, Mrs Leonora 80–2, 84
David family 231
De Bèze (Beza), Théodore 25, 187
De Bever, John 67, 68
De Bose, Pierre 179
De Bostaquet, Isaac Dumont 194–5,
    222
De Brissac, Peter Abraham 134
De Brosse, Salomon 188
De Champaigne, Henri 189
De Champaigne, Philippe de 189
Declaration of Indulgence 107
De Coninck, François 75
decorative arts 113
Dedieu, Joseph 14
defence duties 67
De Gassion, Jean 185
De Guernier, Louis 189
De Heule, Abraham 136
Deheulle family 130
De la Beque, Jean 58
De la Crose, Jean Cornand 21–3
De la Fosse, Charles 114
De Lamerie, Paul 105, 108
De Larrey, Isaac 10, 14
De Lasaux, Peter 139n.19
De Laune, Gideon 47, 50
De Laune, William 47
De l'Epine, Isaac 136
Delme, Philippe 66
Delobel, Simon 114
De Lorme, Jacques Amproux 182
De Maintenon, Madame 116
De Mauclerc, Paul-Emile 11
De Mayerne, Sir Theodore 47
De Missy, César 25, 38n.41
De Moivre, Abraham 28–31
Demoor, Jean Henri 97
Denbeck, abbé de 6
De New, James 69
Denis, Philippe 230
Denis, St 222
denization 46, 80, 93, 98, 99, 103, 107,
    129

De Retz, Cardinal 199
Derignée or Deringer, Robert 119
Dernocour, Josiah 138n.19
De Rosemond, J.B. 28
De Rue, Thomas 68
Desaguliers, Jean Theophilus 30–1
De Sales, St François 190
De Schickler, Baron 220, 230
Des Loges, Madame 178–9, 191
Desmaizeaux, Pierre 22, 31–4
Desormaux family 134
De Thou, Jacques-Auguste 25
Devon 222
Devonshire Ewer and Basin 100, 108
Deyon, Solange 176
D'Harcourt, Comte 185
Die 185–6
Dieppe 66
divorce 84
doctors 47
Dodwell, Henry 22
Dort, Synod of 187
Dover 62, 223
dragonnades 180, 213
Drayton, Northamptonshire 117–18, 120
Drelincourt, Charles 184
Driver, Christopher 223
Du Bois, John 58
Du Bose, Pierre 180, 184
Duchemin, Paul 121
Dufee, Rebekah 117
Duffour, Renée 121
Dugdale, William 43, 47
Du Maresq, Richard 156n.19
Dumont de Bostaquet, Isaac 194–5, 222
Du Moulin, Pierre 146–7, 147–8, 184, 186, 187
Du Moulin, Pierre junior 154n.13
Dunham Massey, Cheshire 106, 118–19
Du Perron, Cardinal 146
Duplessis-Mornay 186
Durand, David 14
Du Ry, Charles 188
Dutch: Almshouse 51; Church 50–1, 75, 93, 220; commercial network 75; Republic 204–6; traders 73, 83; United Provinces 96
Duthoit, Stephen 133
Duthoit family 130, 134, 138n.17.
Dyrham Park 116, 119

East India Company 78, 84; shares in 81–2

Eastland Company 75, 82
ecclesiology, Anglican 147
Edict of Nantes 96–7, 143, 158–60, 162, 163, 165, 175–6, 186, 191; irrevocability of 158–9; revocation of xvii, 99, 101, 150, 158, 177, 214–16, 232
education 135
Edward VI, King 93, 145
Elizabeth I, Queen 58, 93–4, 143
Elizabethan era 42–5
Elles family 189
employment, restrictions on 49–50
engineers 47
English attitudes 67–8, 91, 136, 219, 222
English hatred of foreigners 224
English language, Huguenot knowledge of 144
Enover, Lucas 90
episcopacy 148
Erddig 121
Eton College Collection 111n.60
Eudes, St Jean 179–80
Europe, imports 73
European Economic Community 226
Evil May Day riot 91
exports to France 80

Fagel, Francis 9
Farren, Thomas 105
Feke, Robert 134
Ferry, Paul 184
financial affairs 229
fines 49–50, 68
fire insurance 129
firescreens 121
fishing 56
Flamar, Ephraim 136n.2
Flanders 43, 181; French invasion of 204–7
Flemish craftsmen 91
flowered silk 133, 135
Fondimare, Peter 137n.2
Fontaine, Jacques 222
Fontainebleau: court school 94; Edict of 152, 214
Formey, Jean Henri Samuel 28
Formont, Nicholas 182
Formont brothers 182
Fouquet, Nicholas 182
France: Calvinists in 174 (map), 175–80, 182–91; 193–4; [conversions from Catholicism 183–4; numbers of 179; pastors criticised 184]; Catholic [Church 177, 216;

immigration 181–2; nobility 15]; English alliance with 193; exports to 80; Huguenots in 143, 160–3, 175–6, 184, 186, 187, 190, 192–3, 202, 208–9, 216 [conversion of 201, 203, 207–8, 208, 210–12, 213–16; craftsmen 97; *députation générale* 163; deputies 163–4; enlisting abroad 215; enterprise encouraged 199, 202–3; grievances of 162; harassment of 203–4, 209, 212; loyalty 200; misunderstanding of English affairs 144, 147; persecution of 205–6; radical leadership 164; rebellion 165–7; restrictions on 193, 199–200, 202–3, 209, 210–12; soldiers 206, 211, 214, 214–15; wealthy 207]; invasion of Flanders 204–7; municipal control 182; naval contracts 181; Navy, Protestant officers 211; news of England in 144; pacification edicts 160; political issues 161, 166; power in 205; Protestant foreigners invited to 202, 207–8; Protestants in 132–3, 144, 176–7, 179–84, 188–9, 192–3 [academies 185–6; emigration of 215; foreign 206–8, 211, 215; payment of pastors 161; soldiers 206; tax discrimination against 213; wealthy 181–3]; Protestants in, emigrating 211–13; Reformed Churches 143, 147–8, 148, 152, 187; tax exemption [for conversion 207, 210, 213; for large families 203]; war with Dutch Republic 204; *see also* Edict of Nantes
Franjoux, Paul 26
Franks 11
fraud by gold and silversmiths 89
Frederick, Jane 84
Frederick, Leonora 79
Frederick, Sir John 79
Frederick, Thomas 79, 80, 81, 84
Frederick the Great 5
Frederick *v.* David case 81–3
freemasonry 218
freemen *see* City of London
free trade 21
Fremoult, Samuel 139n.19
French in England: church consistories 232; churches 75, 83, 89, 93, 103, 107, 130, 136, 145, 151,

221–2, 232 [archives 43; baptisms 62–3; becoming anglican 149, 152; bequests 77; consistories 231; deacons 61; deacons, accounts 63, 64; leadership of 230–1; number of 234n.24; *reconnaissances* 232; *Témoignages* 232; *see also* Canterbury; London]; church registers 220, 222; integration into English society 151–2; misunderstand situation 145–7; pastors taking Anglican orders 148–51; Protestant 75–6, 83, 89, 91, 94, 96–7, 102, 104; weavers 127, 129
French furniture 114
French Hospital (La Providence) xxi, 221
French language 58
French silks, campaign against 127
Friendly Societies 218, 229
Frondes 192–3, 200, 210
furniture, French influence on 114, 117–21
Futchett, John 48

Galland, John 52
Gansel, Anne 84
Gansel, David 82–3
Gansel, Lieutenant-General William 84
Gant, James 139n.20
Garnier, Daniel 106
Garnier, Suzanne 107
Garrett, Captain George 140n.34
Garrett, Matthew 48
Garrisson, Janine 176
Garthwaite, Anna Maria 133–5, 137n.5, 138n.8, 140n.32
gauze-weaver 129
Geneva 147, 185–6, 189
Gentleman's Journal 24
George I, King 13
Germain, Lady Betty 105
Germain, Sir John 106, 117
Germans 8
Gibbon, Edward 5
Gibson, Bishop Edmund 14
girdle prayerbook 93
Gleane, Sir Peter 95
Gleane Cup 94–5
Gobee, Daniel 137n.5
Godiere, Peter 139n.19
Godin, James 137n.5

goldsmiths 89–90, 91–3, 93–4, 94–5, 96:
in France 212; Huguenot 98–108
Goldsmiths' Company 89–92, 94, 96,
96–100
Golle, Catherine 120
Golle, Cornelius 120
Golle *or* Gole, Pierre 119–20
Goodman, Bishop Geoffrey 154n.10
Gostling, William 130
Grand Tour 20, 186
Grave, Noe 61
Great Wardrobe 114
Gribelin, Simon 104
Grimthorpe Castle 113
Grotert, Roeloff 134
Grotius, Hugh van Groot 187, 192
Guernier, Suzanne 190
Guerrard, John 139n.19
Guibert, Philip 117
Guilbaud, John 121
Guilliband, John 113
Guillotin 117
gun-making 218
Gwynn, Nell 97
Gyllam, Anthony 48

Haase, Erich 5, 18n.1
Haddon Hall 119
hallmarks 90, 92–3, 95, 109n.5
Ham 118
Hamburg 72, 74, 75
Hamilton Palace 115, 120
Hampton Court 118–19, 121
Hand in Hand Insurance
Company 128–9
Harache, Pierre 98–102, 103
Harache, Pierre II 100
Hardwick 116
Harison, John 48
Hauduroy, Samuel 116
Heal, Ambrose 103
Heidelberg 147
Heinsius, Grand Pensionary 12
Hemard, Peter 129
Henri IV, King 143, 159–63, 164–5, 200
Henry III, King 89
Henry VIII, King 90
Hérault, Louis 145
Hervart, Barthélemy 177, 182, 190, 192
Hervey, John, Earl of Bristol 101
Hessels, J.H. 220, 230
Het Loo palace, Holland 116, 120
Hewitt, Henry 54n.38
Hinde, John 127

historians: attitude to
Huguenots 217–22, 226–7, 229;
Huguenot 4, 6, 15, 28, 33–4
historical fiction on Huguenots 225,
226, 228
historical method 12
histories of Huguenots 220–1, 229–32
Hobbema, Anne 104
Holbein the Younger, Hans 91, 93
Holland 5–6, 9, 21, 30, 35, 108, 189
Holland, Canon Francis 60
Holland, Henry 121
Holme Lacy, Herefordshire 116
Holyroodhouse 115
Hooker, Sir William 74
Hopetoun House 120–1
Hornby Castle 117
Hornenagel, William 56–7
Hoskins, W.G. 225
hospitals, bequests to 84, 135
Hotman, François 11
Houblon family 83
Houghton 117
householders 53n.27
Howzer, Wolfgang 97
Huguenot: definition of 45–6, 53n.6; as
derogatory 191; loyalty 135,
192–3; silversmiths 91; societies
abroad 228; Society xxi–xxiii, 43,
113, 218–20, 223–4, 228, 232; *see also*
France, Huguenots in
Hume, David 17
Hunter, Dr Michael 27

Ickworth 119
immigrants 72: changing religious
inclinations 229; church
membership 45; English attitude
to 91; families 48, 56–7;
naturalised 72, 74–5 [*see also*
denization; naturalisation;
naturalised immigrants]; number
of 218–20, 228; occupations 47–9,
66, 218; origins of 44–6, 58; waves
of 230; *see also* Canterbury;
London
immigration, reasons for 44, 94, 222–3,
227
imports 26–7, 73, 80, 96, 114
indulgence policy 145
informers 50–1
inheritance, law of 77; *see also*
bequests; subterfuges
Innocent XI, Pope 215

intermarriage 48, 130, 136, 202, 210, 219
Invalides, Paris 206
Ireland 11, 227
Italian church in London 45
Italians 8
Ivry, battle of 217

Jacobean plate 95
James I, King 49, 146
James II, King 6–7, 107, 114–15, 145, 227
Jansenism 199, 203
Jebb, Samuel 16
Jenkins, Thomas 107
Jensen, Gerrit 120
Jervis, Mr 140n.34
Jesuits 14, 182, 186, 194
Jeudwine, Abraham 137n.8
Jones, J.R. 224
Jordan, John 139n.20
Journal des Savants 21
journalism 21–2, 31–2, 34
Joutard. P. 234n.24
Joye, Peter 75, 76–7, 78–9, 80
Julins, Simon 134, 135
Jurieu, Pierre 3, 155n.17
Justel, Henri 28

Kelsham, Peter 59
Kennett, White 219
Kensington Palace 117, 119
Kenyon, J.P. 224
King's Bed 114
Kinsale 6–7
Kiveton, Yorkshire 117
Kneller, Sir Godfrey 26
Knole 114–15, 118–21

Labrousse, Elisabeth 18n.2, 176, 177
Lady's Journal 24
La Feauté Club 9
Lambert family 130
Lambeth Palace 149–50
Lamplugh, Bishop 222
Lamport 119
Landon, John 139n.20
Langhemans, François 105
Languedoc 167, 186, 201, 212, 216; Lower 183–4, 193
Lapière, Francis 115–18, 120
Larchevesque, John 129
Lardant, Mr 140n.34
Lardant family 33, 130
Lardau family 130

La Rochelle 164–7, 176, 177, 180–2, 192; peace of 167
Laud, Archbishop 45, 68, 70, 145
Lavie, German 137n.8
Le Blan *alias* White, Elizabeth 67
Le Brun 189
Leclerc, Jean 3–5, 6, 9, 12, 21–2
Le Clercq, Gilles 67
Le Duchat 25
Legendre, Thomas 75, 83
Lefevre, Nicholas 136
Legrew, James 137n.8
Le Griel, David 75
Le Hook, Peter 133
Leiden 147
Lekeux, Captain Peter 134
Le Keux, James 69
Lekeux, John 129
Lekeux, Peter 127, 129, 134, 137n.5
Le Lew *alias* Wolfe, John 68
Leman, James 127, 132, 133–5, 137n.3,5, 140n.32
Leman, Peter 129, 137n.3
Le Nain, Louis 189
Lennoxglove 120
Le Noble, Pierre 69
Léonard, E.G. 176, 178, 180, 183–6
Le Pellison, Jeanne 5
Le Pellison, Paul 5
Le Pléïade Club 9
Le Sage, John 108, 119
Le Scallet, John 129
Lesoeuf, James 137n.8
Le Tellier family 205–6, 214
Le Thieullier, Jan 73
Lethieullier, John 75, 78
Lethieullier, John I 73, 83
Lethieullier, John II 73, 77
Lethieullier, Leonora 74, 77–82, 84
Lethieullier, Samuel 81
Lethieullier, Sir John 81
Lethieullier family 73–4, 76, 83, 231
Levant Company 78, 80
Le Vassor, Michel 27
Lewis (Louis?), John 137n.8
Lewknor, John 81
Lewknor, Mrs Jane 81, 84
lexicography 33
L'Heureux family 130, 133
librarians 28–9
Liège 97
Liger, Isaac 106
Lille 107
Limburg, Germany 97
Limerick, assault on 6

Locke, John 7
London 42–4, 83; Assay Office 92;
  attitude to aliens in 91; French
  Church in 221–2, 231–2;
  Hospital 135; Huguenots
  in 128–9, 229; immigrants 72;
  membership of stranger
  churches 45, 94; mercers 132;
  south bank 51–2; weavers
  in 128–30, 132, 135–6; *see also*
  City; Metropolis; Westminster
looms 133; Dutch 69
Loudun, Peace of 164–5
Loudun Synod 193
Louis, Jean 99
Louis Quatorze style 113, 121
Louis XIII, King 159, 162–7, 200
Louis XIV, King 3, 6–7, 12, 21, 25, 119,
  150, 179, 189, 193, 198, 205–6,
  208–9, 213–16; *mémoires* 199–204
Louvois, Marquis de 205–6, 208–9, 211,
  213–15
Low Leyton, Essex 75, 78, 84
Luneray 133, 135, 139n.25
lutestring 132, 133
Luther, Martin 200
Lutherans 143, 152
Luxembourg Palace 188
luxuries 73, 78
Luynes, Duc de 165
Lyon 130, 132, 135, 181

Macaré, Abraham 139n.20
Macaulay, Thomas Babington 17, 217
Magen, Beate 230
Maidstone 58
Maillard family 134, 135
Mamacher, Hans 93
Manckey, Ben 133
Manneke, Benjamin 132
Manneke, Philip 132
Mannerism 94–5
Marescoe, Charles 74, 76–7, 81, 84;
  daughters of 75, 81–2, 84;
  parents 75; sisters 75, 78
Marescoe, James 77–8
Marescoe, Leonora II 79
Marescoe, Mrs Leonora 77–9
Marescoe, Peter 74, 75, 77, 129
Marescoe family 231
Margas, Jacob 107, 108
Margas, Samuel 107, 111n.51
Marie, Alfred 119
Marillac, Intendant 212–13
market trading 68–9

Marlborough, Duchess of 106
Marmoy, Charles 221
Marot, Daniel 113–21
Marrowe, Bryan 54n.38
Mary I, Queen 91, 93
mathematicians 28–9
Maty, Matthew 5, 29
Maubert, Elizabeth 103
Mayo, Ronald 229
Mazarin, cardinal Giulio 177–8, 188,
  192–3, 195, 198
Maze family 130
Mazell, Peter 134
Maze and Steer 134
Medici, Marie de 163–4, 188
medicine 218
Melbourne, Derbyshire 119
Melville, 1st Earl of 116
Melville Bed 113
Merchant Adventurers 78
merchants 47, 48, 75
Merchant Taylors' Company 133
Mersenne 194
Methodism 229
Methodist Church 218
Methuen, Sir Paul 100
Metropolis, strangers in 42–55;
  composition of stranger community
  in 47–8; occupation of strangers
  in 48–9; places of origin of 44
Mettayer, Louis 103–4, 111n.60
Mettayer, Samuel 103
Metz 103–4, 184
Meyerbeer's *Les Huguenots* 225, 227–8
Meynell, Isaac 78
Michelet, J. 177, 217, 228
Michelin, Jean 189
Mill, Dr John 22
Millor, Barget 48
Minet, Isaac 223
Moisant de Brieux, Jacques 180, 185,
  191
Moisset, Jeanne 182
Monnier, Abraham 69
Monnoyer, Jean-Baptiste 119
monsieur, significance of 51
Montagu, Charles, Earl of
  Halifax 11–12
Montagu, Ralph 114, 119–21
Montagu House 118–20
Montauban 166, 182–4, 186, 192, 204
Montesquieu, baron de 16
Montpellier 190, 194, 216
Morley, Sir Henry xvi
Morris, Peter 47

Mortimer's Directory 135
Moscow 72
Motteux, Pierre 23–7, 38n.41
Murray, James, Duke of Atholl 84
Mylde, Jasper 90
Myller, Barthu 90

Nantes 181–2; *see also* Edict of Nantes
Narva 72
National Synod of Charenton 143
naturalisation 235n.25
Naturalisation Act 46, 98, 102
naturalised immigrants 72, 74–5, 80, 129
Navy, profit from supplies to 74–5, 80
needlewomen 117
Neff, Félix xvi
Netherlands 75, 93, 94
newsletters 35
Newton, Sir Isaac 29–30
Nijmegen settlement 209
Nîmes 177, 183–4, 186–7, 191, 194
Noailles, duc de 216
Norfolk, Duchess of 117–18
Normandy 128–9, 132–3, 144, 179–80, 185
Norwich 61, 95
Nouailles, Peter 135

Oakley, Anne 139n.21
Ogier, Lewis 137n.8
Ogier, Peter 134, 137n.8
Ogier, Peter Abraham 140n.34
Ogier, Thomas Abraham 127, 135, 137n.8
Ogier family 132
Ogier, Vansommer and Triquet 134
Olmius, Hermann 83
Oman, C. 109n.5
Orphans Court of City of London 77, 81
Oufrey, Daniel 136n.2
Oursel, Robert 75–6, 83
Ouvry family 133
Ouvry, John 140n.34
Oxford Children's History 224
Ozell, John 25

package, scavage and porterage 50
Pagès, Louis 182
Paisley 129
Palfar, Anthony 68
Palladian Revolution 121
Pallavicino, Sir Horatio 47
Pantin, Essaie 103

Pantin, Simon 102–3, 108
Papenbroek, Daniel 22
paper-making 218, 229
Papillon, George 83
Pardoe, Jean 121
Paris 119, 188–91, 194; Huguenots' return to 178
Paris, Pierre 136
Paris, Stephen 137n.8
Parisels, Marie 113
parliamentary constitution 15–16
parliamentary news 34–5
Patents of Denization 46
Paudevin, Jean 115
Pays de Caux 132–3
Pays de Gex 201
Payton, James 135
Peck, John 140n.34
Peiresc of Provence 194
Péladin, Isaac 194
Pelletier, Jean 121
Pelletier, Renée 121
Pelletier, Thomas 121
Pellissari, Georges 181
Pellisson, Paul 191
Penshurst Place 117–18, 121
pepper 73
Pepys, Samuel 73–4
Peregol (Peregal), John 138n.8
Perizonius 33
Petit, Samuel 194
Pettegree, Andrew 230
Petworth 119, 120, 134
Peyrard, Jean 114
Philosophical Transactions 21, 23
Picardy 129
picture frames 121
Piedmont xxi
Pilleau, Pezé 108
Pilon, Nicholas 139n.20
piracy 58
plague 61–2
Platel, Claude 107
Platel, Pierre 107–8, 108
plush-weaver 129
poetry, English 32–3
Poitou 132, 134
Political State of Great Britain 34–5
Politic Men 60–1, 66
Pomert, Andrew 90
Pons, Jean 108, 112n.62
Poole, Reginald Lane xxi, 220
poor relief 63, **64**, 66, 68, 102, 130, 136, 218, 229
popery 144, 150

Popish plot 83
Porte St Antoine 192
Portland, Duke of 100
Postlethwaite, M. 140n.32
Poussin, Nicholas 190
poverty of refugees xxi, 32, 231
Presbyterian Church 229
Prestwich, Menna 151
prices, fall in 73
probability theory 29–30
property, purchase of 67
Protestants *see under* France; French in England
Psalms, modernisation of 151
Public Record Office 222
Pyne, Benjamin 105
Pyrenees, Peace of 193
Pyrrhonism, historical 4

Rabelais, François 24–5
Rambouillet, Nicholas 181
Rambouillet family 181
Rapin, Daniel de 6
Rapin, Jacques 5
Rapin, Salomon 6
Rapin de Thoyras, Paul 5–9, 32; criticism of 16–17; history of England 10–18
Rawlinson, Thomas 16
religious disinterest in West 227
religious history, works on 228
Renaissance 94
Renard, Mardoche 69
Reneu, Hillaire 83
Reneu family 231
Renialme, Ascanius 50
rents 67
research into Huguenots 221–3, 230
Returns of Aliens 43, 94
Revocation of the Edict of Nantes *see under* Edict
revolution, English 7
Richardson, John 54n.38
Richelieu, cardinal 160, 166, 177–8, 181–2, 188, 191, 193
Robelon, Henry 136n.2
Roberts, Thomas 115
Rochefort 211
Rochester Cathedral silver-gilt tazze 92–3
Rococo 108, 134
Rocroi, battle of 185
Rohan, Benjamin de 164
Rohan, duc Henri de 164, 167, 175, 176
Rohan, M. de 193

Rohan, wars of 183
Rollos, Phillip 108; (Philip) 119
Rollos, Phillip II 108, 112n.61
Rome 190
Romilly, Sir Samuel xxi
Roseveare, Henry G. 231
Rotolp de la Devèze, Abel 9
Rou, Jean 9–10, 18n.8
Roubiliac, sculptor 223
Rouen 75, 83, 103, 107, 177, 182
Royal African Company 75
Royal Bounty 46–7, 231
Royal Chapels 97
Royal Society xvii, 27–8
Royal Society of Arts 135
RPR, *religion prétendu réformée* 200, 202, 203, 206, 209
Runer, Lucien 67–8
Rushbrooke, Suffolk 118
Russell, Edward 25
Russia Company 72
Rutland Ewer and Basin 95
Ruvigny, Marquis de 7
Rymer, Thomas 11–12
Ryswick, Treaty of 7

Sabatier, John 135, 138n.8, 140n.34
St Alphege Church 59
St Bartholomew Massacre 178
St Dunstan in the East, Church of 75
Sainte-Foy assembly 163
St George's Chapel, Windsor 96
St Margaret Pattens Church 78
St Martin-in-the-Fields 51
St Nicholas Acon Church 90
St Peter Mancroft Church 95
St Petersburg Academy of Sciences 28
Salome, Roger 66–7
Sandwich, Kent 56, 89
Saumur 186–8, 191, 194; assembly of 164
Savell, Bryan 54n.38
science 218; and God 29–31; popularisation of 30–1
Scottish Kirk 147–8
Scouloudi, Irene xxii–xxiii, 221, 224
Sedan 186
Séguier, Chancellor 179, 188–9
separation of powers 15
serge-weaving 136
Shelley, Charles 97
shopkeeping 49, 59, 68
Shoulder, journeyman 132
Shrewsbury, Earl of 47
Shuter, Sir John 98

Sidney, Algernon 6
silk, demand for 132
silk industry: branches 132; Huguenots
   in 132–3, 135; specialisation
   in 135; silk-lustering 132;
   silk-weaving 48–9, 74, 130, 134–6,
   229
silver bed 97
silver-gilt 92–4, 94–5, 105–6
silver plate 92, 95, 104
silversmiths 89, 91, 94, 96–7, 108, 119
Silvestre, Pierre 28
Sisterhood of Loyalists 27
Smiles, Samuel xxi, 218, 220, 222, 227
Smith, Bishop Miles 153n.10
Smith, Dr Thomas 33
social mobility, upward 84
Somner, W. 59, 62. 130
Sophia Charlotte, Queen 5, 10
Soubise 166
Southampton 222
South Sea Company 105
Spitalfields xxi, 132, 135
Stanhope, Lord Philip 104
state beds 114–18
Stationers' Company 50
Statute of Artificers (1563) 50–1
Stauffer, Richard 186
Stone, Lawrence 47
Stop of the Exchequer 79
Stow, John 42
strangers 72; legal position of 46–7;
   see also immigrants; naturalisation;
   Naturalisation Act; naturalised
   immigrants
Strype, Rev. John 84
Stuart period 45
Subsidy Rolls 63
sugar 73
Sully, Duc de 177, 188
sultan 133
Sun Insurance Company 128
surgeons 28
Sussex, Duke of 100
Synod of Dort 143

Tallemant, Gédéon 181, 190
Tallemant, Pierre 181
Tallemant des Réaux 181
Talman, William 117
Tanqueray, David 104
Tar Company 74, 78, 80
taxation 50, 67, 68–9; *see also* France:
   Huguenots in, Protestants in, tax
   exemption

television programmes, Huguenot xxii
Temple Newsam 117
Testelin, Louis 189
Thames, River 42–3
theatre 218; English 32–3
theology, English 32
Thiery, Robert 49
Thirsk, Joan 230
Thirty Years War 165–6
Thornton, Peter 125
Tillotson, John 32
Tipper, William 50
tithes 68
tobacco 73
Tongerlo Abbey 93
Torbay, landing at 6
Toulouse 201–2, 216
Tours 212
trade, intellectual 31
traders: Dutch 74–5, 83;
   Huguenot 75–6, 223
translators 22–3, 26, 28–9, 32–4
transubstantiation 148
Trequet, P. 138n.8
Trevaux, Jesuits of 14
Trevor-Roper, H.R. 229
Trianon de Porcelaine 116
Trinquand, Charles 83
Trinquand family 231
Triquet, Charles 138n.8
Troches, Willyn 54n.38
Trumbull, Sir William 26
Tullibardine, Marquess of 115–16
Turenne, General 192–3
Turner, Robert 140n.34
Turner, Stuart 128, 132
Turner, Thomas 140n.34
tutors 20, 33

Unitarian Church 218
upholsterers 113–17
Urquhart, Sir Thomas 24
Utrecht, Treaty of 12

Vals 193
Van Os, Adrian 67
Van Paets, Hadriaan 145
Van Robais 203
Vansommer, John 133–4, 140n.32
Van Vienen, Christian 96
Vatinel, Denis 133, 139n.24
Vaudois xxi
Vautier, Daniel 134–5
vegetable dyes 73
Vermuyden, Sir Cornelius 47

Verneuil-sur-Oise 188
Versailles 119, 214
Vertue, G. 119
Vickson, Elizabeth 117
Victoria and Albert Museum 119
Viénot, J. 170n.41, 45
Vigne, Randolph xxiii
Viner, Sir Robert 97
Vintners' Company 100
Voltaire 3, 14–16, 31
Von Antwerpen, Hans von (John of
    Antwerp) 90–1
Von Lottum, Count 13
Vouet, Simon 189
Vrouling family 83

Waller, James 6
Waller, Sir Hardress 6
Walloon Church 130, 145; bequests
    to 67
Walloons 57–8, 89, 96, 229
Walpole, Sir Robert 117
Warburton, William 14
Ware, Isaac 121
Ware, John 69
War of the Grand Alliance 7
Warrington, 1st Earl of 118
Wars of Religion xxi, 175–6
watch-making 218
weavers 137n.8; anti-French
    feelings 136; French 127, 129;
    Huguenot 129–30, 132–4, 136;
    journeymen 136
Weavers' Company 49, 69, 135;
    Huguenots in 125, **126**, 127–9;
    membership losses 127–8

weaving 117
weddings 79–82
weighing 50
Wesel 10–13
Westminster 49, 51, 96, 129
Wetken, Hermann 75, 83
Wharton, Philip, Lord 8, 20–1
Whigs 15, 145; and Tories, Rapin
    on 13
Whitehall Banqueting House 114, 115
Wilding Bequest 102, 104–5, 107,
    110n.37
Willaume, Anne 104
Willaume, David 103–6, 111n.60, 117
Willet, Humphrey 83
William, Prince of Orange 6–7, 227
William III, King 9–10, 12, 28, 33,
    100–1, 106–7, 113, 115–16;
    Huguenots in army of 217–18, 229
Willing, Mrs Charles 134
wills 47, 66–7, 77, 81–2
Winchelsea 58, 62
Windsor Castle 117
women: interest in science 30;
    journalism for 24
wood-carvers 119
Woodstock, Lord 7–9
Wootton, Nicholas 58
world trade 73
Wyndham Ewer 94

Youge, Remyge 90
Young Pretender 135

Zurich 97